Popular Science

WOODWORKING PROJECTS

1986 Yearbook

Published by **Popular Science Books**

Distributed to the trade by **Rodale Press, Inc.**

Published by

Popular Science Books
Times Mirror Magazines, Inc.
380 Madison Avenue
New York, NY 10017

Distributed to the trade by

Rodale Press, Inc.
33 East Minor Street
Emmaus, PA 18049

Designed by Linda Watts, Bookworks, Inc.

ISBN: 0-943822-57-2

Manufactured in the United States of America

Introduction

As we put together the *Popular Science Woodworking Projects 1986 Yearbook*, we decided to try something a little different. Most books are written by writers, and most woodworking books are written by writers who know something about woodworking. But this year, we went looking for some honest-to-goodness woodworkers (most of whom knew nothing about writing) and helped them to tell their own stories.

You'll be pleased with the results, we know. There are several new folks for you to meet, accomplished woodworkers who have never before been in print. A few of them are professionals. Both David Wakefield and Judy Ditmer own their own woodworking businesses. David makes wooden toys; Judy makes custom-designed furniture.

Others teach woodworking. Rude Osolnik taught wood arts at Berea College in Kentucky, and now conducts seminars for lathe turners. Dick Belcher tutors woodcarvers.

And still others are accomplished amateurs. Dan Gabriel doesn't even count himself as a woodworker. "I just like to piddle around in my shop," Dan told me. (For an idea of what Dan considers piddling, take a look at the rocking horse on page 64.)

The varied backgrounds and interests of the contributors enhance the variety of projects in this year's yearbook. You'll find something from every part of the woodworking spectrum: classic, contemporary, indoors, outdoors, simple, and involved. Some projects in this book can be built in a few minutes. Others will take you the better part of a year. You'll be finishing up just in time for the next yearbook!

Want something quick for a birthday or Christmas gift? The "Cassette Racks" will be big hits under the tree next holiday season. David Wakefield's "Animated Toys" are a treat for a favorite niece or nephew. Or make a half-dozen of the "One-Piece Boxes" at a time, and keep them on hand to give away whenever an occasion arises.

Or perhaps you'd like to take your time and create something very special. If your tastes run to modern furniture, Phil Bacon's "Contemporary Cabinet" might look nice in your living room. Or if you'd rather have a copy of a fine antique, take a look at the "Serpentine Dresser" or the "Federal Period Sideboard". The originals that these projects were patterned after are now worth hundreds of thousands of dollars!

How about something that looks good outside your home? The "Hexagonal Picnic Table" is an attractive setting for those summer barbecues. And afterwards, you can lay back and soak up the rays in the "Rocking Lawn Chair".

If you're a practical woodworker, you'll appreciate projects like the "Quick-and-Easy Shelves". With this simple butt-jointed system, you can build any number of good-looking storage projects in next to no time. The "Reorganized Closet" is another project in this same vein — simple and useful. And if you want the ultimate in practicality, try your hand at the "Rolltop Desk". Maybe you think of a rolltop as a piece of fine furniture, but believe us, there was never a more useful piece of fine furniture. Just shovel your bills into the pigeonholes, shut the rolltop on the mess, and forget about it. Out of sight, out of mind.

As you can see, there are lots of great projects in this year's *Woodworking Projects Yearbook* from many excellent woodworkers. But in all my searching, there's one thing we didn't find: A perfect woodworker. All of us make mistakes, and there's every chance that somewhere in this book someone gave us a wrong measurement that we didn't catch. We checked over all the numbers thoroughly, but there's no such thing as a perfect editor, either. So, once again, we want to warn you to *check and doublecheck all the measurements* **before** *you cut wood.*

It's considered good woodworking practice to sit down with a pad, a pencil, and a calculator to add up the numbers before you jump into a project. Not only does this save you time and lumber if there's a wrong measurement somewhere, but it forces you to trace the thoughts of the craftsman who originally designed the piece. You see how he or she fit the parts together and why. This in-depth understanding of a project saves you time and frustration in the shop. Your woodworking goes smoother and the results are more satisfying.

In short, a little planning and doublechecking helps insure that you'll enjoy this yearbook as much as we enjoyed putting it together for you.

With all good wishes,

Nick Engler

Nick Engler

Contributors

Phil Bacon ◆ Phil portrays himself as a contemporary wood designer. "I like new designs, new things that you can do with wood," says Phil. While he respects traditional woodworking forms, he much prefers state-of-the-art designs and methods.

He started out by just puttering around. "I was always building something," he recalls. Then his high school industrial arts teacher pointed him towards a career in woodworking. Phil earned a Bachelor of Fine Arts from the prestigious Rochester Institute of Technology, and went on to do professional cabinetmaking and millwork.

Today, he's the Craftsman/Designer for *The Woodworker's Journal*, which publishes out of New Milford, Connecticut. Phil builds many of the projects you see in that magazine.

Dick Belcher ◆ Dick started carving wood when he joined the Boy Scouts. Thirty-one years later, he's one of the most successful professional woodcarvers in America.

For many years, Dick considered carving as just a hobby. He was an executive for an international company; and carving, he found, helped relieve the pressure associated with his job. But one day he decided to quit and become a full-time carver. Today, he not only carves; he teaches woodcarving and judges woodcarving exhibitions. He has been to Europe several times to lecture and participate in international woodcarving shows. When he's not on the road, he's carving in his shop in Dayton, Ohio.

If that weren't enough, he's also a Director on the board of Affiliated Woodcarvers Limited, an organization for professional woodcarvers. "We're trying to get woodcarving recognized as an art, not just a craft," says Dick. "We want carving to gain the recognition that it should have."

Judy Ditmer ◆ All during her school years, Judy tested extraordinarily high in mechanical aptitude. But none of her teachers knew what to make of it. "Those days, girls weren't supposed to be good with machinery," she recalls. So Judy never took a shop course.

Then, while attending the Kansas City Art Institute, she discovered woodworking. "I tried and tried to get a cabinetmaking apprenticeship, but I was just laughed at because I was a woman," says Judy. Undaunted, she saved up her money for many years, bought her own tools, and taught herself woodworking. Today she owns and operates her own cabinetmaking shop, *Heartwood*, in Tipp City, Ohio. Judy still encounters a few prejudices from time to time, but her woodworking skills quickly dispel any doubts that a woman can handle the machinery.

Nick Engler ◆ Nick founded the woodworking magazine, *HANDS ON!*, and managed the publication for several years. During that time, he helped to publish not only the magazine, but over 100 projects plans, books, manuals, and a syndicated newspaper column for woodworkers.

Today, he is the co-owner of *Bookworks, Inc.*, a firm in West Milton, Ohio, that specializes in the production of how-to books. Nick and the staff at Bookworks put together this edition of the *Woodworking Project Yearbook* for Popular Science.

Dan Gabriel ◆ When we asked Dan to describe what kind of woodworker he is, he told us: "Very lucky. I've done exactly four projects and they all turned out wonderful."

Dan is a professional photographer, owner of Dayton Commercial Studios in Dayton, Ohio. While he was photographing woodworking tools, he became interested in woodworking. So he bought some equipment and rebuilt two cabin sailboats, inside and out. (In his spare time, Dan likes to sail.) He also remodeled his bathroom and built the rocking horse on page 64. Does he have any plans for future woodworking projects? "If my luck holds out," says Dan.

Jim McCann ◆ Jim has been woodworking ever since he can remember. His father taught him the basics when he was a kid, then he got formal training at Eastern Kentucky University. The three-legged stand you see on page 124 was a project that Jim built for a final exam in a class on woodworking technology.

He joined the staff of *HANDS ON!* in 1979 as a craftsman and designer. During his stay at the magazine, he put together over 100 projects and wrote the "Ask Smitty" column, offering advice and tips to woodworkers. Today Jim works in the engineering laboratory of Shopsmith, Inc., helping to design power tools for home shops. He's also inherited his father's tools and has set up shop in Trotwood, Ohio.

Rude Osolnik ◆ Rude taught wood arts at Berea College for 40 years and was Chairman of the Industrial Arts Department before he retired a few years ago. But Rude didn't stop teaching when he retired; now he conducts seminars in lathe turning all over the United States.

Rude remains a prolific woodturner. He sells his bowls and other turnings through various art galleries across the country. He and his wife operate their own gallery, *Benchmark*, in Berea, Kentucky. Benchmark not only features his own turnings, but many other examples of fine woodworking from some of Rude's former students.

Dale Nish lists this former professor in his book, *Master Woodturners*, where he calls Rude "the most versatile turner in America."

John Shoup ◆ John started woodworking in his father's shop, then worked for a friend making furniture and repairing antiques. "I more or less taught myself," says John.

For many of his working years, woodworking was just a hobby. But then he joined H. Gerstners & Sons, a manufacturer of fine wooden toolboxes in Dayton, Ohio. John quickly learned the finer points of small case construction and worked his way up to foreman of the assembly section.

Later, he joined the staff of *HANDS ON!* magazine as head craftsman.

Today, John is retired and is enjoying his shop in Waynesville, Ohio. He remains a prolific woodworker, designing and building custom furniture and accessories.

David Wakefield ◆ David is a native of Australia, and the son of Oliver Wakefield, a famous English comedian. His family traveled extensively, but David eventually came to rest in Yellow Springs, Ohio, where he started *Howling Wolf Woodworks*.

At first, David produced acoustical guitars. But later he expanded his line to include custom furniture and wooden toys. The toys proved to be his most popular designs, and today he produces them almost exclusively. He gets as involved in his toymaking as any one toymaker can get. "I take my toys from the tree to the finished project," says David. He cuts his own timber, cures it, and builds his toys from it.

In 1980, David moved his business to Athens, Ohio, where he bought some land. He's built two houses on his property, one of them a treehouse. When he isn't making toys or tramping about his forest, David is working on a book of his toy designs for Popular Science.

And Others... ◆ It takes more than a few woodworkers to put together a book of woodworking projects. We'd also like to recognize Linda Ball, Adam Blake, Betty Buchelt, Donna Cheshire-Engler, and Mary Jane Favorite.

And special thanks to Sotheby Parke Bernet for allowing us to publish some of their materials.

Contents

Projects

Techniques

PROJECTS

Rolltop Desk

A timeless design is at home in modern, classic, or country surroundings.

ate in the eighteenth century, craftsmen began to use 'tambour' doors in their designs. The word "tambour" originally referred to cloth stretched over a wooden frame. In cabinetmaking, a tambour door came to mean slender strips of word glued to a cloth backing. The strips, or tambours, ride in grooved frame, 'rolling' around a curve like a single piece of flexible wood.

Federal Period designers in the early nineteenth century, such as Sheraton and Hepplewhite, were the first

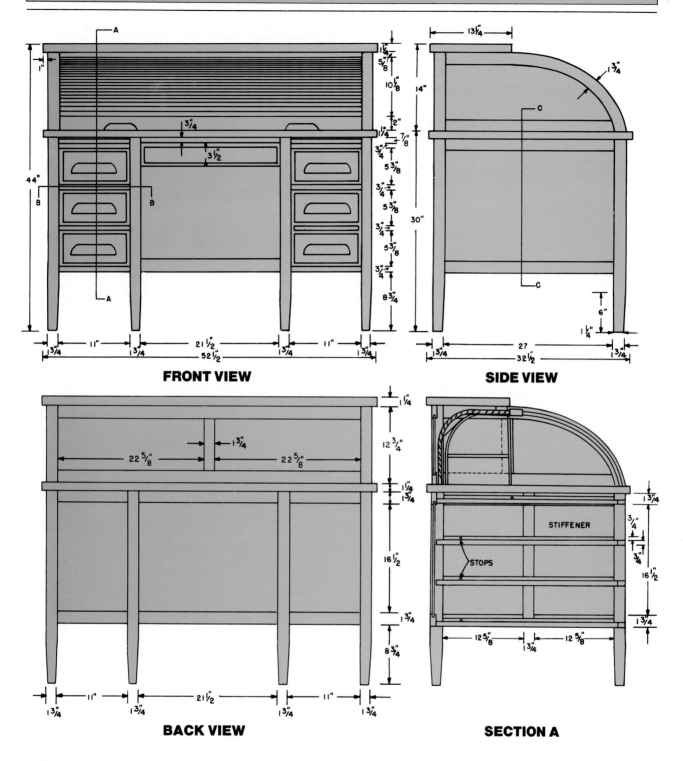

FRONT VIEW

SIDE VIEW

BACK VIEW

SECTION A

craftsmen to incorporate these doors into desks. The tambours were usually mounted vertically, so that the doors rolled from side to side. But, a few craftsmen experimented with a single tambour door that mounted *horizontally*, so that it rolled up and disappeared into the frame. This design quickly gained popularity and soon became known as the 'rolltop desk'.

By the late nineteenth century, the rolltop desk began to assume the classic proportions you see here. Two large chest of drawers or 'pedestals' support a thick top. This top is fitted with a framework of 'pigeonholes', and covered with

a single long tambour door. Rolltops were manufactured with two different curves: The tambours of a 'waterfall' rolltop follow a classic S-curve. The 'cylinder' rolltop, such as the one you see here, follows a simple arc.

While the waterfall shape is more commonly associated with the rolltop, the cylinder shape offers certain advantages to a craftsman. The cylinder rolltop is easier to build because the tambours only need to bend in one direction, the clearances in the rolltop aren't as critical. And finally, the cylinder rolltop is less susceptible to changes in humidity and temperature.

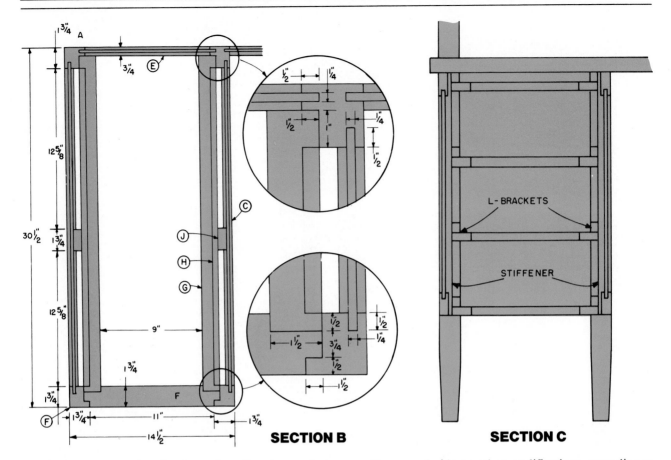

SECTION B

SECTION C

But, no matter what the shape, the rolltop is a project that will stretch your talents. It requires careful planning and accurate work. But, as you can see, the results are well worth the effort.

Choosing the Materials

The traditional wood for a rolltop desk is oak. This is because so many desks were mass-produced between 1880 and 1930. During that period, oak was inexpensive and available in huge quantities. It was also well suited for mass production techniques. Once it was properly cured, it didn't change shape overmuch. Furniture factories could set up to make huge runs of one part or another, then store these parts away until needed.

Despite the tradition, many rolltops were also made of finer woods — walnut and cherry, particularly. The earliest rolltops from the Federal Period were made of mahogany. So you really have your choice.

Whatever wood you decide to use, use a cabinet-grade plywood for the large panels. Some of these panels are quite wide, and plywood will add both strength and stability to the finished desk. You can special-order plywoods already covered with birch, oak, walnut, or cherry veneers from your local lumber store.

Making the Pedestals

The pedestals are simple frame-and-panel construction, with the legs serving as the vertical stiles of the frames. Inside the pedestals, L-brackets suspend the drawers. Both pedestals are essentially the same, though one has an extra-deep drawer for files.

You may decide on other modifications, according to your needs. You could make *both* pedestals with file drawers for twice the file storage. Or, you could eliminate the drawers in one pedestal completely and hinge a door to the outside leg. This would make a cabinet in which you could store large pieces of artwork, etc. If you want more ideas, look through a reproduction copy of the "1901 Sears & Roebuck Catalogue". You'll find a tremendous variety in desk pedestals — some might suit your purposes a lot better than what you see here.

Begin by cutting the joinery in the legs. The rails are mortised into the legs, as you can see in the working drawings. The front rails sit in blind dadoes, while the side and back rails sit in the same grooves that the panels ride in. The middle front rail that joins the pedestals is dovetailed into the middle front legs.

Cut the blind dadoes in two steps. First, cut as far as you can with a dado cutter on your table saw. Then, square off the blind end with a chisel. (See Figure 1.) To make the

Figure 1. To make the blind dadoes in the legs, first cut as far as you can with a dado cutter. Then, square off the ends with a hand chisel.

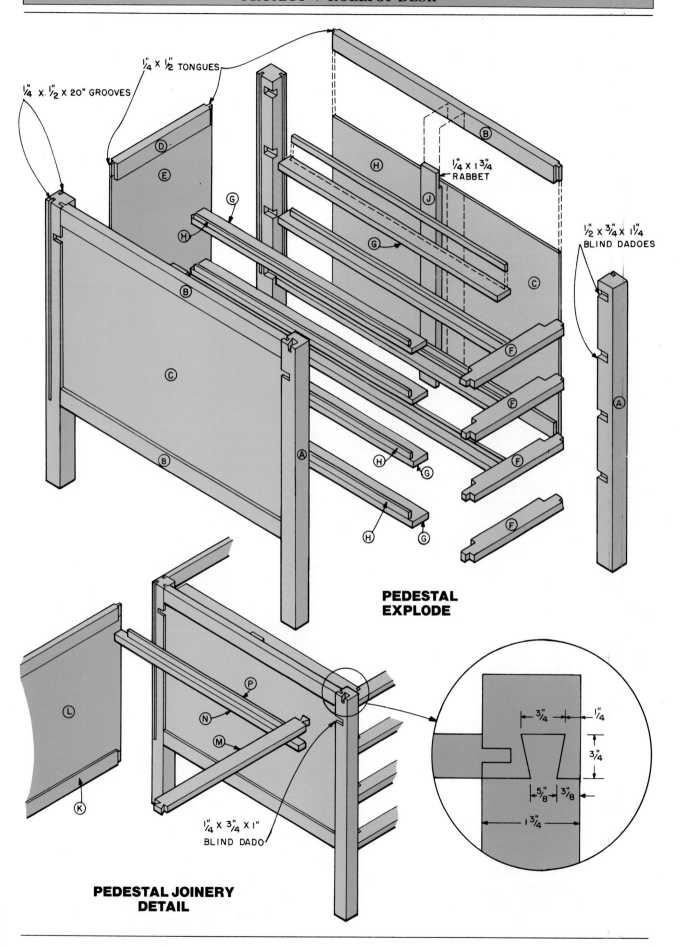

¼" X ½" TONGUES

¼" X ½" X 20" GROOVES

¼" X 1¾"
RABBET

½" X ¾" X 1¼"
BLIND DADOES

D

E

G

H

B

C

A

B

H

J

G

F

F

H

G

F

H

G

**PEDESTAL
EXPLODE**

L

K

P

N

M

¼" X ¾" X 1"
BLIND DADO

**PEDESTAL JOINERY
DETAIL**

¾" ¼"

¾"

⅝" ⅜"

1¾"

grooves, first clamp the leg *securely* to your benchtop. Cut the groove with a hand-held router and a 1/4″ straight bit. (See Figure 2.) Don't try to rout this groove all in one pass. Take small bites, routing just 1/8″ deeper with each pass until you reach the proper depth. Finally, cut dovetail slots in the upper ends of the two inside front legs. Make these slots by drilling a stopped hole, then cutting the dovetail shape with a hand chisel. (See Figure 3.) When you've cut all the joinery, taper the bottom ends of the legs slightly on a bandsaw or table saw.

Notch the front rails and cut the dovetails in the middle front rail on a bandsaw. You'll have to hand-fit these dovetails to the slots, then plainly mark which dovetail fits in which slot. Cut the tenons on the back and side rails with a dado cutter. You can also cut the grooves in the edges of the rails with a dado cutter. (See Figure 4.)

Dry assemble the legs, rails, and panels *temporarily* to check the fit. Use band clamps and bar clamps to hold the assembly together.

While the pedestals are assembled, fit the brackets for the drawers and sliding shelves. For the most part, these brackets are notched only on the back ends. The front fits

into the blind dadoes in the front legs, behind the front rails. Only the brackets for the middle drawer are notched on both ends. Attach these rails to the insides of the pedestals with flathead wood screws.

> **Tip ◆** Be sure to countersink the wood screws in the brackets so that the heads of the screws won't interfere with the sliding action of the drawers.

Making and Fitting the Drawers

While the pedestal is still assembled, make and fit the drawers. These drawers are simplicity personified. Both the front and the back are dovetailed to the sides, while the bottom rides in a groove near the lower edge of the other drawer parts. There is no complicated joinery or drawer glides to worry about. The only parts that need a little extra attention are the drawer fronts.

Cut the drawer joinery *before* you shape the drawer fronts. The easiest way to make the half-blind dovetails is with a router and a dovetail jig. (See Figure 5.) Cut the grooves for the drawer bottoms with a dado cutter. Temporarily assemble the drawers and fit them to the pedestals. Position the drawer stops so that the drawer fronts are flush with the front rails when the drawers are completely closed.

When you're satisfied that the drawers fit properly, disassemble them. Mortise those drawer fronts where you want to install locks. Then, shape the drawer fronts with a dado cutter. Arrange the knives to cut a 1/2″ wide rabbet, just 3/16″ deep all around the outside of the drawer front. (See Figure 6.). This will give the drawers the appearance of small 'raised' panels in the pedestal. Notice that the file drawer front has two 3/16″ x 1/2″ dadoes cut across the middle, to give the drawer the appearance of being two separate drawers. This extra decoration is not necessary, but it adds symmetry to the finished pedestals.

Figure 2. Cut the grooves in the legs with a hand-held router. Make sure the legs are clamped securely to the benchtop before you start to rout.

Figure 3. To make a dovetail slot, first drill a stopped hole. Then, cut the dovetail shape with a hand chisel.

Figure 5. The easiest way to cut the joinery for the drawers is with a router and a dovetail template.

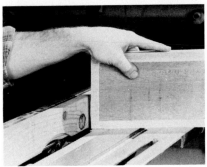

Figure 4. Cut the grooves in the rails with a dado cutter.

Figure 6. Cut a shallow rabbet all the way around the edge of the drawer fronts. This will give them the appearance of raised panels.

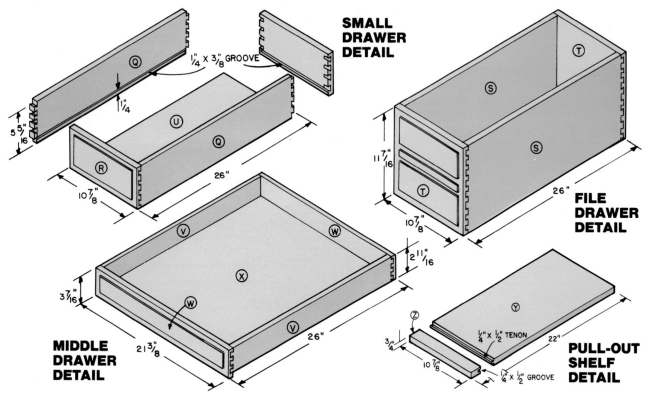

SMALL DRAWER DETAIL

FILE DRAWER DETAIL

MIDDLE DRAWER DETAIL

PULL-OUT SHELF DETAIL

Finally, make the sliding shelves. These shelves have just two parts — the shelf and a shelf facing, joined by a tongue-and-groove joint. The facing is added so that you won't see the end grain of the shelf. With a 'core box' router bit, cut finger grips in the underside of the shelves, near the front edge. Lay the shelves in place in the pedestal, and position the stops for the shelves so that they stick out 1″ past the drawer fronts when the shelves are pushed all the way in.

When all parts of the pedestals fit properly, disassemble and sand all the individual pieces. Be careful not to sand the panels too much; you may wear through the veneer. Reassemble the pieces with wood screws and glue. *Do not* glue the panels in place. Allow these parts to 'float' free in the grooves. This will help keep the pedestals square.

Tip ◆ Wipe off any extra glue with a *very* wet rag. This will raise the grain slightly, but, it will cut down on the amount of work you have to do when it comes time to finish the desk.

Making and Fitting the Top

The top of the desk, as shown in the working drawings, is 1-1/4″ thick. You could glue this up from solid wood, but we don't recommend it. The top is 32″ wide. A slab of wood this massive may expand and contract as much as 1/2″ with changes in temperature and humidity. This will almost certainly affect the fit of the drawers, the shelves, and the tambour door. They may start to 'stick' during certain times of the year.

Instead of solid stock, glue up two sheets of plywood — 1/2″ and 3/4″ thick — to make a single 1-1/4″ thick slab. Plywood is much more stable than solid wood. The top sheet should be veneered with wood that matches the wood

in the pedestals. You'll also have to veneer the edges of the slab to hide the plies.

There are several ways to attach the top to the pedestals. You could drill screw pockets on the inside of the upper side rails and sink screws through the rails into the underside of the top. However, the easiest way is to use small metal brackets screwed to the insides of the rails and the underside of the desk top. You don't need many of these brackets; just 4-6 will hold the top secure.

Making the Rolltop

So much for the easy part. Now comes the rolltop — the part that gives most craftsmen fits. However, it needn't be as difficult as it looks. As we mentioned before, just work carefully, and make sure all your setups are dead-on accurate.

Tip ◆ It is especially important to use lumber with a clear, straight grain when making the pieces for the rolltop. It's hard to be accurate and build a square case with figured wood.

Let's begin with the hardest part — the paneled side sections to the top. The insides of these sections are grooved to hold the tamboured top. And, in order for that top to slide properly, the groove must be smooth and consistent. Also, these sections are constructed with *two* panels each — so that the inside looks as good as the outside.

Tip ◆ You'll find it's a good idea to cut out the parts for *three* side sections, even though you only need two. It makes it easier to check your setups — and you have some extra stock to practice on when it comes time to rout the tambour groove.

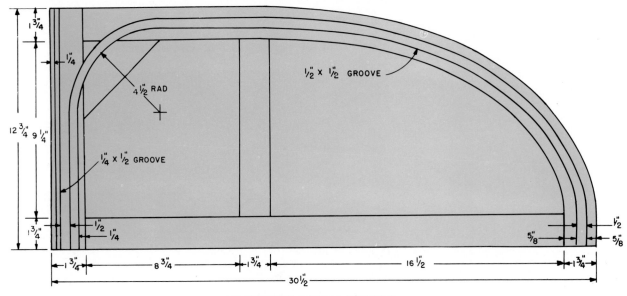

ROLLTOP SIDE LAYOUT

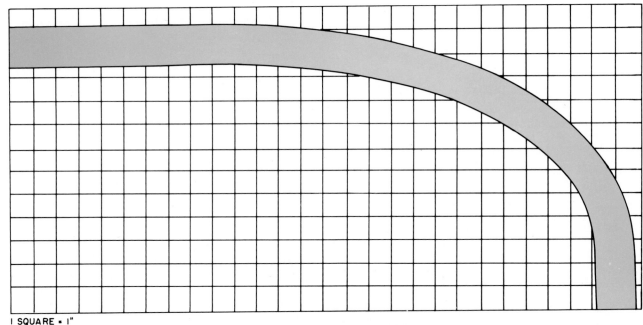

I SQUARE = 1"

CURVED RAIL PATTERN

Cut the curved rails from 1-3/4″ thick stock on a bandsaw. Cut a little wide of the line, then sand down to the line to remove the mill marks. Cut the 1/4″ panel grooves on the inside of the curve with a shaper cutter. (See Figure 7.) Remember that there is a *left* and a *right* curved rail. These two parts are mirror images of each other.

Also cut the lower rail and stiles. Use the same shaper setup to cut the grooves in these parts as you used to cut the grooves in the curved rails. Note that the long stiles need a single groove on the inside faces to hold the back panels and rails. With a dado cutter, make both the double and single tenons in the ends of those parts that need them. (See Figure 8.) Finally, cut the panels and the triangular glue blocks. Dry assemble all of these pieces to check the fit. If you're satisfied, glue them up.

Figure 7. Make the grooves in the cabinet top rails and stiles with a shaper cutter.

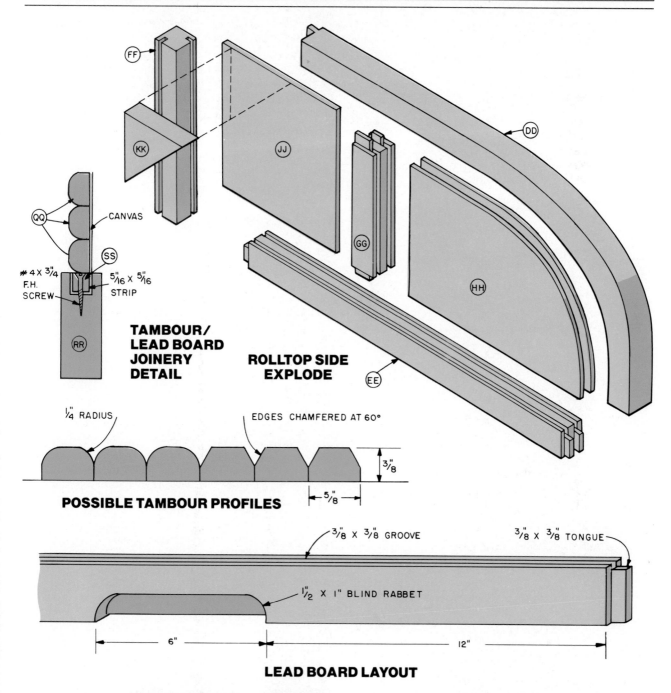

FF

KK

JJ

DD

GG

HH

EE

QQ
CANVAS

SS
5⁄16″ X 5⁄16″
STRIP

#4 X 3⁄4″
F.H.
SCREW

RR

**TAMBOUR/
LEAD BOARD
JOINERY
DETAIL**

**ROLLTOP SIDE
EXPLODE**

1⁄4″ RADIUS

EDGES CHAMFERED AT 60°

3⁄8″

5⁄8″

POSSIBLE TAMBOUR PROFILES

3⁄8″ X 3⁄8″ GROOVE

3⁄8″ X 3⁄8″ TONGUE

1 1⁄2″ X 1″ BLIND RABBET

6″

12″

LEAD BOARD LAYOUT

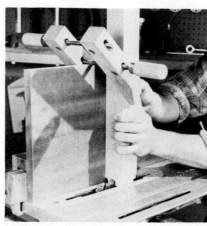

Figure 8. You can cut both the single and the double tenons in this project with a dado cutter. A 'tenoning jig' helps hold the boards square to the knives.

To cut the tambour groove, build a template from hardboard, as shown in the working drawings. The long, curved slot in the template must match the curve of the grooves you want to cut in the side sections. However, this slot should be 5/8″ wide. The finished grooves will be 1/2″ wide. You must be able to use *both* sides of this template, so that you can cut *matching* grooves in both the side sections.

Clamp the template down to the side section, and tack it in place with small brads. Mount a 1/2″ straight bit in your router, and attach a 5/8″ guide bushing to the base plate. This bushing will ride in the slot of the template, guiding the router. (See Figure 9.) Make several passes with the router to cut the slot, cutting just 1/8″ deeper with each pass. Detach the template, turn it over, and repeat this procedure for the other side section.

Once the side sections are completed, make the back rails, stile, panel, and cabinet top. All of these parts fit together in exactly the same way the pedestals and desk top fit together. As with the desk top, we suggest you make the thick slab for the cabinet top out of plywood and veneer the edges.

Making the tambour door for a rolltop can be the ultimate test of your patience. Those that make it through the deal are candidates for sainthood. To make a single tambour, you need to rip strips of *absolutely* straight lumber, then pass them through a shaper twice. You'll have to discard some of the strips because they bow after you rip them; other strips will break up in the shaper. In the end, you'll make two to three times as many tambours as you actually need just to get enough usable ones.

Figure 9. To cut two matching grooves for the tambours, use a hardboard template, a hand-held router, and a guide bushing.

Figure 10. If you make your own tambours, use two or more feather-boards to guide the thin strips of wood past the shaper cutters. This will keep your fingers out of danger.

We've provided the drawings you need to make and shape your own tambours, if you're so inclined. But, there is an easier way to get past this step. Some woodworking supply houses now sell ready made tambours for rolltops, already glued to canvas strips. Write:

The Woodworker's Store
21801 Industrial Blvd.
Rogers, MN 55374

> **Tip** ◆ If you insist on making your own tambours, use two or more featherboards to guide the wood past the shaper. (See Figure 10.) This will keep your fingers out of danger.

Cut the 'lead board' to length, and make 3/8" tenons on both ends. Also, cut blind rabbets on the outside bottom edge of this board, as shown in the working drawings. These rabbets form hand-holds, so that you can easily open the rolltop. Also, mortise the board for the desk lock. These locks are available from several sources, including the Woodworker's Store, mentioned earlier. Here's another source:

The Wise Company
6503 St. Claude Ave.
Arabi, LA 70032

Attach the lead board to the tambours with canvas strips and glue. When the glue dries, insert the tambours in their grooves from the *bottom front* of the rolltop cabinet. Temporarily, sit the cabinet on the desktop and check the rolltop action. The tambours should slide back easily, stopping just before they disappear under the cabinet top. If everything works as it should, attach the rolltop cabinet to the desktop with metal bracket and screws. *Don't* glue it in place.

> **Tip** ◆ Rub the ends of the tambours with paraffin wax. This will help them slide easier. But, *don't* apply this wax until after you have completely finished the desk.

Making the Pigeonholes

The most intriguing part of a rolltop desk is the tambour door. But, the most useful parts are the pigeonholes, in which to organize bills and correspondence.

The pigeonholes shown here are fairly standard for a large rolltop. At one point, the U.S. Post Office issued guidelines to desk manufacturers, dictating the proper proportions for these pigeonholes. Our design follows these proportions fairly closely. However, if you can think of a better arrangement that suits your own tastes and needs, by all means, build it. The Post Office doesn't need to know.

As you can see, the pigeonholes are just a miniature set of shelves, built from 3/4", 1/2", 1/4", and 1/8" thick wood. All these parts fit together with simple dado or rabbet joints. Cut all the partitions and shelves to follow an arc that matches the curve of the tambour top as it disappears into the cabinet. Make the back of the pigeonholes by 'kerfing' a sheet of 1/4" plywood, then bending this sheet to match the arc. (See Figure 11.)

Position the finished pigeonholes inside the cabinet, and check to see that they don't interfere with the sliding

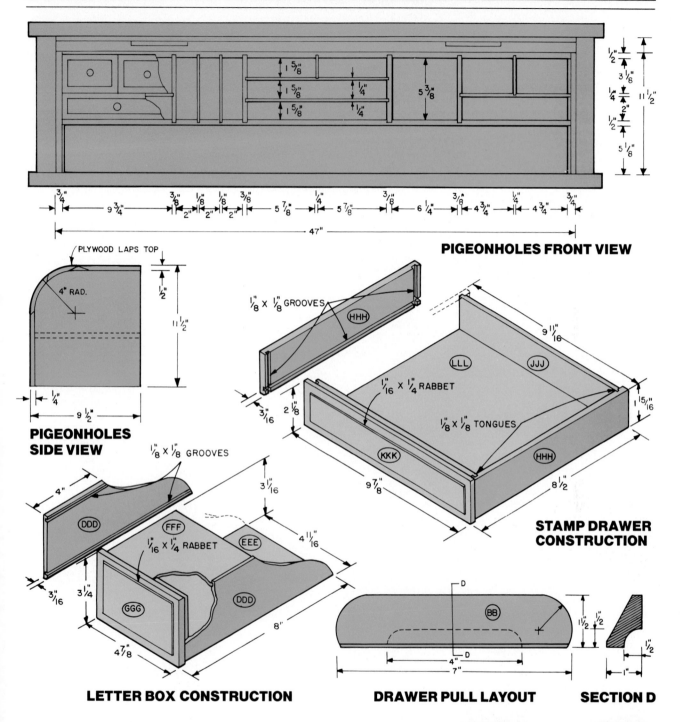

PIGEONHOLES FRONT VIEW

PIGEONHOLES SIDE VIEW

STAMP DRAWER CONSTRUCTION

LETTER BOX CONSTRUCTION

DRAWER PULL LAYOUT

SECTION D

actions of the tambour door. Then, attach the pigeonholes to the rolltop by passing flathead screws through the sides into the lower rails.

Tip ◆ Don't glue the pigeonholes in place. If something goes wrong with the tambour door, you'll want to remove this assembly so that you can fix it.

Some of the pigeonholes are fitted with small drawers, doors, or letter boxes, as shown in the working drawings. The fronts of all these *overlap* the front edges of the pigeonholes. Cut 1/4″ wide, 3/16″ deep rabbets around the front edges of all box, door, and drawer fronts to give them the same 'raised-panel' look as the drawer fronts in the pedestals.

Figure 11. Cut a series of kerfs in the plywood back for the pigeonholes. This will allow you to bend the sheet as needed.

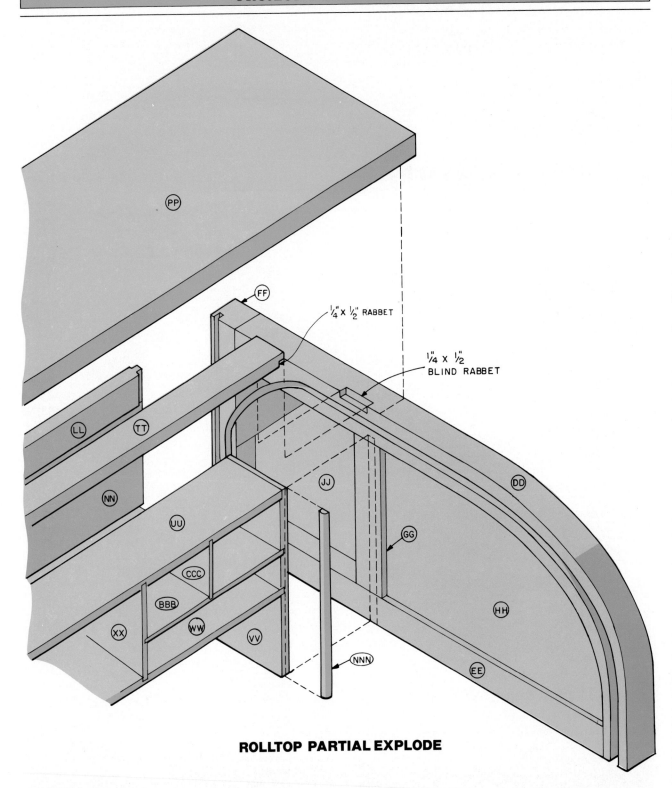

¼" x ½" RABBET

¼" x ½"
BLIND RABBET

ROLLTOP PARTIAL EXPLODE

Finishing Touches

Install all the hardware on the desk — locks, door hinges, and drawer pulls. Mark the desktop where the rolltop lock meets it, and mortise the top for the female portion of the lock. Also, cut any mortises needed in the rails for drawer locks.

The pulls for the drawers in the pedestals are made from wood. These are available from the Woodworker's Store, mentioned earlier, or, you can make your own. Cut a

long strip of wood 3/4" thick and 1-1/2" wide. Mark this wood into 7" lengths, allowing for the saw kerfs. In the middle of each 7" length, cut a 5" long cove with your shaper. (See Figure 12.) Cut the board into 7" lengths, then cut a wedge from the front of each board on your bandsaw. Finally, round the ends.

When you have completed the rolltop, take a minute to admire your handiwork. Then, disassemble the cabinet top, desk top, tambour top, pigeonholes, and pedestals. Remove all the hardware and finish sand all assemblies. If you're working with an open grain wood such as oak, fill it with wood filler. Apply a good building finish to both the inside and the outside of all parts — we recommend spar varnish mixed with tung oil, 1:1. Two or three coats should be adequate; don't build up the finish too thick, especially on the tambours.

When the finish dries, rub the entire project down with #0000 steel wool and paste wax. Reassemble all the parts. Then, fill the drawers and pigeonholes with all the papers you've been keeping in shoeboxes all these years.

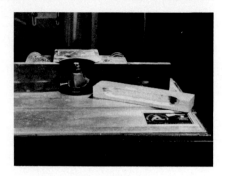

Figure 12. Cut the hand-holds in the wooden drawer pulls with a cove cutter on your shaper. Make the cove at least 1/2″ x 1/2″.

BILL OF MATERIALS — Rolltop Desk

Finished Dimensions in Inches

Pedestals

A.	Legs (8)	1-3/4 x 1-3/4 x 28-3/4
B.	Side Rails (8)	3/4 x 1-3/4 x 28
C.	Side Panels (4)	1/4 x 17-1/4 x 27-3/4
D.	Back Rails (4)	3/4 x 1-3/4 x 12
E.	Back Panels (2)	1/4 x 17-1/4 x 11-3/4
F.	Front Rails (7)	3/4 x 1-3/4 x 12
G.	Bracket Bottoms (14)	3/4 x 1-1/2 x 28-1/2
H.	Bracket Sides (14)	1/2 x 3/4 x 27
J.	Stiffeners (4)	3/4 x 1-3/4 x 20
K.	Middle Back Rails (2)	3/4 x 1-3/4 x 22-1/2
L.	Middle Back Panel	1/4 x 17-1/4 x 22-1/4
M.	Front Middle Rail	3/4 x 1-3/4 x 23
N.	Middle Bracket Bottoms (2)	3/4 x 1 x 29
P.	Middle Bracket Sides (2)	1/4 x 3/4 x 27

Drawers and Shelves

Q.	Small Drawer Sides (8)	3/4 x 5-5/16 x 25-1/4
R.	Small Drawer Ends (8)	3/4 x 5-5/16 x 10-7/8
S.	File Drawer Sides (2)	3/4 x 11-7/16 x 25-1/4
T.	File Drawer Ends (2)	3/4 x 11-7/16 x 10-7/8
U.	Drawer Bottoms (5)	1/4 x 10-1/8 x 25-1/4
V.	Middle Drawer Sides (2)	3/4 x 2-11/16 x 25-1/4
W.	Middle Drawer Ends (2)	3/4 x 3-7/16 x 21-3/8
X.	Middle Drawer Bottom	1/4 x 20-5/8 x 25-1/4
Y.	Sliding Shelves (2)	3/4 x 10-7/8 x 20-3/4
Z.	Shelf Facings (2)	3/4 x 1-3/4 x 10-7/8
AA.	Drawer/Shelf Stops (8)	3/8 dia. x 1″
BB.	Drawer Pulls (6)	1 x 1-1/2 x 7

Rolltop

CC.	Desktop	1-1/4 x 32-1/2 x 52-1/2
DD.	Curved Rails (2)	1-3/4 x 1-3/4 x 29-1/4
EE.	Bottom Rails (2)	1-3/4 x 1-3/4 x 28
FF.	End Stiles (2)	1-3/4 x 1-3/4 x 12-3/4
GG.	Middle Side Stiles (2)	1-3/4 x 1-3/4 x 10-1/4
HH.	Curved Panels (4)	1/4 x 10 x 17-1/4
JJ.	Back Side Panels (2)	1/4 x 9-1/2 x 10
KK.	Corner Blocks (2)	1-1/4 x 5 x 5

LL.	Upper Back Rails (2)	3/4 x 1-3/4 x 48
MM.	Middle Back Stile	3/4 x 3/4 x 10-1/4
NN.	Upper Back Panels	1/4 x 10 x 23-3/8
PP.	Rolltop Top	1-1/4 x 13-1/4 x 52-1/2
QQ.	Tambours (32)	3/8 x 5/8 x 47-3/4
RR.	Lead Board	3/4 x 2 x 47-3/4
SS.	Attachment Strip	5/16 x 5/16 x 47
TT.	Top Brace	5/8 x 2 x 48

Pigeonholes

UU.	Sides (2)	3/4 x 9-1/4 x 11-1/2
VV.	Top Shelf	1/2 x 5-1/4 x 46-1/4
WW.	Bottom Shelf	1/2 x 9-1/4 x 46-1/4
XX.	Dividers (4)	3/8 x 5-7/8 x 9-1/4
YY.	Middle Shelves (2)	1/4 x 9-1/4 x 12-3/8
ZZ.	Middle Shelf Divider	1/4 x 1-7/8 x 9-1/4
AAA.	Letter Partitions (2)	1/8 x 5-7/8 x 9-1/4
BBB.	Letter Box Shelves (2)	1/4 x 9-1/4 x 10
CCC.	Letter Box Dividers (2)	1/4 x 3-3/8 x 9-1/4
DDD.	Letter Box Sides (8)	3/16 x 3-1/6 x 7-3/4
EEE.	Letter Box Bottoms (4)	1/8 x 4-9/16 x 7-3/4
FFF.	Letter Box Tops (4)	1/8 x 4 x 4-9/16
GGG.	Letter Box Fronts (4)	1/2 x 3-1/4 x 4-7/8
HHH.	Stamp Drawer Sides (4)	3/16 x 1-15/16 x 8-1/4
JJJ.	Stamp Drawer Backs (2)	3/16 x 1-15/16 x 9-9/16
KKK.	Stamp Drawer Fronts (2)	1/2 x 2-1/8 x 9-7/8
LLL.	Stamp Drawer Bottoms (2)	1/8 x 8 x 9-9/16
MMM.	Compartment Door	1/2 x 5-1/2 x 6-3/8
NNN.	Pigeonhole Moldings (2)	1/2 x 1/2 x 11-1/2

Hardware

#8 x 1-1/4 Flathead Wood Screws (2 dozen)
#4 x 3/4″ Flathead Wood Screws (6-8)
Small Brackets and Mounting Screws (4-6)
24″ x 48″ Canvas or Heavy Cotton Duck
Small Drawer Pulls (6)
Compartment Lock (optional)
Drawer Locks (optional)
Rolltop Lock

Designed and built by Phil Bacon

Contemporary Cabinet

This modern cabinet serves as an audio or video center, liquor cabinet, or display case for your collectibles.

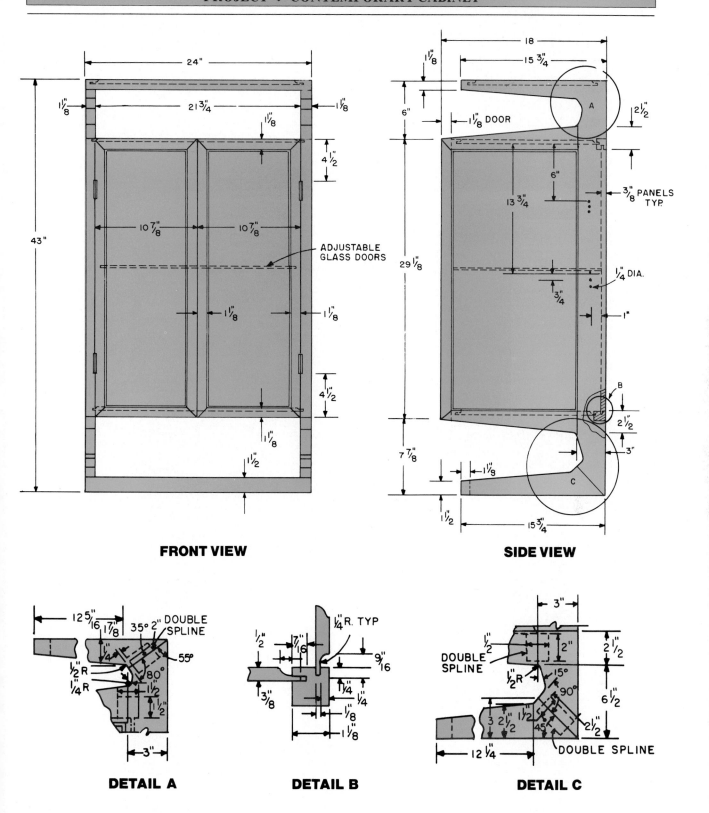

FRONT VIEW

SIDE VIEW

DETAIL A

DETAIL B

DETAIL C

When Phil Bacon was attending the Rochester Institute of Design, his professor assigned his class the task of making either a blanket chest or a liquor cabinet. Unfortunately, Phil would have preferred not to make either one. What he really needed at the time was a rack for his stereo system.

What he came up with was a contemporary cabinet with the versatility to serve as either a dry bar *or* an audio center. If you wish to use it as a liquor cabinet, there is plenty of room underneath the cabinet for bottles, while glasses and condiments can be kept under or on top of the shelf. As a liquor cabinet, the shelf will support a turntable, while an amp fits nicely under the shelf. Inside the cabinet there's room for a tape deck, tapes, and records.

By expanding the width and the depth so that the cabinet could house a portable television, you could also use this cabinet as a video center. There's plenty of extra room for a VCR, video disc player, video game unit, etc.

Cutting the Parts

Once you have settled on a use for Phil's cabinet, decide on the stock. Phil made the frame of the cabinet out of cherry, and the panels out of oak. However, almost any combination of contrasting hardwoods would be attractive —walnut and maple, mahogany and birch, rosewood and teak.

Tip ◆ When mixing woods in a project, make sure that if one wood has a strong grain pattern (such as oak), then the other has a more subtle pattern (such as cherry). If you mix two or three woods, all of which have bold grains, the project design will seem too busy.

Cut the panels from 3/8″ stock. These panels are fitted into 1/8″ grooves in the frame, and are raised 1/4″. Perhaps the easiest way to raise the panels is with a router. Cut a rabbet all the way around the panels first with a straight bit, then make a second pass with a core box bit to form the cove. (See Figure 1 and the working drawings.) Use either a router table or a router arm. If you must use a hand-held router, be certain the panel is clamped securely to the table while you work.

Tip ◆ If you're going to use this cabinet as either an audio or video rack, drill a line of 3/4″ holes near the top of the back panel for ventilation. You'll also have to drill one or more 1-1/4″ holes at other locations in the panel for power cables and speaker wires.

Plane down the stock for the frame parts from 5/4 stock. 'Five-quarters' wood isn't an off-the-rack thickness that you can pick up at any lumberyard, but most large suppliers of hardwoods will carry it. Or you may be able to have a sawmill custom cut it for you. If you can't find it in your area, resaw 1-1/2″ stock.

Cut the square ends of the framing parts, then taper those parts that need it. There are several ways to taper a board, but perhaps the quickest and the most accurate is to use a tapering jig on your table saw. (See Figure 2.) Be sure to plainly mark the flat or 'un-tapered sides'. You will need to refer to these marks from time to time when cutting other joints or assembling the pieces.

Next, make the miters. All the miters in this project are cut at 45°, with one notable exception — where the shelf ends and the sides come together. The shelf ends are cut at 35°, and the top ends of the sides are cut at 55°. (Refer to the working drawings.) When cutting the miters, be sure that you have positioned the flat, *un-tapered* side of the framing piece against the fence or miter gauge.

Figure 2. The easiest way to cut the tapers in the framing pieces is to use a tapering jig on your table saw.

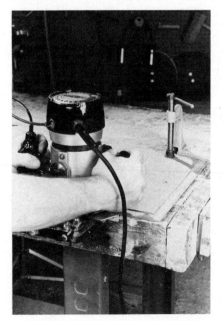

Figure 1. Make the cove cut on the raised panels with a core box bit. If you're using a hand-held router, be sure the panel is clamped securely to your workbench.

Figure 3. Cut the tenons in the stretchers with a dado cutter. A stop block helps you cut the tenon to the proper length.

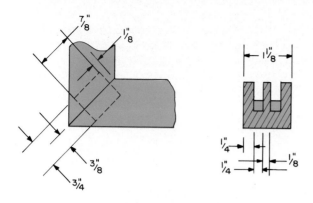

TYPICAL DOUBLE SPLINE DETAIL

holes with a chisel. If you have a horizontal boring machine, or a multipurpose tool with the horizontal boring mode, you can accomplish this task without making a sliding jig — just use the worktable and the miter gauge. (See Figure 5.)

Phil made a jig for his router table. A guide board holds the work at the proper angle, while a stop block determines the length of the dado. To use this setup, lower the framing piece carefully onto a 1/4″ plunge-cut straight bit, then slide the guide board forward until it stops. (See Figure 6.) Whatever method you decide to use, remember that *most* of the dadoes are cut in simple 45° mitered faces, but you'll have to adjust your jig and/or your tools to cut the pieces that are mitered at 35° and 55°.

Saw the splines from 1/4″ cherry, and temporarily put the framing parts together to check the fit. Remember that

> **Tip** ◆ *Do not* try to cut out the shapes where the sides join the base ends and shelf ends right now. Wait until *after* you've actually joined these pieces.

Cut the mortises in the frame parts with a mortising attachment for your drill press, or by drilling a series of holes and then squaring up the sides with a chisel. *Do not* cut the mortises for the back top stretcher, not just yet. This mortise straddles the miter joint between the shelf end and the sides, and must be cut *after* these pieces are assembled. However, you can cut all the tenons in the stretchers at this time. Use a dado attachment on your table saw or radial arm saw. (See Figure 3.)

Make the spline dadoes in the mitered ends of the sides, shelf ends, base ends, shelf front, and base front. There are several ways to make these joints, and most of them require that you build a jig for your power tools. Perhaps the easiest way is to turn your drill press table vertically, and make a sliding jig to hold the pieces while you drill a double line of holes. (See Figure 4.) Afterwards, clean up the edges of the

Figure 5. You can also cut the spline dadoes on a horizontal boring machine.

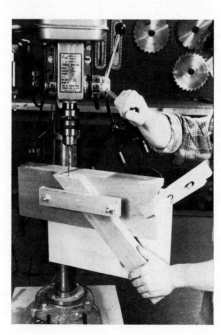

Figure 4. To cut the spline dadoes on your drill press, first make a sliding jig to hold the framing pieces. Then drill a double line of 1/4″ holes. Clean up the sides of the holes with a chisel.

Figure 6. If you use a router table to cut the spline dadoes, you'll have to make a jig to hold the framing pieces and stop the cut when the dado reaches the proper length. Use a 1/4″ plunge-cut straight bit.

the grain of the splines should run perpendicular to the face of the miter.

While you've got the frames together, mark the sides that will hold the panels. Then disassemble the framing pieces, and cut the panel grooves. These 1/8″ grooves can be easily made with a table saw blade. Note that some grooves are cut 7/16″ deep, while others need only be 1/4″ deep. The reason for this is that wood moves *across* the grain to a much greater degree than it does with the grain. A 12″ wide oak panel may expand or contract up to 1/4″ across the grain with changes in humidity and temperature, but it will barely move 1/64″ with the grain.

To make sure that one side of a panel doesn't slip out of a groove as it contracts, Phil includes 'panel centering' dowels in his design. Drill 1/8″ holes in the panel grooves where needed, then notch the panel for the dowels. It is quite important that you fit these dowels to the shelf, side, back, top, and bottom panels, since these are quite wide. However, they are optional on the door panels.

Finally drill 1/4″ holes, spaced 1″ apart in the inside of the sides and stiles. These holes will be used to hang the glass shelves on the inside of the cabinet.

Assembly

As you begin the assembly, remember to go through a dry run first, to be sure that all parts fit correctly. Hold the pieces together temporarily with web clamps or bar clamps and work out all the problems *before* you start to actually glue up the parts.

Put together the two side assemblies first. Be careful *not* to glue the panels in place. These must 'float' freely in the frames so that they can expand and contract. After the glue has set up, cut the shapes near the bottom and top of the sides. Drill 1/2″ holes at each bend to make the 1/4″ radii, then bandsaw in between the holes. (See Figure 7.) Also, make the mortises for the upper back stretcher.

Assemble the remaining stretchers, ends, and panels to the cabinet sides. Check that the cabinet is square after you clamp it up, and adjust the clamps if it is not. While the glue is drying on the cabinet, put together the door frames.

Mortise the door frames and the cabinet frame stile to accept the door hinges. You'll also have to cut mortises for the ball catches. Finally, drill holes in the cabinet base to accept four T-nuts and levelers. The butt hinges are available at most hardware stores, and all the other hardware you need for this project is available from:

Craft Products Company
2200 Dean Street
St. Charles, IL 60174

Tip ◆ Since there are no cabinet door handles on this project, you might consider using magnetic Tutch Latches® inside of ball catches. These ingenious catches open the door for you after you gently press against the door front.

Have the glass shelves custom made at a glass shop. You could use acrylic plastic and cut the notches yourself, but plastic scratches easily as you take things on and off the shelves. Hang the shelves on movable shelving supports. (See Figure 8.) These little ledges fit in the 1/4″ holes you drilled in the sides and stiles.

How you finish this cabinet will depend on what you want to use it for. If you're using it as a liquor cabinet, you'll probably want to apply some sort of a water-proof 'building' finish, such as spar varnish, so that you can easily wipe up spills. If you're using it to store electronic components, apply a 'penetrating' finish — Danish oil, for example — that won't be affected by the heat. Whatever finish you use, be certain to apply just as many coats to the inside of the cabinet as you do to the outside. Otherwise, the panels may warp.

Figure 7. Cut the shapes near the top and bottom of the sides by drilling 1/2″ holes, then cutting between those holes on a bandsaw.

Figure 8. Hang the glass shelves on movable shelving supports. These supports fit into 1/4″ holes drilled on the inside of the cabinet.

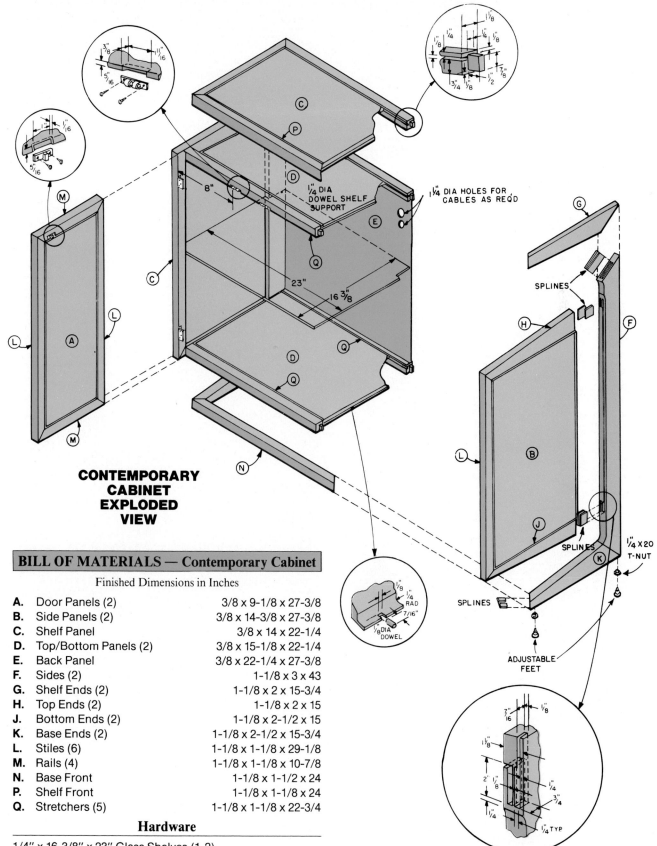

**CONTEMPORARY
CABINET
EXPLODED
VIEW**

BILL OF MATERIALS — Contemporary Cabinet

Finished Dimensions in Inches

A.	Door Panels (2)	3/8 x 9-1/8 x 27-3/8
B.	Side Panels (2)	3/8 x 14-3/8 x 27-3/8
C.	Shelf Panel	3/8 x 14 x 22-1/4
D.	Top/Bottom Panels (2)	3/8 x 15-1/8 x 22-1/4
E.	Back Panel	3/8 x 22-1/4 x 27-3/8
F.	Sides (2)	1-1/8 x 3 x 43
G.	Shelf Ends (2)	1-1/8 x 2 x 15-3/4
H.	Top Ends (2)	1-1/8 x 2 x 15
J.	Bottom Ends (2)	1-1/8 x 2-1/2 x 15
K.	Base Ends (2)	1-1/8 x 2-1/2 x 15-3/4
L.	Stiles (6)	1-1/8 x 1-1/8 x 29-1/8
M.	Rails (4)	1-1/8 x 1-1/8 x 10-7/8
N.	Base Front	1-1/8 x 1-1/2 x 24
P.	Shelf Front	1-1/8 x 1-1/8 x 24
Q.	Stretchers (5)	1-1/8 x 1-1/8 x 22-3/4

Hardware

1/4" x 16-3/8" x 23" Glass Shelves (1-2)
2" x 1-1/2" Butt Hinges and Mounting Screws (2 pair)
Ball Cabinet Catches and Mounting Screws (2)
Movable Shelving Supports (8)

This project first appeared in The Woodworker's Journal,
September/October 1984.

Designed and built by Nick Engler

Jacob's Ladder

This traditional folk toy provides hours of entertainment — even for adults!

I wish I had a nickel for every one of these 'Jacob's Ladders' I've made for my younger friends. Better yet, I wish I had one of the Jacob's Ladders. This is one children's toy that you hate to give away. I usually compensate by spending a few hours "breaking it in" after I've made it, then delaying until the last possible minute before wrapping it up.

The toy is so intriguing perhaps because it's so simple. A small clothespin-like 'angel' bounces and bumps down the ladder in a most un-heavenly manner. If you have two angels, they can race. With three angels, the action becomes positively addicting.

To make the ladder, cut two 1/4″ grooves in the edges of a scrap board. Then rip 1/2″ wide strips from each edge. (See Figure 1.) These grooved strips will become the rails for the ladder. Fasten the rungs in the grooves with glue and small brads. (See Figure 2.)

Cut and drill the angels as shown in the working drawings. Then begin to carefully 'fit' the angels to the ladder —slightly round the rungs of the ladder, smooth the slots in the clothespins, widen the chamfers at the bottom of the slots. It will take some patience and some handwork to get everything just right. But when you're finished, the results will be worth it.

ANGEL DETAIL

2 3/4"
15/16" 7/8" 15/16"
11/32"
5/16"
1"
11/32"
7/16" DIA.
CHAMFER AT 45°

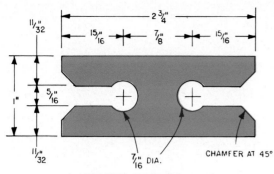

SAMPLE ANGELS

Figure 1. Cut two grooves in the edge of a board, then rip strips from the board. These strips will form the ladder rails.

Figure 2. Fasten the rungs in the grooves with glue and brads. The brads will keep the rungs from slipping out of position should the glue bond ever weaken.

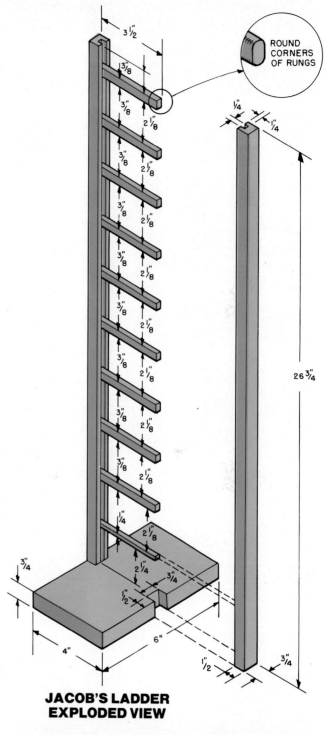

ROUND CORNERS OF RUNGS

3 1/2"
3/8"
3/8"
2 1/8"
3/8"
2 1/8"
3/8"
2 1/8"
3/8"
2 1/8"
3/8"
2 1/8"
3/8"
2 1/8"
3/8"
2 1/8"
3/8"
2 1/8"
1/4"
2 1/8"
3/4"
2 1/4"
2 1/4"
3/4"
1/2"
4"
6"
1/2"

1/4"
1/4"
26 3/4"
3/4"

**JACOB'S LADDER
EXPLODED VIEW**

BILL OF MATERIALS — Jacob's Ladder	
Finished Dimensions in Inches	
A. Ladder Rails (2)	1/2 x 3/4 x 26-3/4
B. Ladder Rungs (9)	1/4 x 3/8 x 3-1/2
C. Bottom Rung	1/4 x 1/4 x 3-1/2
D. Base	3/4 x 4 x 6
E. Angels (2-3)	1 x 1 x 2-1/2

Hardware

5/8" Wire Brads (20)

Designed and built by Judy Ditmer

Infant Organizer

Here's a baby's chest designed with Mom and Dad in mind.

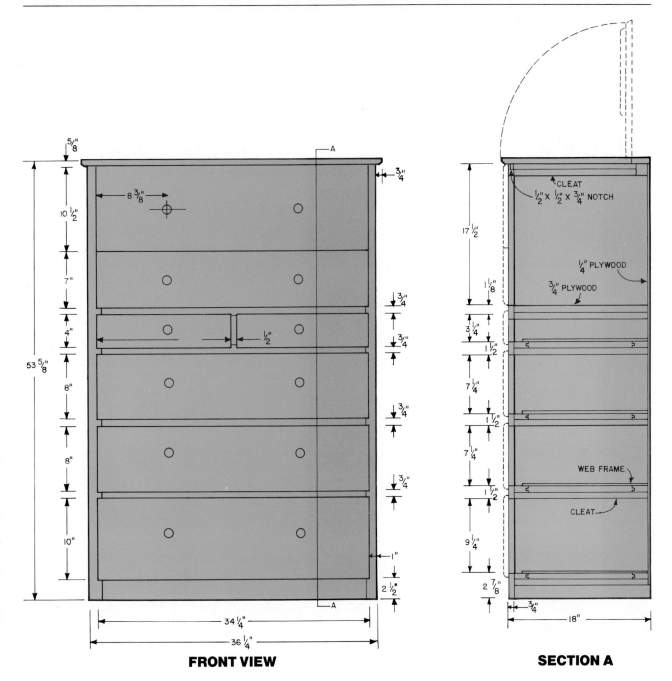

FRONT VIEW

SECTION A

Once upon a time — not so very long ago — a very organized young business woman gave birth to a daughter. She was very fond of her daughter, but she was also fond of her job. So she decided to take her daughter to work with her, at least while her daughter was very young and needed her every hour on the hour.

Now, there's nothing like a baby to disorganize your life. Many of us have had a lot to do with babies, and a good many more of us have actually been babies. So you all know what I'm talking about. This young business woman's office looked like an explosion in a diaper factory.

Fortunately, this story has a happy ending. The new mother commissioned Judy Ditmer, a designer and builder of one-of-a-kind furniture, to clean up the mess. Judy's solution was this ingenious 'Infant Organizer'. It looks like a handsome chest of drawers, but the top folds out to make a changing tray for the infant. And there's plenty of room beneath the tray to hide diapers, bottles, toys, and all that baby stuff. Just close the lid and you hardly know there's a baby around — until he or she needs to be changed again.

Making the Case

For the most part, this project is built like a traditional chest of drawers. Web frames and side panels form a case for five drawers of different sizes. Only the top of the chest departs from normal construction procedures.

Start by cutting and assembling the web frames. The web frame stiles have tenons that fit into grooves in the web frame rails, as shown in the working drawings. Three of the dust panels have a single stile in the center, the fourth — the frame that supports the two small drawers — has two extra

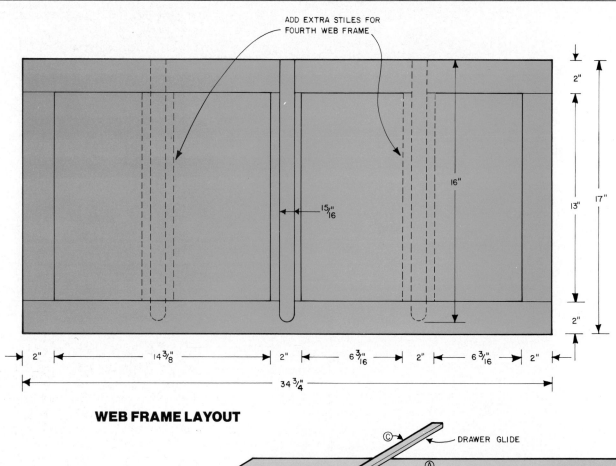

ADD EXTRA STILES FOR
FOURTH WEB FRAME

WEB FRAME LAYOUT

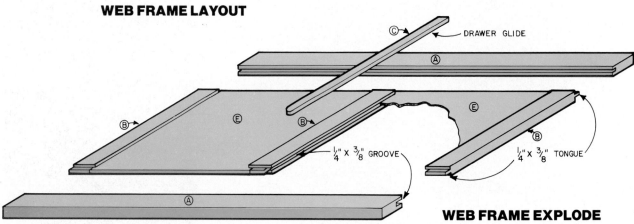

DRAWER GLIDE

1/4" x 3/8" GROOVE

1/4" x 3/8" TONGUE

WEB FRAME EXPLODE

Figure 1. If you wish, you can insert dust shields in the web frames, as shown. These are optional.

stiles. Judy cut grooves in the stiles as well as the rails so that she could install dust shields in the top three frames. (See Figure 1.) However, these dust shields are optional.

Each web frame is fitted with one or more drawer glides. While the frames can be made from inexpensive pine, the glides will get quite a bit of wear and tear. Therefore, they should be made of something harder — rock maple, oak, or beech.

While the glue on the web frames is drying, make the side panels and changing tray. Judy elected to use solid wood for these parts, but you might give considerable thought to using veneered plywood. Eighteen-inch wide planks of solid wood will expand and contract 1/4″ or more with changes in humidity. Plywood is more stable.

Fortunately, the joinery allows for wood movement. As you make the cleats that hold the frames to the side panels, notice that they all have one slotted hole. This lets

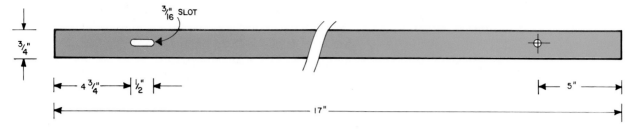

3/16" SLOT

3/4"

4 3/4"   1/2"   5"

17"

CLEAT LAYOUT

the wood in the case change shape without warping or checking. (See Figure 2.)

Attach the cleats to the side panels with roundhead wood screws, but *don't* glue them in place. Then attach the web frames to the cleats with flathead wood screws. Attach the changing tray to the cleat with roundhead screws that pass up through the cleats and into the tray from *underneath*. This way, you won't have to cover any screw holes.

> **Tip ◆** If you make the changing tray out of solid wood, the screw holes in the cleat must also be slotted. Refer to the working drawings.

Clamp facing rails to the fronts of the web frames so the tops of the rails are flush with the top surface of the frame. Then clamp the facing stiles in place, and mark for dowel joints. Drill the dowel holes in the ends of the rails and the edges of the stiles with a doweling jig. Then reassemble the facing rails and stiles with glue and dowels, and glue the entire frame to the front of the case.

> **Tip ◆** If you have a milling attachment for your drill press, you'll find that this makes a super-accurate doweling jig. (See Figure 3.)

To finish the case, install the back panel in the rabbets in the rear of the sides. This panel must also fit flush against the web frames, as shown in the drawings. Use cabinet-grade veneered plywood, good on one side, for this piece. The back will be seen frequently, every time you open the top to expose the changing tray.

Fitting the Drawers

The drawer construction and materials are unique. Judy elected to use a highly figured wood — bird's-eye maple — on the drawer fronts. This stock was given to her by the woman who commissioned the project, a slab of wood that had belonged to the baby's grandfather, who was also a woodworker. As you can see, the maple is beautiful. Unfortunately, there wasn't enough of it to build the entire piece. Judy decided to save it for the drawer faces and doors *only*.

The drawer fronts, backs, and sides are made from inexpensive pine, like the web frames. Attach the drawer fronts to the sides with 1/4" finger joints, and set the drawer backs in the sides with simple dadoes. These dadoes should be at least 1/2" forward from the rear of the drawer sides. The reason for this inset is that if you attach the drawer back flush with the sides, and the back warps; then the drawer may not fit properly. (See Figure 4.)

There's some more joinery to worry about: Fit the drawer bottom in a groove that runs around the front, back

Figure 2. The cleats have one slotted hole to allow the wood on the side of the case to expand and contract with changes in humidity and temperature. Make these slots with a router.

Figure 3. If you have a milling attachment for your drill press, you can use it as a doweling jig. The drill press table must be rotated to the vertical position in order to drill end grain.

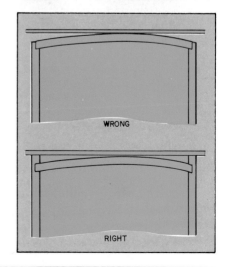

Figure 4. The drawer backs should be set slightly forward from the rear of the case, *not* up against it. If the backs butt against the case and they happen to warp or bow, the drawers will no longer fit properly.

WRONG

RIGHT

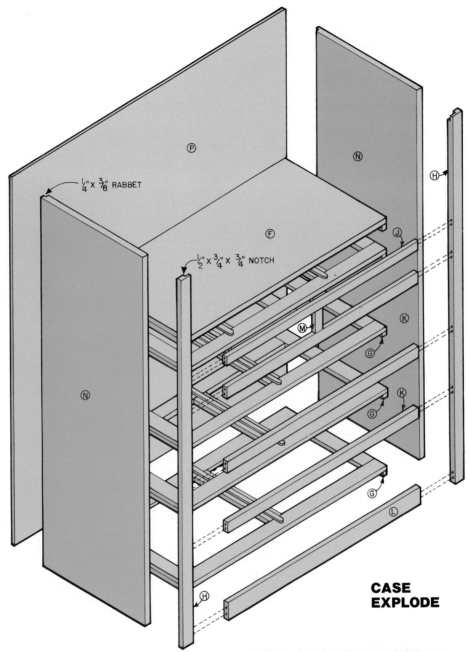

$\frac{1}{4}" \times \frac{3}{8}"$ RABBET

$\frac{1}{2}" \times \frac{3}{4}" \times \frac{3}{4}"$ NOTCH

**CASE
EXPLODE**

and sides. And notch the underside of the drawer back to match the groove in the drawer guides. These guides are glued underneath the drawer bottoms as shown in the working drawings. They fit over the drawer glides and keep the drawer properly aligned when you push it in or pull it out.

Tip ◆ Consider making the drawer bottoms out of 1/4″ cedar closet lining. It's not expensive, and it keeps the baby's things smelling fresh.

When you've assembled the drawers, cut the drawer faces 1/2″ bigger than the drawer fronts all the way around. Chamfer the edges of the fronts on the jointer. (See Figure 5). Then attach them to the drawers with glue and screws. Be sure to sink the screws from *inside* the drawers, so the screwheads don't show. When you fit the drawers in the case, the drawer faces should overlap the front rails and stiles.

Figure 5. Chamfer the edge of the drawer fronts and doors on a jointer.

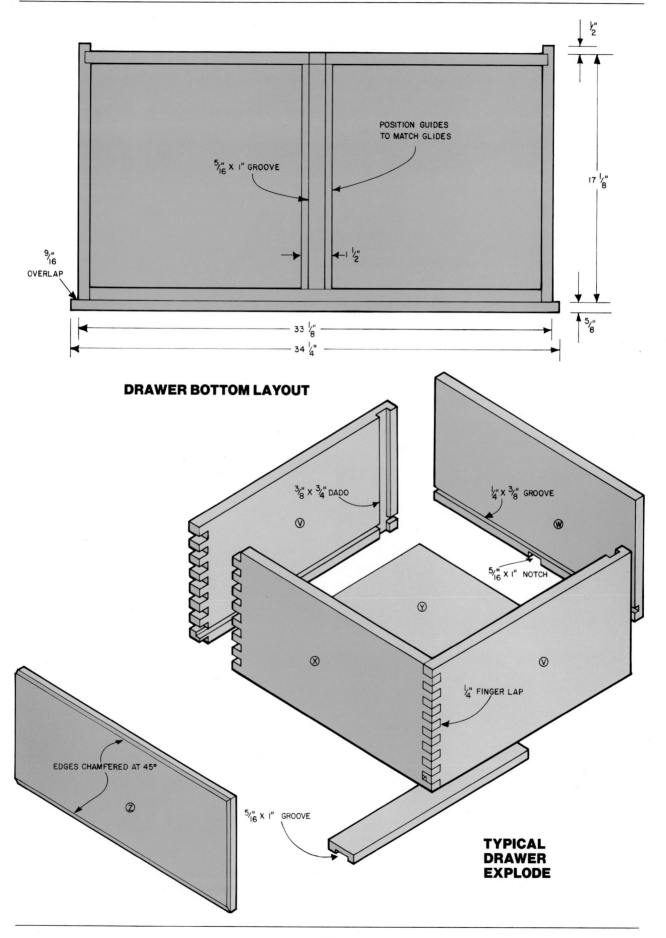

DRAWER BOTTOM LAYOUT

POSITION GUIDES
TO MATCH GLIDES

$\frac{5}{16}$" X 1" GROOVE

$1\frac{1}{2}$"

$\frac{1}{2}$"

$17\frac{1}{8}$"

$\frac{9}{16}$"
OVERLAP

$33\frac{1}{8}$"

$34\frac{1}{4}$"

$\frac{5}{8}$"

$\frac{3}{8}$" X $\frac{3}{4}$" DADO

$\frac{1}{4}$" X $\frac{3}{8}$" GROOVE

$\frac{5}{16}$" X 1" NOTCH

$\frac{1}{4}$" FINGER LAP

Ⓥ

Ⓦ

Ⓨ

Ⓧ

Ⓥ

EDGES CHAMFERED AT 45°

Ⓩ

$\frac{5}{16}$" X 1" GROOVE

TYPICAL
DRAWER
EXPLODE

After you are certain that the drawers fit the case properly, install small blocks or 'kickers' underneath each web frame, just above the drawer sides. (Refer to the working drawings.) These kickers keep the drawers from tilting forward when you pull them out.

Fitting the Doors

What appear to be drawer fronts on the top of the chest are actually two doors. The top lifts up, and the upper door folds back and rests on cleats attached to the sides. The lower door folds out to extend the working space of the changing tray. (See Figure 6.)

To fit these doors, you first need to attach the side cleats and the top brace. Also, notice that the facing stiles have a blind notch on the *inside*. The upper door has matching notches on both upper corners. The notches on the doors fit around the blind notches in the stiles when the doors are folded back. To make a blind notch, rout out the stock with a router, then square the corners with a chisel. (See Figure 7.)

Attach the top flush with the back of the case, then hinge the lid to the top. Attach friction lid supports to *both* sides of the lid so that it won't bang down on your head — or the baby's — when it's in the raised position.

Hold the upper door in place and mark where it meets the lid. Then remove the lid and attach the upper door to it

with a piano hinge. Replace the lid with the door attached and check the action. The door should lay flat against the front of the case, then fold back and slip easily into the rabbet.

Important: The upper corners of the upper door have to be notched slightly to fit around the end on the blind rabbet. Without these notches, the upper door will *not* fold back into the rabbets in the sides. Refer to the working drawings.

Hinge the lower door to the changing tray with butler's tray hinges. (See Figure 8.) These hinges are especially designed so that they will hold a board vertical or horizontal to the floor with no need for catches, folding braces, etc. When the lower door is properly fitted, glue a small facing strip to the inside. This facing strip matches the other facing rails, and makes the doors look like the other drawer front. It also serves as a lip for the changing tray. By the way, butler's tray hinges are available through the mail from:

The Woodworker's Store
21801 Industrial Blvd.
Rogers, MN 55374

Woodworker's Supply
5604 Alameda N.E.
Albuquerque, MN 87113

Finishing Up

How you finish this piece is pretty much up to you. You'll probably want to make pads for the changing tray, as shown in the photo. You'll probably want to apply some sort of water-resistant, washable finish with low toxicity — tung oil mixed with varnish is a good choice.

But there's one finish touch that's not an option; it's a must. You *must* install a safety strap. If you have to leave the baby on the changing tray, even for a moment, it must be strapped in so that it can't roll off. These straps can be easily made from belt webbing and friction buckles — a Cub Scout belt makes an attractive safety harness that's easy to fasten and unfasten.

Judy Ditmer is the proprietor of Heartwood, a woodworking studio in Tipp City, Ohio. She asked us to remind our readers that the design for the infant organizer is her copyrighted property. Judy has kindly allowed Popular Science to publish the design so that you may reproduce it for your own use or as a gift. Readers are warned that reproduction for sale or profit is forbidden by law.

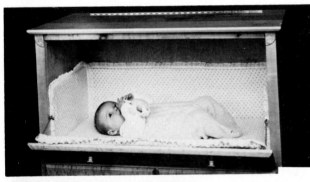

Figure 6. The upper door folds up into the case and sits in a rabbet, while the lower door folds out to extend the working space.

Figure 7. To make a blind notch, rout out as much stock as you can with a router, then square the corner with a hand chisel.

Figure 8. Butler's tray hinges will hold a piece of wood in either a vertical or horizontal position with no need for any other hardware.

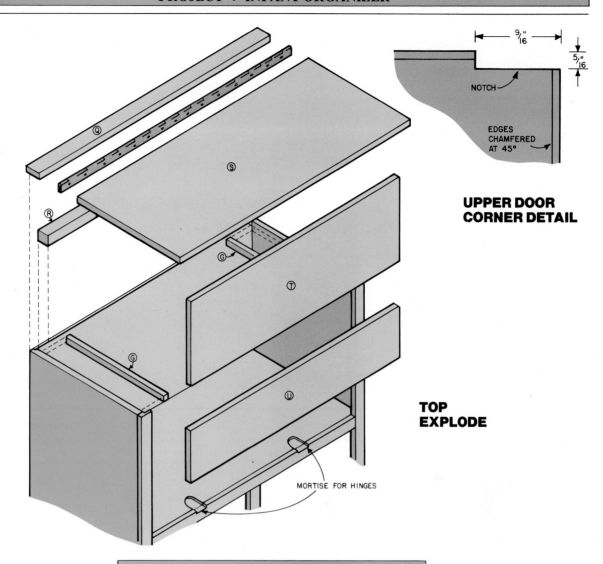

UPPER DOOR CORNER DETAIL

NOTCH

EDGES CHAMFERED AT 45°

TOP EXPLODE

MORTISE FOR HINGES

BILL OF MATERIALS — Infant Organizer

Finished Dimensions in Inches

A.	Web Frame Rails (8)	3/4 x 2 x 34-3/4
B.	Web Frame Stiles (14)	3/4 x 2 x 13-3/4
C.	Drawer Guides (5)	1/4 x 15/16 x 16
D.	Small Dust Shields (2)	1/4 x 6-7/8 x 13-5/8
E.	Large Dust Shields (6)	1/4 x 13-5/8 x 15
F.	Tray	3/4 x 17 x 34-3/4
G.	Cleats (12)	3/4 x 3/4 x 17
H.	Facing Stiles (2)	3/4 x 1-1/2 x 53
J.	Top Facing Rail	3/4 x 1-1/8 x 33-1/4
K.	Middle Facing Rails (3)	3/4 x 1-1/2 x 33-1/4
L.	Bottom Facing Rail	3/4 x 2-7/8 x 33-1/4
M.	Short Facing Stile	3/4 x 1-1/2 x 3-1/4
N.	Sides (2)	3/4 x 17-1/4 x 53
P.	Back	1/4 x 35-1/2 x 53
Q.	Top	5/8 x 2 x 37-3/4
R.	Top Brace	1-1/2 x 1-1/2 x 34-3/4
S.	Lid	5/8 x 16-5/8 x 37-3/4
T.	Top Door	5/8 x 10-1/2 x 34-1/4
U.	Bottom Door	5/8 x 7 x 34-1/4
V.	Top Drawer Sides (4)	3/4 x 3-1/8 x 17-5/8
W.	Top Drawer Backs (2)	3/4 x 3-1/8 x 15
X.	Top Drawer Fronts (2)	3/4 x 3-1/8 x 15-3/4
Y.	Top Drawer Bottoms (2)	1/4 x 15 x 16-3/8
Z.	Top Drawer Faces (2)	5/8 x 4 x 16-7/8
AA.	Middle Drawer Sides (4)	3/4 x 7-1/8 x 17-5/8
BB.	Middle Drawer Backs (2)	3/4 x 7-1/8 x 32-3/8
CC.	Middle Drawer Fronts (2)	3/4 x 7-1/8 x 33-1/8
DD.	Middle Drawer Faces (2)	5/8 x 8 x 34-1/4
DD.	Bottom Drawer Sides (2)	3/4 x 9-1/8 x 17-5/8
EE.	Bottom Drawer Back	3/4 x 9-1/8 x 32-3/8
FF.	Bottom Drawer Front	3/4 x 9-1/8 x 33-1/8
GG.	Bottom Drawer Face	5/8 x 10 x 34-1/4
HH.	Drawer Bottoms (3)	1/4 x 32-3/8 x 16-3/8
JJ.	Drawer Glides (5)	1/2 x 1-1/2 x 15-5/8

Hardware

Drawer Pulls (12)
Butler Tray Hinges (1 pair)
#8 x 1-1/4" Flathead Wood Screws (6-12)
#10 x 1-1/4" Roundhead Wood Screws and Washers (2 dozen)
Lid Supports (2)
1-1/2" x 33" Piano Hinge
1-1/2 x 36-1/4" Piano Hinge
Infant Safety Strap

Designed and built by Nick Engler

Rocking Lawn Chair

This collection of sticks forms an ingenious chair that looks good indoors or out.

Some projects are a delight to make because they're so clever. This rocking lawn chair is doubly so. It's delightful because it's so simple to make — it's really just a collection of 1x2's with the simplest of joinery. And it's a delight to use. You'll have trouble believing that a pile of sticks could be so comfortable and soothing to sit in.

Cutting and Shaping the Sticks

Start by ripping the stock. A single chair requires about 258 linear inches of stock 1-3/4″ wide, 44 inches of stock 3-1/2″ wide, and 36 inches of stock 4″ wide. You may have to cut more than this, depending on the length of the boards you're ripping.

We suggest you use a good hardwood, such as oak, maple, or beech for this project. Remember, these slender sticks must support your weight. If you'd rather use softwood, increase the width of the front and back stretchers somewhat.

Drill 1/4″ holes in each piece, as shown in the working drawings. Tape all 'double' parts together and pad drill them — this helps assure that both sides of the project are exactly the same. (See Figure 1.) Using a dado accessory on your table saw, make 1/4″ x 3/4″ rabbets on both ends of the braces, headrest, and footrest. Enlarge the pattern for the arm and cut it on a bandsaw. Finally, round the corners of the stretchers, struts, armrest, and arm where indicated in the drawings. (See Figure 2.)

And that's it for joinery! There's nothing left to do but assemble the pieces.

> **Tip ◆** To save time and work, sand all parts after you shape and drill them, but *before* you assemble them.

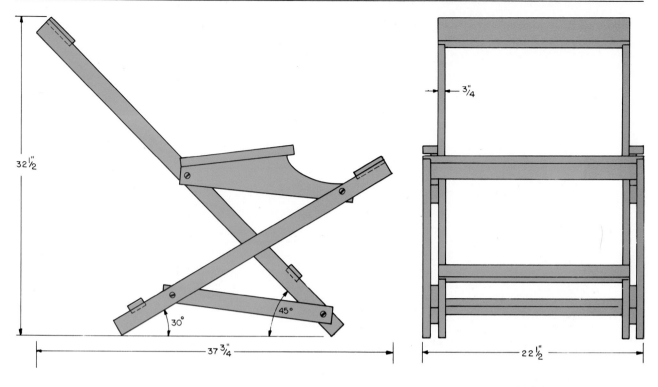

SIDE VIEW

FRONT VIEW

Assembling the Sticks

The chair is actually two frames hinged together by the arms and struts. You want to assemble the frames first, then add the other parts.

Assemble the 'inside' frame by attaching the headrest and the front brace to the back stretcher, as shown in the working drawings. Make the outside frame by assembling the front stretcher, footrest, and back brace in the same manner. Use #8 x 1-1/4″ flathead wood screws for these assemblies, but *do not* glue the headrest or footrest to the stretchers. You'll need to remove these parts in a later step.

Attach the armrests permanently to the arms. Then bolt the arms and struts *between* the frames, as shown in the drawings. (See Figure 3.) Use 1/4″ x 2″ flathead stove bolts and self-locking nuts. Countersink the head of the bolt on the inside of the frames, and put the nuts toward the outside,

Figure 1. Pad drill the matching or 'double' parts (such as the stretchers) to insure that both sides of this project are exactly the same.

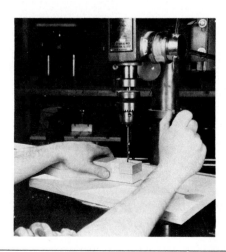

Figure 2. Round the corners of the stretchers, struts, armrests, and arms with a disc sander. Also, round over all hard edges.

Figure 3. Bolt the chair together, inserting the struts and arms between the inside and outside frames.

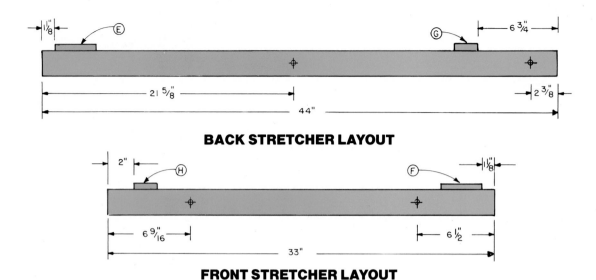

BACK STRETCHER LAYOUT

FRONT STRETCHER LAYOUT

where they won't interfere with you getting in and out of the chair. (See Figure 4.) Put at least two washers between the frame and the arms or struts, so that all parts pivot smoothly without rubbing.

> **Tip ◆** Don't tighten the nuts too tight on the bolts. This will cause the parts to bind.

When you've assembled all the parts and you're sure the frames rock together correctly, apply a liberal coat of a penetrating finish such as tung oil or Danish oil. *Don't* use varnish or polyurethane; that will just gum up the pivots.

Making the Seat

While you're waiting for the finish to dry, sew the sling seat (or get someone you know to sew the seat). This is sewing at its simplest — all you need is a long strip of cloth with two loops on either end. Use a brightly colored canvas duck or some other heavy material. If you wish, you can also make a small pillow to cover the headrest.

Remove the headrest and the footrest, insert them in the loops on the sling seat, and reattach them to the frames. (See Figure 5.) If you've elected to make a pillow, attach it to the top of the headrest with upholstery tacks.

And that's it! What could be easier? Or more comfortable?

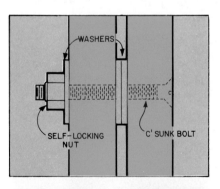

Figure 4. Each pivot joint is held together with a flat-head bolt and self-locking nut. Countersink the head of the bolt toward the inside of the stretcher, and put two washers between the stretcher and the other part.

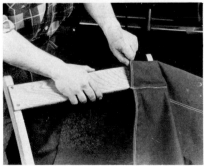

Figure 5. Hang the sling seat on the chair by inserting the headrest and footrest through the loops you've sewn in the cloth.

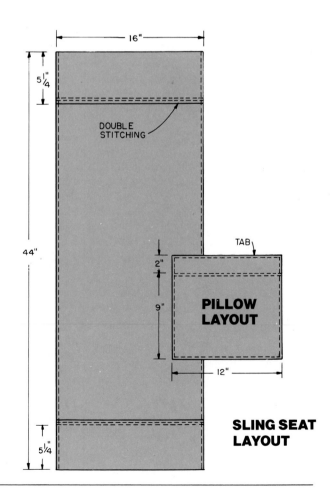

SLING SEAT LAYOUT

PILLOW LAYOUT

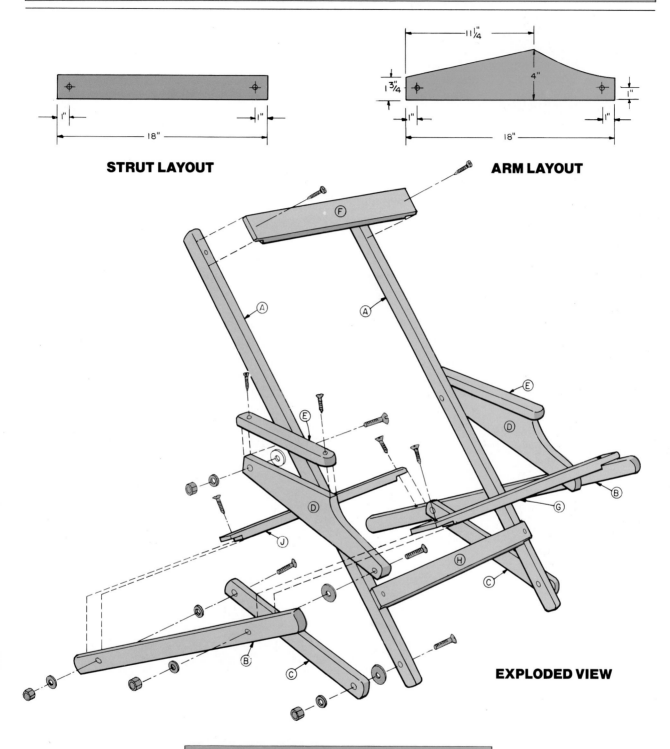

STRUT LAYOUT

ARM LAYOUT

EXPLODED VIEW

BILL OF MATERIALS — Rocking Lawn Chair

Finished Dimensions in Inches

A.	Back Stretcher (2)	3/4 x 1-3/4 x 44
B.	Front Stretcher (2)	3/4 x 1-3/4 x 33
C.	Struts (2)	3/4 x 1-3/4 x 18
D.	Arms (2)	3/4 x 4 x 18
E.	Armrests (2)	3/4 x 1-3/4 x 12
F.	Headrest	3/4 x 3-1/2 x 19
G.	Footrest	3/4 x 3-1/2 x 22-1/2
H.	Front Brace	3/4 x 1-3/4 x 19
J.	Back Brace	3/4 x 1-3/4 x 22-1/2

Hardware

Heavy Cotton Duck (1 to 1-1/2 yards depending on width of bolt)

#8 x 1-1/4″ Flathead Wood Screws (16)

1/4″ x 2″ Flathead Stove Bolts (8)

1/4″ Self-Locking Nuts (8)

1/4″ Washers (24)

Shredded Foam Rubber (optional — for pillow)

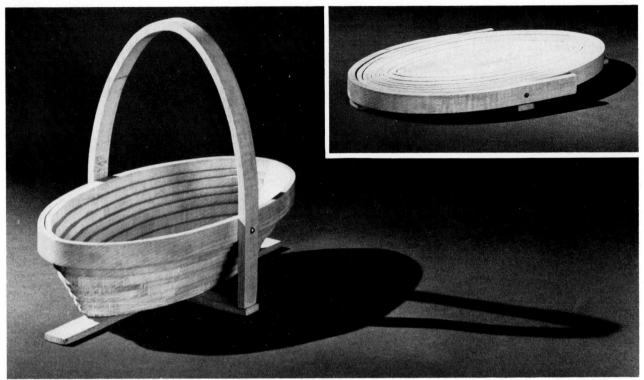

Designed and built by Nick Engler

Folding Basket

Use an old turner's trick to make this curious basket.

Y ou've probably seen the 'drinking cup' trick illustrated in books on lathe turning. Or perhaps you've tried it yourself.

To perform this trick, cut concentric rings from a board with the worktable of your jigsaw set at a slight angle. If you pull these rings apart from the 'top', where the tops of the rings are at their largest diameter, the rings come apart easily. But if you try to pull them apart from the *bottom*, where the rings are smaller due to the cut angle, the rings will wedge against each other forming a cup shape. (See Figure 1.) If you want to turn this shape, you can glue the rings together permanently.

You can also use a variation on this trick to make the collapsible basket you see here. First, cut the curved handle, 1/4″ thick, from an oval-shaped board. Then, instead of cutting concentric rings, cut a *spiral* in the board, with the jigsaw table tilted at 3°. (See Figure 2.) Each turn of the spiral should be approximately 1/4″ smaller than the previous turn, as shown in the drawings.

Attach braces to the bottom of the spiral in a cross shape. These braces keep the basket flat when it's collapsed. Assemble the handle to the sides of the spiral with small roundhead screws so that the handle pivots easily to lay flat or stand up on the braces. With the handle upright, the spiral will partially uncoil, forming a basket.

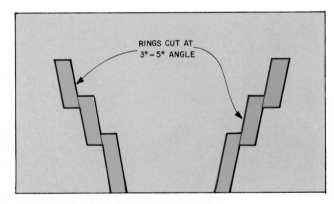

RINGS CUT AT
3° – 5° ANGLE

Figure 1. To perform the 'drinking cup' trick, cut concentric rings at a slight angle. When these rings are pulled apart from the proper direction, they will wedge against each other and form a cup shape.

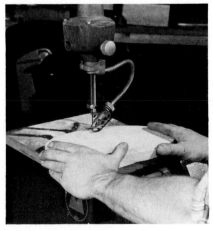

Figure 2. To make the basket, cut a spiral in the oval board with the table of your jigsaw tilted at 3°.

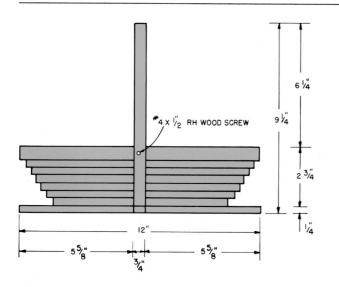

#4 x 1½" RH WOOD SCREW

6 ¼"

9 ¼"

2 ¾"

¼"

12"

5 ⅝"

5 ⅝"

¾"

**SIDE VIEW—
OPEN**

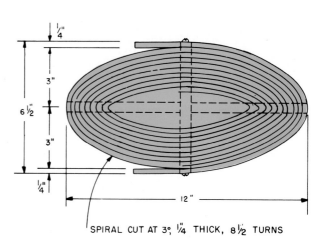

¼"

3"

6 ½"

3"

¼"

12"

SPIRAL CUT AT 3°, ¼" THICK, 8½ TURNS

**TOP VIEW—
COLLAPSED**

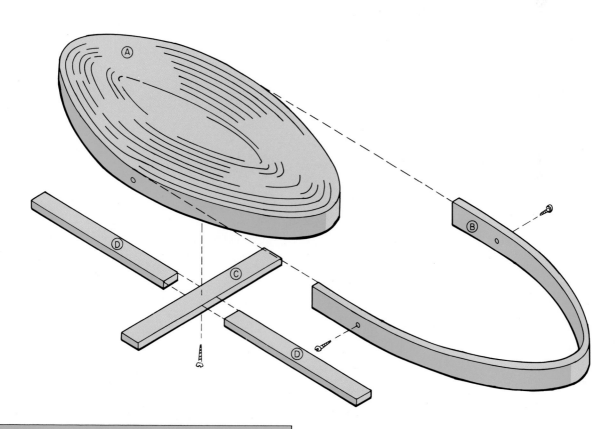

EXPLODED VIEW

BILL OF MATERIALS — Folding Basket	
Finished Dimensions in Inches	
A. Basket	3/4 x 6 x 12
B. Handle	3/4 x 6-1/2 x 9
C. Side-to-Side Brace	1/4 x 3/4 x 6-1/2
D. Front-to-Back Braces (2)	1/4 x 3/4 x 5-5/8

Hardware

#4 x 1/2" Roundhead Wood Screws (2)

Designed and built by George Frank Davis

Ten-Gun Cabinet

Safely store and display your firearms and other hunting equipment in this classic cabinet.

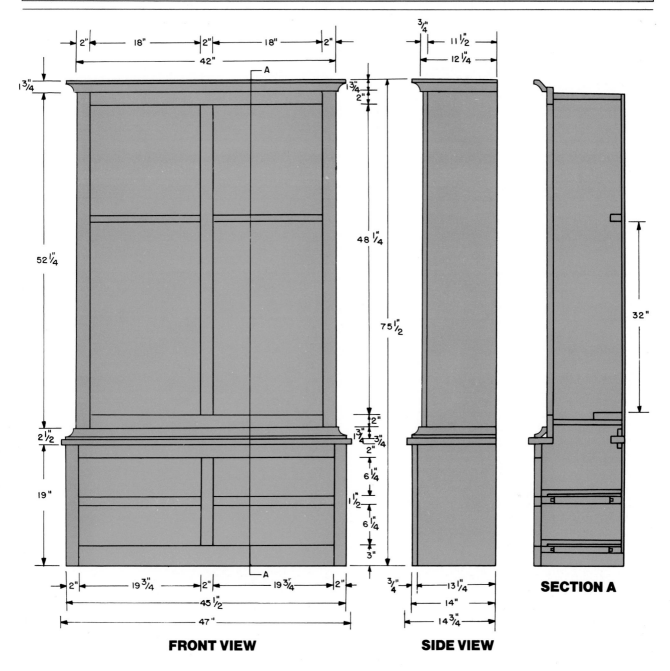

FRONT VIEW   **SIDE VIEW**   **SECTION A**

I t's a pleasure to look at a well-maintained rifle. So it's easy to understand why many gun collectors and hunting enthusiasts prefer to keep their hardware on display.

Displaying your guns, however, poses two problems — safety and security. Rifles, shotguns, handguns and ammunition must be kept out of reach of children and people who don't know how to properly handle firearms. And your guns must be secure. Gun theft hurts both the gun owner *and* the victims of crimes that may be committed with the stolen guns.

The gun cabinet shown here solves both those problems. There are locks on the drawers so that you can keep your ammunition locked up. And the guns are double-secure. First, there are locks on the cabinet doors. Second, a steel bar locks in place in front of the gun barrels to keep people from removing the guns from the case in the event that the glass doors are broken.

Adjusting the Design

As designed, the cabinet will hold ten rifles or shotguns. However, if your gun collection is smaller or larger than that, you may wish to adjust the horizontal dimensions of the cabinet. Lay your guns on the floor, spacing them out so there's about 2"-3" between each gun. Then measure across the gun barrels to see how wide your collection is. Add about 6" for the space needed on either side of the cabinet for the security bar mounts. Also, add space for any new additions to your collection that you may be planning for the future.

If you want to display your handguns, you have two choices: You can shorten the upper and lower rifle racks, and mount the handguns on the back wall of the cabinet. Or you can hang them on the side walls of the cabinet. Wherever you choose to mount them, remember that they should

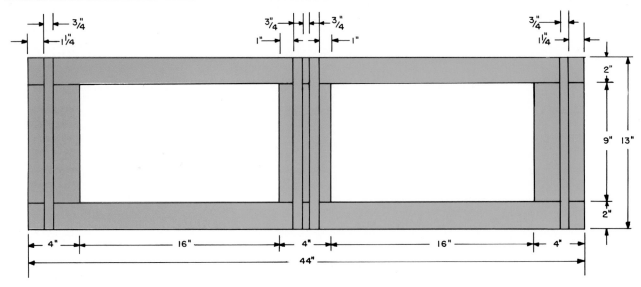

WEB FRAME LAYOUT

also be double-secured. A simple, secure handgun mount is shown in Figure 1 and in the Handgun Mount Detail.

Building the Lower Chest

The gun cabinet is built in two parts — a chest of drawers, which serves as a foundation for the upper cabinet. As with any large project, it's always best to start at the bottom:

Make two web frames to support the drawers, as shown in the Web Frame Layout and Detail. These are simple pieces, put together with tongue-and-groove joinery, and made from utility wood (since they won't show). Use a dado blade on your table saw to make both the tongues and the grooves. (See Figures 2 and 3.)

While the glue is drying on the web frames, construct the chest front frame and the chest top frame. These assemblies should be made of good lumber, since they'll show. They're held together with dowels, as shown in the exploded view. There's nothing tricky about dowel joinery; a good doweling jig will help you properly line up the holes, even on the mitered faces of the top frame parts. (See Figure 4.)

Once you've assembled the frames, it's a simple matter to assemble the chest. We suggest you do a 'dry assembly' first, using screws to hold the parts together. When you're sure all the parts fit together, disassemble the chest, spread glue on the mating edges, and reassemble. Cover the screw heads with wooden plugs and sand the plugs flush to the surface.

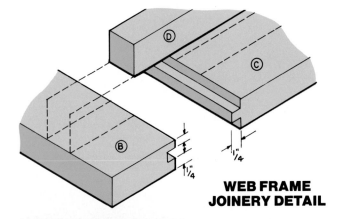

WEB FRAME JOINERY DETAIL

Figure 2. Cut a groove on the inside edge of the web frame rails by passing it across a dado cutter.

Figure 3. Using the same dado setup, cut mating tongues in the ends of the web frame stiles. A tenoning jig helps hold the board straight up and down.

Figure 1. By drilling a hole in the end of a dowel, you can lock a handgun on its mount.

38

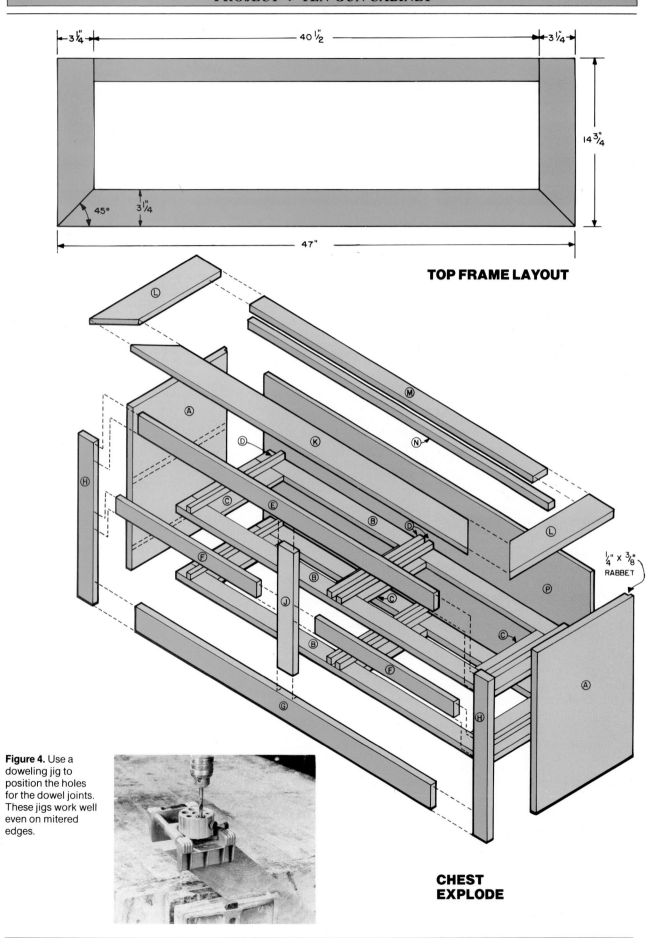

TOP FRAME LAYOUT

Figure 4. Use a doweling jig to position the holes for the dowel joints. These jigs work well even on mitered edges.

CHEST EXPLODE

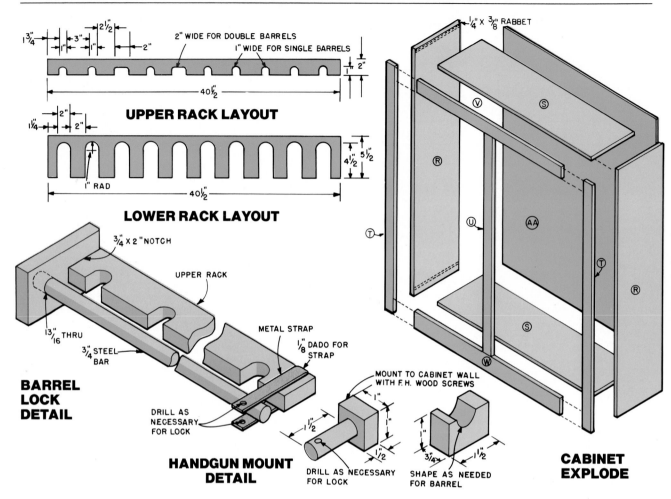

UPPER RACK LAYOUT

2" WIDE FOR DOUBLE BARRELS
1" WIDE FOR SINGLE BARRELS

40½"

LOWER RACK LAYOUT

1" RAD
40½"

BARREL LOCK DETAIL

¾ X 2" NOTCH
UPPER RACK
13/16" THRU
¾" STEEL BAR
METAL STRAP
⅛" DADO FOR STRAP
DRILL AS NECESSARY FOR LOCK

HANDGUN MOUNT DETAIL

MOUNT TO CABINET WALL WITH F.H. WOOD SCREWS
DRILL AS NECESSARY FOR LOCK
SHAPE AS NEEDED FOR BARREL

CABINET EXPLODE

¼" X ⅜" RABBET

Building the Upper Cabinet

The upper cabinet is much simpler than the lower chest. There's only one frame to make — the cabinet front frame. Like the chest front frame, this is doweled together.

Make the parts for the cabinet and dry assemble them, as you did the chest. Then set the cabinet on top of the chest to make sure that it fits properly. When you're satisfied that it does, reassemble the cabinet with screws and glue.

We suggest that you *do not* glue the cabinet to the chest. Simply screw them together, passing the screws up through the top frame of the chest into the bottom of the cabinet. Then, if you ever want to move the cabinet, you can break it down into two easy-to-handle parts.

Cut out the upper and lower racks on a bandsaw. (See Figure 5.) The purpose of these racks is to keep the guns vertical in the cabinet. The size of the slots in the bottom rack will be the same for all guns. But the slots in the upper rack may differ from gun to gun, depending on the width of the barrel. We suggest cutting 1" slots for single-barrel rifles and shotguns, and 2" slots for double-barrel, side-by-side shotguns. Line the interior of these slots with felt to protect the guns.

Before you attach the upper rack in the cabinet, remember to attach the metal strap for the barrel lock, as shown in the Barrel Lock Detail. If you wish, you can blue this metal so that it blends in with the barrels of the guns. Gun blueing is available at any gun shop or sports equipment store.

You may also wish to add a light to the cabinet. Buy a small, flat fluorescent fixture, no more than 2-1/2" high. Cut a hole in the top of the cabinet and screw this fixture to it. (See Figure 6.) After you apply the top molding, the fixture will be completely hidden.

Figure 5. Cut the slots in the upper and lower racks on a bandsaw. On the upper rack, cut slots 1" wide for single barrel rifles, and 2" wide for double barrel rifles.

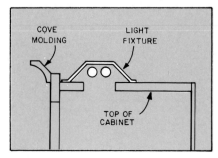

COVE MOLDING
LIGHT FIXTURE
TOP OF CABINET

Figure 6. If you want to illuminate your guns, mount a flat fluorescent fixture to the top of the cabinet. This fixture will be hidden by the top molding.

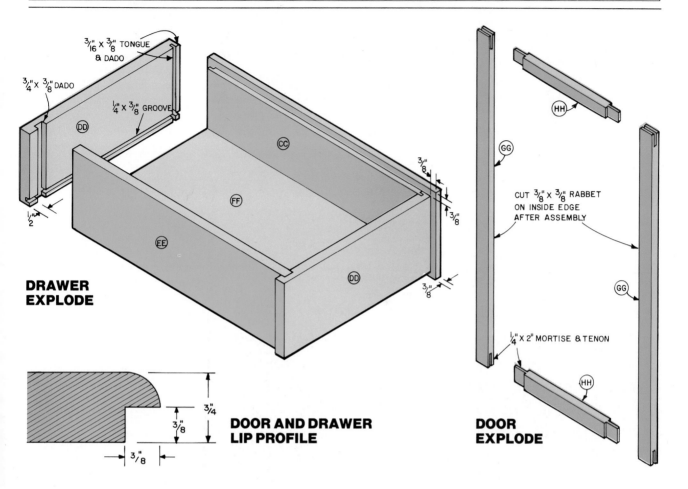

DRAWER EXPLODE

DOOR AND DRAWER LIP PROFILE

DOOR EXPLODE

Doors and Drawers

Both the doors and the drawers in this project overlap the front frames. There are several ways to make this overlap. The easiest is to use a cabinet lip cutter on your molder, shaper, or router. (See Figure 7.) This cutter shapes the lip in one pass. If you don't have a cabinet lip cutter, you can make the lip in two steps. First, cut a rabbet in the back edge of the boards to form the overlap. Then round over the front edge.

When making the doors, remember to cut a rabbet on the inside back edge for the glass. Make the rabbet deep enough so that you can hold the glass in place with 1/4″ x 1/4″ wood strips. Avoid using glazing points to mount the glass in these large doors. Glazing points don't provide the

security you want. Besides, the glass tends to rattle every time you open the door.

Both doors and at least one drawer should lock. There are many different types of locks you can choose from, but perhaps the most secure (and the easiest to mount) are the cam locks. These locks have a large cam that flips around to catch on the case to prevent you from opening the door or drawer. To mount these, you simply drill a hole in the door front or drawer front, insert the lock, and tighten down a nut to hold it in place. (See Figure 8.) They are available from many hardware stores, or you can also order them from:

The Woodworker's Store
21801 Industrial Blvd.
Rogers, MN 55374

The Wise Company
6503 St. Claude Ave.
Arabi, LA 70032

Figure 7. Shape the drawer fronts and door frames with a cabinet lip cutter. This cutter makes and shapes the overlap in one pass.

Figure 8. The strongest lock you can use for both the drawers and the doors is a cam lock. It's also the simplest to install.

Tip ◆ You can get by with putting a lock on just one door if you outfit the other door with an elbow catch. In order to release this catch, you first have to open the locked door, then reach inside the cabinet.

Finishing Touches

To finish off the project, add cove molding to the top and bottom edge of the cabinet. You can make this molding yourself with a cove cut on your table saw. Just run the molding across the saw at an angle to make the cove. (See Figure 9.) Don't try to cut the whole cove at once! Make several passes, cutting 1/8″ deeper with each pass. Then chamfer the edges of the molding on your jointer or table saw. (See Figure 10.)

Attach the molding to the cabinet by running a screw through the case from the inside, into the back of the molding, as shown in the details. That way, the screws will be hidden and you won't have to worry about covering them up. *Do not* attach the bottom molding to the chest. Just

attach it to the cabinet. That way, you can detach the chest and cabinet without a lot of trouble.

Finally, remove all glass and hardware from the project, sand all the pieces down, and apply the finish of your choice. Be sure to apply an equal number of coats to both the inside and the outside of the chest and cabinet. This will help prevent warping.

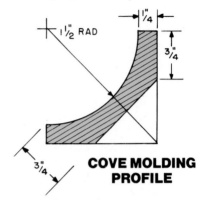

COVE MOLDING PROFILE

Figure 9. To make the cove molding, first cut a cove in the face of the stock. Pass the wood over the blade at a 23° angle. Take small bites, just 1/8″ (or less) per pass until you've cut the cove as deep as you want it.

Figure 10. To finish the molding, chamfer the edges at 45°. If you do this chamfering on a jointer, be sure to tilt the fence *towards* the blade.

BILL OF MATERIALS — Ten-Gun Cabinet

Finished Dimensions in Inches

Lower Chest

A.	Chest Sides (2)	3/4 x 13-1/4 x 19
B.	Web Frame Rails (4)	3/4 x 2 x 44
C.	Web Frame Stiles (6)	3/4 x 4 x 9-1/2
D.	Drawer Guides (8)	3/4 x 3/4 x 13
E.	Front Frame Top Rail	3/4 x 2 x 41-1/2
F.	Front Frame Middle Rails (2)	3/4 x 1-1/2 x 19-3/4
G.	Front Frame Bottom Rail	3/4 x 3 x 41-1/2
H.	Front Frame End Stiles (2)	3/4 x 2 x 19
J.	Front Frame Middle Stile	3/4 x 2 x 14
K.	Top Frame Front Rail	3/4 x 3-1/4 x 47
L.	Top Frame Side Stiles (2)	3/4 x 3-1/4 x 14-3/4
M.	Top Frame Back Rail	3/4 x 2 x 40-1/2
N.	Back Cleat	3/4 x 3/4 x 44
P.	Chest Back	1/4 x 16-3/4 x 44-3/4
Q.	Dowels (28)	1/4 dia. x 2

Upper Cabinet

N.	Back Cleat	3/4 x 3/4 x 44
Q.	Dowels (12)	1/4 dia. x 2
R.	Cabinet Sides (2)	3/4 x 11-1/2 x 54-3/4
S.	Cabinet Top/Bottom (2)	3/4 x 11-1/4 x 40-1/2
T.	Cabinet End Stiles (2)	3/4 x 2 x 54-3/4
U.	Cabinet Middle Stile	3/4 x 2 x 48-1/4
V.	Top Cabinet Rail	3/4 x 2-3/4 x 38
W.	Bottom Cabinet Rail	3/4 x 3-3/4 x 38

X.	Upper Rack	3/4 x 2 x 40-1/2
Y.	Barrel Lock Mount	3/4 x 2-3/4 x 4-1/2
Z.	Lower Rack	3/4 x 5-1/2 x 40-1/2
AA.	Cabinet Back	1/4 x 41-1/4 x 54
BB.	Cove Molding (Total)	3/4 x 2-1/2 x 147

Drawers

CC.	Drawer Fronts (4)	3/4 x 7 x 20-1/2
DD.	Drawer Sides (8)	3/4 x 6-1/8 x 13
EE.	Drawer Backs (4)	3/4 x 6-1/8 x 18-7/8
FF.	Drawer Bottoms (4)	1/4 x 12-1/8 x 18-7/8

Doors

GG.	Door Stiles (4)	3/4 x 2 x 49
HH.	Door Rails (4)	3/4 x 2 x 18-3/4
JJ.	Glazing Strip (Total)	1/4 x 1/4 x 251

Hardware

#8 x 1-1/4″ Flathead Wood Screws (7-8 dozen)
Offset Cabinet Door Hinges and Mounting Screws (2 pair)
3/4″ dia. x 40-1/4″ Steel Bar
1/8″ x 3/4″ x 9-3/4″ Steel Strap
Padlock
Cam Locks (2 — at least)
Elbow Catch (optional)
Felt
Fluorescent Light Fixture (optional)

Designed and built by Nick Engler

Hall Tree

A few hours on the lathe is just about all it takes to produce this turn-of-the-century heirloom.

Jackets and hats prefer the wide open spaces of a hallway or entrance way, I'm convinced. They don't like dark closets (would you?); they want to be out where the action is, casually draped over a piece of furniture, acting cool. As often as I hang up my clothes, they always seem to escape the closet and head straight for freedom — and my favorite chair.

Since it's not good form to let your jackets and hats roam the house in gay abandon, I decided to build them a hall tree. It's a place where they can congregate out in the open, enjoy the fresh air, and still manage to appear 'hung up'.

The hall tree is also a great lathe project. Like many woodworkers, I particularly enjoy the lathe because you can begin *and* finish a project on the same machine. There's no need to be overly concerned about accuracy, and the sanding is a snap. All the parts of the hall tree (except the legs) can be made on the lathe. Furthermore, all of the parts must be made in either duplicate or triplicate, so this is a good opportunity to rationalize that lathe duplicator you've had your eye on.

Turning the Spindles

The first step in making the hall tree is to glue up the stock for the main spindle. There's nothing particularly hard about this, *except* that the stock must have six sides.

To make this hexagon, start with stock 1-1/2″ thick and at least 4″ wide. Set the blade of your table saw at 30°, and rip one edge of the stock. Turn the stock end for end, set the rip fence, and rip the second edge. (See Figure 1.) Cut the stock in four 3′ lengths and laminate the pieces together to form two hexagons. Each side of the finished hexagon should be 1-3/4″ wide. (Refer to the working drawings.)

> **Tip ◆** Be sure to get a good, even glue bond when you laminate the stock and let the glue dry for *at least* 24 hours before you turn the spindles. Otherwise, the stock may come apart on the lathe.

Mount the stock between the centers of your lathe and turn the shapes shown in the drawings. Or design your own spindles. Note that in our design, the top and bottom parts of the main spindle are exactly the same. This isn't necessary, though it adds a pleasing symmetry to the hall tree. However, suit yourself. Just be sure to leave about 12″ of each spindle *unturned* — don't scrape off the flats. (See Figure 2.) The legs must be doweled to the flat area of the lower part, and the hangers are mounted in the flat area of the upper part.

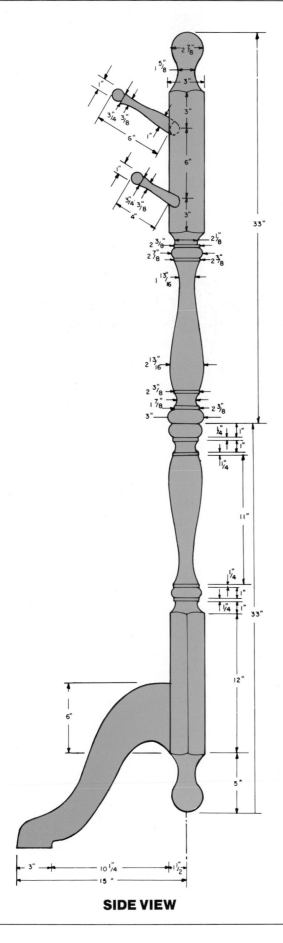

SIDE VIEW

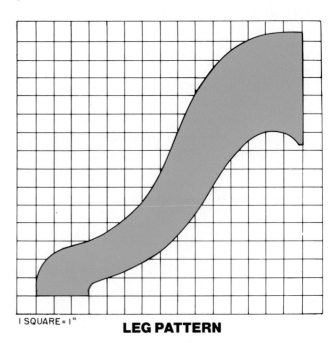

I SQUARE = 1″   **LEG PATTERN**

Also turn the hangers on the lathe. You'll need three hangers approximately 7-1/2″ long, and three more 5-1/2″ long. Once again, you can follow our patterns or design your own hangers. However, remember that these hangers may have to support a heavy load from time to time. (I have a couple of fat jackets.) Don't turn the hangers so that they're too slender. Also, use a set of calipers to insure that you turn the bases of these hangers to a diameter of *precisely* 1″. (See Figure 3.)

Making the Legs

Cut the legs from 1-1/2″ thick stock on a bandsaw. Be careful to orient the leg pattern on the stock so that the grain runs in the same direction as indicated in the drawings. This will give the legs maximum strength. To make all the legs exactly the same, you can tape the stock together and 'pad saw' all three pieces at once. (See Figure 4.)

Remove the millmarks from the legs with a drum sander, then round over the top edges on a shaper. To add some design interest, you may want to cut an ogee or a bead into the edges, instead of just rounding them off. (See Figure 5.) Once again, what we show you here is just a suggestion.

Finish sand the legs after you shape them, *before* you assemble the hall tree. This will save a lot of time later on.

Assembly

All of the parts in this project are doweled together, starting with the legs: Carefully mark both the legs and the lower half of the main spindle where you want to drill. Make sure the marks line up exactly, then drill the dowel holes. Remember, this project has just three legs, set 120° apart.

Drill the holes for the hangers in the upper half of the main spindle. These holes must be bored at a 30° angle. You'll find it easier to be accurate if you clamp the spindle to the table of the drill press before you make the holes. (See Figure 6.) The arrangement of the hangers can be varied to suit your own needs and tastes, but I suggest you create two

Figure 1. Rip the edges of the spindle stock at 30°. When the stock is glued up, each face of the hexagon should be 1-3/4″ wide.

Figure 2. Turn the two halves of the main spindle exactly the same. Be sure to leave approximately 12″ of the stock unturned — don't scrape off the flats.

Figure 4. Tape the leg blanks together and trace the pattern on the top blank only. Pad saw the entire stack at one time.

Figure 3. Use a pair of calipers to insure that the bases of the finished hanger spindles are *exactly* 1″ in diameter.

Figure 5. Shape the top edges of the legs on a shaper, if you have one. You can also use your drill press or a router mounted to a router table.

Figure 6. Before you drill the angled holes in the main spindle for the hangers, clamp the spindle to the drill press table. Otherwise, the spindle may slip as you drill it.

rows with the long hangers on top, and the shorter hangers on the bottom. 'Stagger' the hangers so there's only one hanger per flat. (See Figure 7.)

Finally, join the two halves of the main spindle: Carefully drill 1″ holes, 2-1/2″ deep in the mating ends of the turnings. When drilling end grain, feed the bit very slowly and back it out frequently to clear the chips. Using a bandsaw or table saw, carefully cut a glue spiral in a 1″ dowel. (See Figure 8.) Cut off a 5″ length of the dowel, and test the fit.

> **Tip** ◆ Commercial dowels that you purchase out of the 1″ bin are not always 1″ in diameter. Usually, they shrink slightly after they're manufactured. If you use a dowel that's too small for the main spindle joint, the joint won't last. Instead, drill the holes undersize or turn your own dowels.

Join all parts with a generous amount of glue. Clamping the legs to the main spindle while the glue dries may pose a problem, but you can solve it easily with an old inner tube. Cut the tube in strips, then wrap the strips around the legs and the spindle so that the pressure of the stretched rubber holds the parts in place. (See Figure 9.)

The finish is up to you. But if you've made the hall tree from an open-grain wood such as oak, you might try this trick: Apply a coat of tung oil, and let the finish dry for several hours. Rub on a thin coat of walnut oil stain or walnut Danish oil, then rub it off quickly. The tung oil will prevent the darker oils from penetrating the wood too deeply, but some of the oil will remain in open grains. This will make the grain pattern stand out and give the project an aged look. After the oils dry completely, rub down the entire project with steel wool and paste wax.

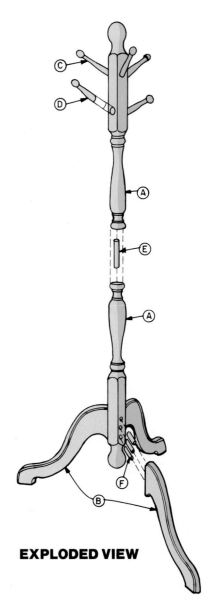

EXPLODED VIEW

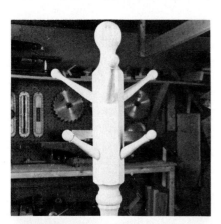

Figure 7. Arrange the hangers in two rows, long hangers on the top, short hangers on the bottom. Only one hanger per side!

Figure 8. To cut a glue spiral, 'screw' the dowel past the blade at a slight angle. The blade should only bite into the dowel 1/8″ or less.

Figure 9. Clamp the legs to the main spindle with strips of an old inner tube, as shown.

BILL OF MATERIALS — Hall Tree		
Finished Dimensions in Inches		
A.	Main Spindles (2)	3 dia. x 33
B.	Legs (3)	1-1/2 x 7 x 22
C.	Long Hangers (3)	1 dia. x 7-1/2
D.	Short Hangers	1 dia. x 5-1/2
E.	Spindle Dowel	1 dia. x 6
F.	Leg Dowels (9)	1/2 dia. x 2

Designed by Rude Osolnik

I SQUARE = 1/4"

VASE PATTERN

Weed Pots

Some of the ugliest wood in the forest makes the prettiest turnings.

Did you ever notice a burl growing out from the side of a tree? These monsterous growths are 'scars', the result of an earlier injury to the tree. They look uncommonly ugly on the outside, but that homeliness is only bark deep. On the inside of a burl is some of the prettiest wood in the tree — curly grain, birds-eye's, sap pockets, all that good stuff.

Unfortunately, there's never a lot of wood in a burl. So any project that you make from burled wood usually has to be quite small. These 'weed pots' get the most out of a burl. The shape shown here is just an example; it can be easily made fatter, skinnier, taller, or shorter to accommodate the shape of a burl.

The first step in making a weed pot is to harvest a few burls. This is best done with a chain saw. To get as much usable wood as possible, cut into the tree with the nose of the saw from several angles, and remove the burl as if it were a plug. (See Figure 1.) If the tree is living, cover the hole with pitch to keep the birds and insects out while the tree grows another burl.

> **Tip ◆** Keep green burls in a plastic bag until you're ready to turn them. This will keep the wood from drying out too quickly and checking.

Mount the burl between the centers of your lathe and turn the shape of a weed pot. Incorporate some of the imperfections in the wood, if you want — knots, cavities, spaults, etc. This will give character to the finished turning. (See Figure 2.) Sand the pot on the lathe, then drill the hole in the neck on your drill press. Finish with a penetrating oil such as tung oil or Danish oil.

Figure 1. Carve a burl out of a tree with the nose of a chain saw. If the tree is living, cover the hole with pitch.

Figure 2. Adjust the shape of each weed pot to fit the shape of the burl. Don't hesitate to incorporate knots, cavities, and other imperfections in the turning; this will add to the uniqueness of the finished pot.

© 1985, Sotheby's, Inc.

Serpentine Chest

A simple curve on the front of this chest of drawers makes it a true classic.

Early in the 1700's, American cabinet makers discovered the *cyma curve* — a graceful S-curve or 'ogee' that became the motif for all furniture design during the Queen Anne and Chippendale periods.

This 'serpentine front' chest of drawers, built in 1770, is a classic example of how the craftsmen of that period applied the cyma curve. The top is edged in an ogee, as is the molding around the base. The cabriole legs flow from the cabinet in a graceful S, then terminate in a traditional ball-and-claw. Even the drawer fronts undulate through two cyma curves laid end-to-end to form the serpent shape.

If you'd like to reproduce a serpentine chest, it's not important that you understand the theory behind designing with a cyma curve, only that you appreciate its grace and its beauty. And despite the fact that some fine craftsmanship obviously went into making this piece, you'll find a serpentine chest is a relatively simple project to build. The only pieces that require a high level of skill are the ball-and-claw feet. And if you feel you aren't up to carving these parts, we've provided plans for simple Chippendale 'bracket feet' that you can substitute.

Building the Case

Glue up wide stock for the top and sides. You may also use plywood for these parts, and attach 1″ wide solid strips to the edges to hide the plies. However, the joinery in this piece is designed to accommodate the movement that occurs with solid wood.

While the glue is drying on the top and sides, make the web frames. The back rails and stiles of these frames can be made out of a cheap utility wood such as pine, but the front rails must be made out of wood that matches the top and sides. Cut the curves in the front rails on a bandsaw. (See Figure 1.) The curve in the front edge follows the same curve as the drawer fronts, while the curve in the side edges should have the same radius as your dado cutter. (You'll understand why when it comes time to fit the frames to the sides.) Note that the front edge of the bottom front rail is *straight* — it has no curve. This rail is also built up with a strip of wood to make it double-wide in the front.

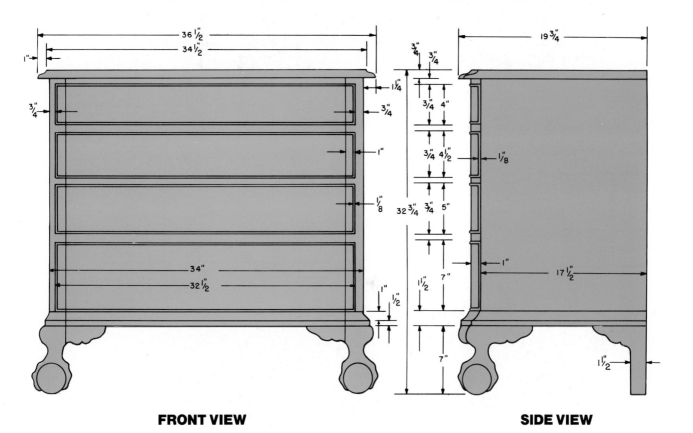

FRONT VIEW   **SIDE VIEW**

Tip ◆ Before cutting the shape in the front web frame rails, make a template from hardboard. Use this template to mark the rails *and* the drawer fronts. That way, the curves will match exactly.

Traditionally, the web frames on a fine chest of drawers were fitted with 'dust shields'. As a wooden drawer rubs back and forth across a frame, it creates a very fine sawdust. Without the shields, this sawdust will sift down into the drawer below. We've drawn the plans to include the dust shields, but they are optional. If you decide to hang the drawer with modern metal or nylon hardware, you won't need them.

Cut the blind dadoes for the web frames in the sides. Cut from back to front, and stop cutting 3/8″ before you get to the front edge. When you assemble the case, you should

not be able to see the dadoes from the front. Also cut a 1/8″ dado near the top edge and a rabbet in the back edge of the sides, as shown in the working drawings.

Tip ◆ If you use a router to make the dadoes for the web frames, then square off the corners of the blind end with a chisel. (See Figure 2.) You'll also have to change the design of the front web frame rails somewhat: Instead of cutting a curve in the side edges, just cut a square notch.

Figure 2. If you cut the dadoes in the sides with a router, square the blind ends with a hand chisel.

Figure 1. Cut the serpent shape in the front web frame rail on the bandsaw. Make a template to mark the stock, so that all the serpent shapes you cut are *exactly* the same.

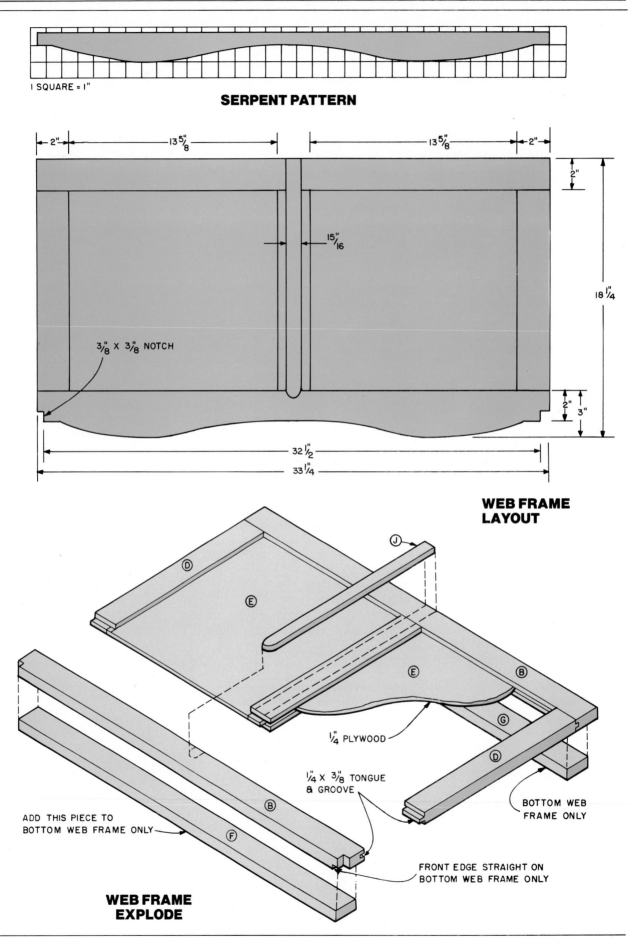

1 SQUARE = 1"

SERPENT PATTERN

3/8" X 3/8" NOTCH

2"

13 5/8"

13 5/8"

2"

15/16"

18 1/4"

2"

2"

3"

32 1/2"

33 1/4"

**WEB FRAME
LAYOUT**

J

D

E

E

B

G

D

1/4" PLYWOOD

BOTTOM WEB
FRAME ONLY

1/4" X 3/8" TONGUE
& GROOVE

B

ADD THIS PIECE TO
BOTTOM WEB FRAME ONLY

F

FRONT EDGE STRAIGHT ON
BOTTOM WEB FRAME ONLY

**WEB FRAME
EXPLODE**

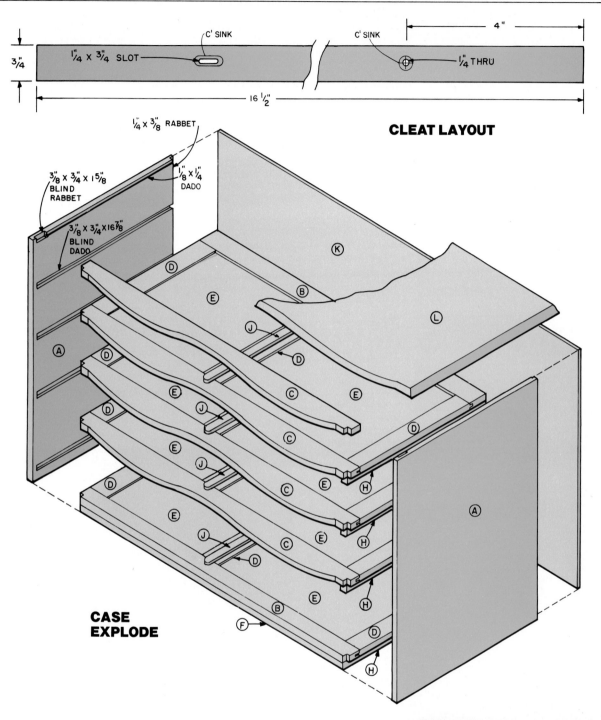

CLEAT LAYOUT

CASE EXPLODE

Make the cleats from utility wood, and drill the holes for screws. Note that the hole nearest the *back* of the case is slotted. This will allow the sides to expand or contract with changes in humidity. There are several ways to make these slots. Either drill a series of holes and clean up the edges with a chisel, or use a router bit in your drill press. (See Figure 3.) If you use your drill press to rout, take the cut very slow and make several passes, cutting 1/16"-1/8" deeper each time.

Screw the cleats to the sides, flush with the bottom of the dadoes. Then insert the web frames in the dadoes and attach the frames to the cleats with glue and screws. *Do not* glue the frames in the dadoes. They must be allowed to 'float' to allow for the movement of the wood.

Figure 3. Use a router bit mounted in your drill press to cut the slotted holes in the cleats. This setup cuts slowly, so have patience.

Secure the top to the cabinet with mirror clips. These clips screw into the underside of the top, then hook into the 1/8″ dado near the top edge. (See Figure 4.) Like the cleats, they allow for the movement of the wood. Finally, attach the back to the case with small wood screws.

Making the Legs

Make the front legs from 3″ thick stock. Start by cutting a cove in the stock 1-1/4″ deep and 2″ wide. This is best done on your table saw, by passing the wood across the blade at 17°. (See Figure 5.) Then round over the top part of the stock with a hand plane. (See Figure 6.) This will form the characteristic cabriole (or cyma) curve.

Cut the stock into 8″ lengths, and miter one end. Cut a 1/4″ groove in the mitered face for a spline, cut a rabbet in the top edge for the corner block, and saw the apron shape on a bandsaw. Glue the leg parts together, reinforcing the miter joint with a spline and a glue block, as shown in the working drawings.

Figure 4. Use mirror clips to attach the top to the cabinet. It's easy, and you can't see the clips after you're done.

Figure 5. To shape the stock for the legs, first make a cove cut on your table saw. Pass the wood across the blade at 17° and take small bites, cutting just 1/8″ deeper with each pass.

Figure 6. Round the top of the leg stock with a hand plane. A hardboard template helps you determine when you've got the proper curve.

Tip ◆ So that the miter joint is as strong as possible, the wood grain of the spline should run *perpendicular* to the face of the miter.

Carving the ball-and-claw requires more patience than skill. It is a simple sculpture, provided you concentrate on one thing at a time, in the proper order. First, trace the pattern on all four sides of the foot. The claw has four talons — one to each corner — so the pattern is going to be precisely the same no matter what direction you view it from. Then remove the stock between the talons, making the ball. (See Figure 7.) Turn the piece frequently as you work, removing a little stock from this side, then a little stock from the next, so that the ball appears to be perfectly round. When you're satisfied that the ball is indeed a ball, round over the talons. Remove a little more stock between the knuckles, as indicated on the pattern, so that the talons appear to have natural joints. (See Figure 8.)

If you don't want to spend the time making ball-and-claw feet, this project will also look nice with simple bracket feet. Follow exactly the same procedure when making the feet, but cut the cove a little shallower and a little wider.

The back legs are made in a slightly different manner, from 3″ stock butted up against 1-1/2″ thick stock. The 3″ stock is shaped to follow the same cyma curve as the front legs, but there is no carving. Note that unlike the front legs, there is a left back leg and a right back leg — don't make them both the same.

Figure 7. Carve the ball in the legs first. Turn the wood frequently, removing a little stock on each side until the ball appears perfectly round.

Figure 8. After you've carved the ball, shape the talons. Remove a little extra stock between each knuckle so that it will look as if each talon is jointed, like a real dragon's foot.

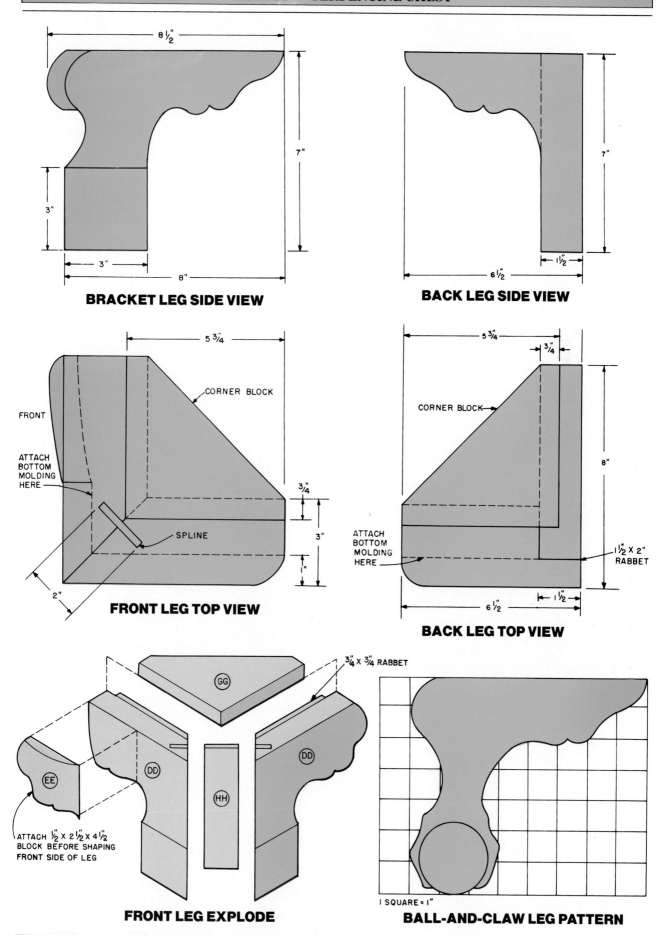

BRACKET LEG SIDE VIEW

BACK LEG SIDE VIEW

FRONT LEG TOP VIEW

BACK LEG TOP VIEW

FRONT LEG EXPLODE

BALL-AND-CLAW LEG PATTERN

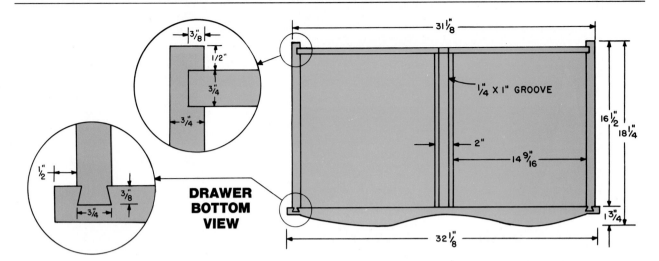

Making and Fitting the Drawers

The drawer construction is standard. The front is attached to the sides with blind dovetails, and the back is attached to the sides with a dado. The drawer bottom rests in a 1/4″ groove in the front, sides, and back. A hardwood guide on the web frame fits in a notch in the drawer back to keep the drawers straight as it slides in and out of the case. (Refer to the working drawings.)

> **Tip ◆** Consider making the drawer bottoms out of cedar. Those things that you keep in the drawers will smell so much fresher.

There are, however, several special considerations. First of all, the drawer sides and back are cut narrower than the drawer front to allow room for the cleats. But don't cut them too narrow; the cleats also serve as guides to keep the drawers from binding when they are pulled out. The sides should clear the cleats by just 1/16″ — 1/8″.

The front is cut from a single solid piece of 1-3/4″ thick wood. The serpent shape is cut with a bandsaw. Most bandsaws have the capacity to cut stock up to 6″ thick, so you'll be able to cut those drawer fronts in one piece. To cut the bottom drawer front, however, you'll have to split the stock in two, cut both pieces, then glue it back together. Don't rip this drawer front to its final width until *after* you cut the shape.

The drawers also get 1/8″ thick 'cock beading' around the fronts. This beading was a decorative touch used by many cabinetmakers in the eighteenth century. To make room for the side beading, you'll have to cut a 1/8″ deep, 3/4″ wide rabbet in the drawer sides *after* they are assembled. The drawer fronts should be narrow enough to accommodate the top and bottom beading with no additional joinery. Cut this beading to overlap the drawer fronts by 3/16″, then round over the front edge with sandpaper. After you've removed the millmarks, the beading should protrude just 1/8″, as shown in the working drawings. Attach this beading to the drawers with brads and glue.

Final Assembly

Make sure the drawers fit properly in the chest. Rub the drawer guides with paraffin wax to help the drawers slide smoothly, then set the drawers aside.

Attach ogee molding to the bottom of the chest, around the sides and the front. You can build this molding up out of two pieces of stock, one shaped and the other square, as shown in Figure 9. Remember that the front molding should be curved to follow the contour of the drawer fronts. You won't be able to cut the slight 'corner' (where the serpent shape begins and ends) on your shaper; you'll have to 'touch up' this part of the molding with hand chisels.

Assemble the legs to the case with large wood screws. Pass these screws up through the corner blocks into the bottom web frame. Use hand chisels to shape the front legs to follow the contour of the bottom molding.

The original chest was fitted with locks for all four drawers. If you want to do the same, brass locks and Chippendale escutcheons are available from:

The Wise Company
6503 St. Claude Avenue
Arabi, LA 70032

This company also sells matching Chippendale drawer pulls.

Finish your chest with a clear 'building' finish — we recommend a mixture of varnish and tung oil. Mix the first two coats, two parts tung oil to one part varnish; and the last coat, three parts varnish to one part tung oil. Rub each coat on with your hands or a soft, clean rag. Finally, rub out the finish with #0000 steel wool and paste wax.

Figure 9. Make the ogee molding in two parts. Shape the top part with an ogee cutter on your shaper or router. The bottom part is just a square strip of wood.

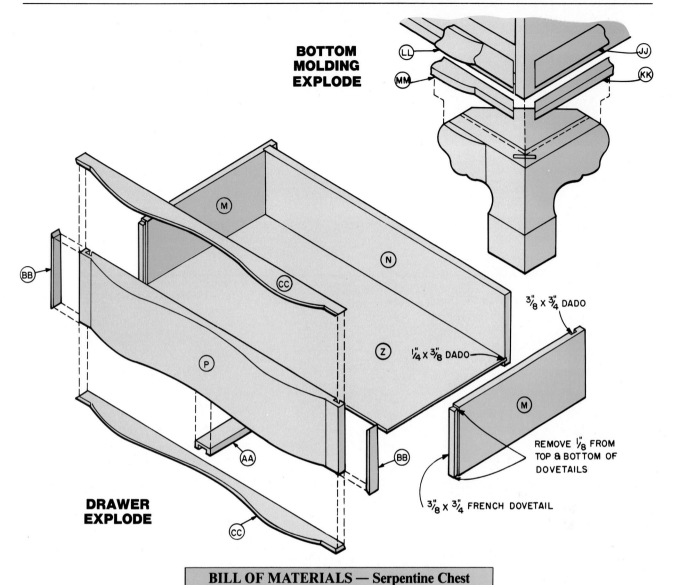

BOTTOM MOLDING EXPLODE

3/8" x 3/4" DADO

1/4" x 3/8" DADO

REMOVE 1/8" FROM TOP & BOTTOM OF DOVETAILS

3/8" x 3/4" FRENCH DOVETAIL

DRAWER EXPLODE

BILL OF MATERIALS — Serpentine Chest

Finished Dimensions in Inches

A.	Sides (2)	3/4 x 17-1/2 x 25	**X.**	Lower Drawer Back	3/4 x 6-7/8 x 30-3/8
B.	Straight Rails (5)	3/4 x 2 x 33-1/4	**Y.**	Lower Drawer Front	1-3/4 x 6-5/8 x 32-1/8
C.	Curved Rails (4)	3/4 x 3 x 33-1/4	**Z.**	Drawer Bottoms (4)	1/4 x 16 x 30-3/8
D.	Stiles (12)	3/4 x 2 x 14	**AA.**	Drawer Glides (4)	1/2 x 2 x 15-1/4
E.	Dust Shields (8)	1/4 x 14-3/8 x 14	**BB.**	Side Beading (total)	1/8 x 7/8 x 41
F.	Front Bottom Brace	3/4 x 2 x 32-1/2	**CC.**	Top/Bottom Beading (8)	1/8 x 1-7/8 x 32-3/8
G.	Back Bottom Brace	3/4 x 2 x 31	**DD.**	Front/Side Legs (6)	3 x 7 x 8
H.	Cleats (8)	7/16 x 3/4 x 16-1/2	**EE.**	Front Leg Blocks (2)	1/2 x 2-1/2 x 4-1/2
J.	Drawer Guides (4)	3/16 x 15/16 x 16-1/2	**FF.**	Back Legs (2)	1-1/2 x 7 x 7
K.	Back	1/4 x 25 x 33-1/4	**GG.**	Corner Blocks (4)	3/4 x 5-3/4 x 5-3/4
L.	Top	3/4 x 19-3/4 x 36-1/2	**HH.**	Splines (2)	1/4 x 2 x 7
M.	Upper Drawer Sides (2)	3/4 x 3-7/8 x 16-7/8	**JJ.**	Side Ogee Moldings (2)	3/4 x 1 x 72
N.	Upper Drawer Back	3/4 x 3-7/8 x 30-3/8	**KK.**	Side Flat Moldings (2)	1/2 x 3/4 x 72
P.	Upper Drawer Front	1-3/4 x 3-5/8 x 32-1/8	**LL.**	Front Ogee Molding	1 x 1-3/4 x 35-1/2
Q.	Upper Middle Dr. Sides (2)	3/4 x 4-3/8 x 16-7/8	**MM.**	Front Flat Molding	1/2 x 1-3/4 x 35-1/2
R.	Upper Middle Dr. Back	3/4 x 4-3/8 x 30-3/8			
S.	Upper Middle Dr. Front	1-3/4 x 4-1/8 x 32-1/8		**Hardware**	
T.	Lower Middle Dr. Sides (2)	3/4 x 4-7/8 x 16-7/8			
U.	Lower Middle Dr. Back	3/4 x 4-7/8 x 30-3/8		#10 x 1-1/2" Flathead Wood Screws (2-3 dozen)	
V.	Lower Middle Dr. Front	1-3/4 x 4-5/8 x 32-1/8		#10 x 1-1/4" Roundhead Wood Screws (2 dozen)	
W.	Lower Drawer Sides (2)	3/4 x 6-7/8 x 16-7/8		Chippendale Drawer Pulls (8-12)	
				3/4" Brads (1-2 dozen)	

Designed and built by Nick Engler

Bathroom Towel and Paper Holders

These modern racks add precious shelving space to your bathroom.

Space is at a premium in every room in your house, but nowhere is it so precious as in the bathroom. Did you ever wonder why the smallest room in the house always seems to be crammed with the most stuff? These towel and paper holders could help relieve some of that congestion. They not only have racks to hang bath towels, hand towels, and toilet paper, but they also provide shelving space above the towels and paper.

The measurements on the working drawings are calculated to hold standard-size towels and paper rolls. However, the number of shelves assigned to each rack and the spacing of those shelves is just a suggestion. Once you study the design, you may want to rearrange these holders to better fit your bathroom.

Construction

There's not much to say about construction; it's fairly straightforward. Cut the parts to size; bandsaw the design in the sides, cut the dadoes for the shelves and drill the holes for the racks. However, there are a few special techniques you may want to try:

The first technique has to do with the racks. We've designed the project so that you can use standard 1″ dowels, straight off a lumber rack. However, most commercial dowels are turned from either beech or oak, and this wood may not match the wood in your holders. You could turn your own dowels on a lathe, but it's difficult to scrape a long, slender spindle to a perfectly uniform diameter. If you want to turn perfect dowels quickly and easily, make your own dowel-maker.

Drill a hole in a 2″ thick block of hardwood the same size as the dowel you want to make — in this case, 1″. Using a gouge or a 'reamer', enlarge the hole in the front of the

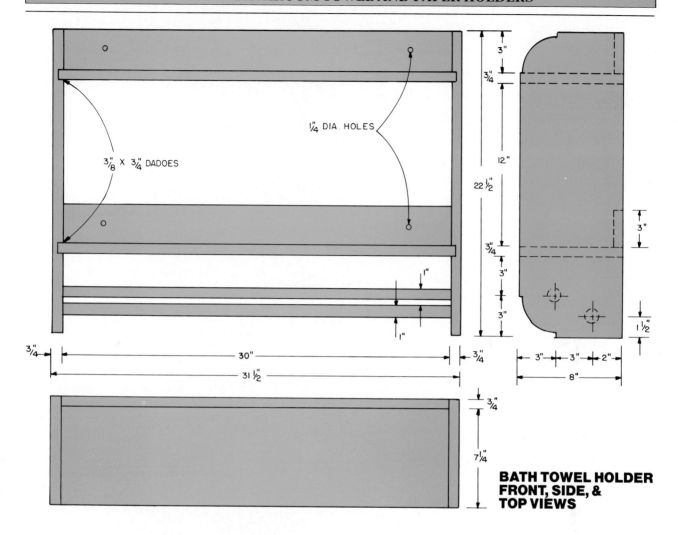

**BATH TOWEL HOLDER
FRONT, SIDE, &
TOP VIEWS**

block so that it tapers slightly from the front to the back. (See Figure 1.) When you're finished, the hole should taper from 1-1/2″ to the original diameter of 1″. (Refer to the drawings.)

Figure 1. Enlarge the hole in the front of the dowel-maker so that the hole *tapers* from 1-1/2″ down to 1″.

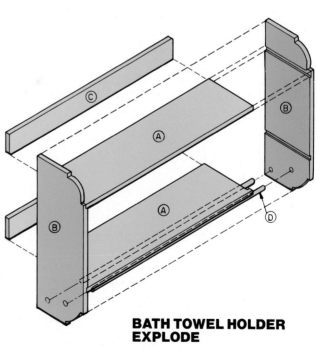

**BATH TOWEL HOLDER
EXPLODE**

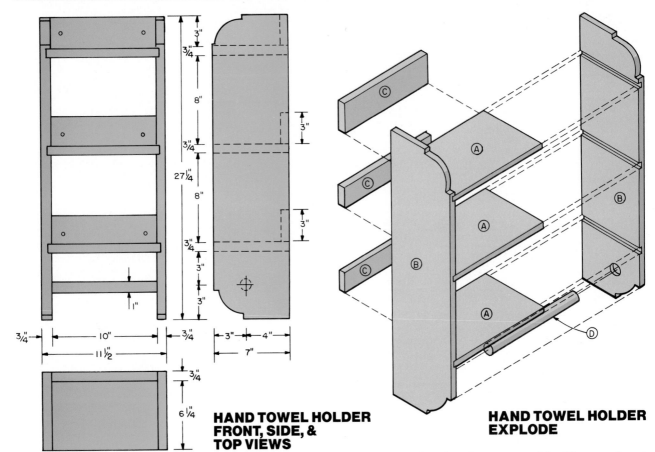

HAND TOWEL HOLDER FRONT, SIDE, & TOP VIEWS

HAND TOWEL HOLDER EXPLODE

Draw a line tangent to the top of the enlarged hole, then make a second line that intersects the circumference of the hole at the tangent, 45° to the tangent line. (See Figure 2.) Cut along this second line with your bandsaw. Since the hole is tapered, tilt the table of the saw to match the taper — about 10° for this dowel-maker.

Make a second bandsaw cut straight down from the top of the hole, along an extended radius line. (See Figure 3.) This will open up a slanted slot in the dowel-maker. Secure a plane iron or a spokeshave knife to the slanted face of the slot with a large roundhead wood screw. (See Figure 4.)

Test your dowel-maker on some 1″ x 1″ scraps. Insert one end of the scrap in the enlarged side of the tapered hole, and slowly turn the scrap against the knife so that it shaves it down. (See Figure 5.) You will probably have to adjust the position of the knife several times before it cuts smoothly and leaves a dowel precisely 1″ in diameter.

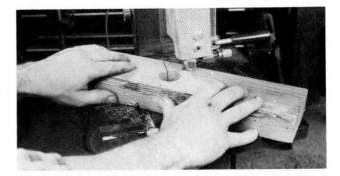

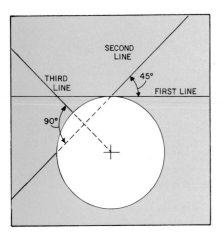

Figure 2. Draw several lines on the front of the dowel-maker: The first line is tangent to the top of the hole. The second line is 45° from the first line, and intersects the first line where the tangent meets the hole. The third line is a radius of the hole, drawn 90° to the second line.

Figure 3. Cut the second and third lines on a bandsaw. Remember to tilt the worktable at the same angle as the taper when you cut the second line.

Figure 4. Attach a plane iron to the slanted face of the slot with a large roundhead wood screw.

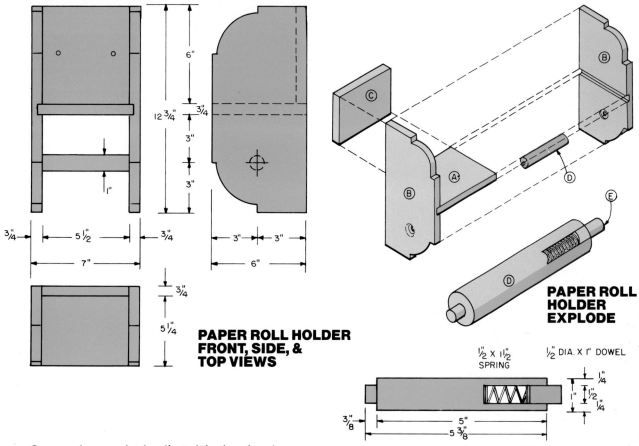

PAPER ROLL HOLDER FRONT, SIDE, & TOP VIEWS

PAPER ROLL HOLDER EXPLODE

½" X 1½" SPRING

½" DIA. X 1" DOWEL

PAPER ROLL HOLDER DETAIL

Once you've completely adjusted the dowel-maker, you can use it on your lathe. Turn the first 2″-3″ of a 1″ x 1″ strip by hand, just as you did the scrap, to get a small start. Then mount the strip between the centers of your lathe with the dowel-maker attached. Keep a tight grip on the dowel-maker and turn the lathe on the run at its *slowest* speed. (Be ready to let go of the dowel maker and turn the lathe off *immediately* should something go wrong.) Once you're sure that the lathe is running smoothly and the stock isn't binding or chattering in the dowel-maker, *slowly* draw the dowel-maker down the length of the strip. (See Figure 6.) The tool will cut a perfect 1″ dowel in a snap.

Tip ◆ You may want to cut the strips 1/16″-1/8″ oversize so there are no flat areas on the finished dowel.

Figure 5. Test the dowel-maker by turning a piece of scrap through it. Adjust the position of the knife so that it cuts the wood smoothly, leaving a 1″ dowel.

Since you've gone to so much trouble to make the racks out of the same wood as the shelves, you'll also want to plug the screw holes in the shelves with a matching wood. To make your own plugs, first select a plug-cutter the same diameter as the counterbore. (If you use a commercial #8 pilot drill, the diameter of the counterbore is usually 3/8″.) Mount the plug cutter in your drill press and drill part way through a scrap of wood from the project. Repeat as many times as necessary to get the number of plugs you need. (See Figure 7.) Cut the plugs free from the scrap on a bandsaw. (See Figure 8.)

Figure 6. To use the dowel maker on the lathe, mount the stock between the centers with the dowel-maker already in place. Turn on the machine and carefully draw the dowel-maker across the stock.

Figure 7. Mount a plug cutter in your drill press, and drill plugs part way through a scrap of wood from the project.

Figure 8. Cut the plugs free from the scrap on a bandsaw.

Figure 9. Use your pocket knife to hold the plugs while you dip them in glue and insert them in the screw holes.

To quickly install the plugs, use your pocket knife like a 'fork'. Stab one end of the plug with the point, then dip the other end in a puddle of glue. (See Figure 9.) Insert the glue end into the counterbore and remove the knife. Tap the plug down into the hole with a mallet. *Be sure* the grain on the plug is oriented in the same direction as the grain in the surrounding wood. When the glue is dry, sand off the plugs flush with the surface of the wood.

Only one other step in the construction requires any special attention: making the paper holder. You may want to use a holder from an old rack or one that you purchase in a plumbing store — this would certainly be easier. But if you're a purist, you can make your own spring-loaded holder. You can purchase the spring you need at most

automotive stores. Just be sure that there is enough clearance so that you can get the holder in and out of the rack easily.

Coat the racks with a water-resistant finish, since this project will have to withstand a lot of moisture. Avoid polyurethane and other 'building' finishes. These will delaminate and peel off the wood after so many months of expanding and contracting with the changing humidity. The traditional water-resistant finish is tung oil — the Chinese still use this penetrating finish to preserve the hulls of their wooden boats. There is also a new product out called "QRB". QRB is a blend of tung oil and several other chemicals that make it impervious to 'spotting'. It's available from QRB Industries, 3139 U.S. 31 North, Niles, MI, 49120.

BILL OF MATERIALS — Bath Towel Holder

Finished Dimensions in Inches

A.	Shelves (2)	3/4 x 8 x 30-3/4
B.	Sides (2)	3/4 x 8 x 22-1/2
C.	Backstops (2)	3/4 x 3 x 30
D.	Racks (2)	1 dia. x 30-3/4

Hardware

#8 x 1-1/4" Flathead Wood Screws (8)
1/4" Hanger Bolts and Molly Anchors (2-4)

BILL OF MATERIALS — Hand Towel Holder

Finished Dimensions in Inches

A.	Shelves (3)	3/4 x 7 x 10-3/4
B.	Sides (2)	3/4 x 7 x 27-1/4
C.	Backstops (3)	3/4 x 3 x 10
D.	Rack	1 dia. x 10-3/4

Hardware

#8 x 1-1/4" Flathead Wood Screws (1 dozen)
1/4" Hanger Bolts and Molly Anchors (2-4)

BILL OF MATERIALS — Paper Roll Holder

Finished Dimensions in Inches

A.	Shelf	3/4 x 6 x 6-1/4
B.	Sides (2)	3/4 x 6 x 12-3/4
C.	Backstop	3/4 x 5-1/2 x 6
D.	Rack*	1 dia. x 5-3/8
E.	Dowel*	1/2 dia. x 1

Hardware

#8 x 1-1/4" Flathead Wood Screws (7-8)
1/4" Hanger Bolts and Molly Anchors (2)
1/2" dia. x 1-1/2" Spring*

*These parts are optional. You need them only if you intend to make your own spring-loaded rack. You can buy ready-made racks at most plumbing supply stores.

Designed and built by Nick Engler

Laminated Nesting Tables

A few materials and methods borrowed from an auto body shop makes these tables sparkle.

During the seventeenth century, oriental craftsmen introduced furniture with a thick, glossy finish made from the resin of the *Rhus vernicifera*, or Asian Sumac tree. This came to be called 'laminated' furniture, because the finish was built up by applying as many as thirty coats of resin. Often, this resin was tinted so the furniture appeared to be made of colored glass.

Today, you can duplicate the appearance of a laminated finish by applying colored enamel paint over a carefully prepared surface. The modern nesting tables you see here were finished in this manner.

Making the Tables

Of course, the first step in making laminated furniture is to build the furniture. (My shop teacher would be proud of me for that bit of wisdom.) The tables are extremely simple —each one is made from just three pieces of plywood. By following the techniques outlined here, you can build all four of them in just a few hours.

Start with the tops. All four tops are exactly the same, as if they were cut from a single plywood circle, 48″ in diameter. You can cut a big circle, then cut it into quadrants, but this would be a waste of time. Instead, temporarily nail four 2′ x 2′ sheets of plywood together. Scribe an arc with a radius of 24″ from corner to corner. (See Figure 1.) Then 'pad saw' all four sheets on a bandsaw. (See Figure 2.)

You can also pad saw the side pieces, two at a time. They can't all be pad sawn together because the radii of the

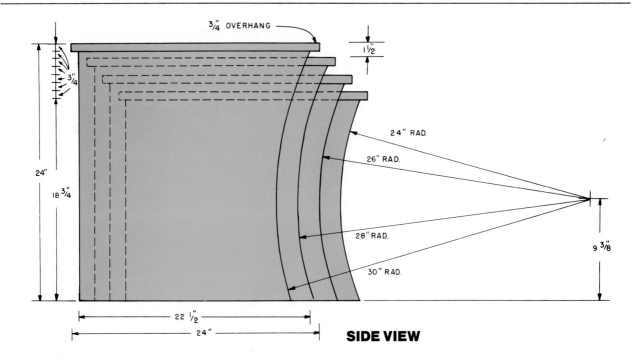

3/4 OVERHANG
1½
3/4
24"
18 3/4"
24" RAD.
26" RAD.
28" RAD.
30" RAD.
9 3/8"
22 1/2"
24"

SIDE VIEW

curves are different. Just remember that on each table, one side is 3/4″ shorter than the other, and stack them together accordingly.

Round over all edges on all pieces, *except* those edges that will butt up against another piece — or the floor. Use a shaper or a router to do the rounding, and round both the top *and* bottom of an edge, removing all hard corners. (See Figure 3.)

After you've machined the parts, assemble them with wood screws and glue. Use plenty of glue, and wipe off the excess with a damp rag. Finally, cover the screw holes and fill any 'voids' in the plywood with wood putty. (See Figure 4.)

Tip ◆ You can also eliminate the voids by using a good cabinet-grade plywood. There are several imports from northern Europe and the Soviet Union that are completely free of voids. These may be available on special order from your local lumberyard.

Laminating

In order to finish these tables, you have to make the surface perfectly smooth. Sanding won't accomplish the smoothness you're after; even the minute openings in the wood grain will dull the finish. Instead, you need to cover up the wood completely.

Spray the tables with gray metal primer to fill in the imperfections in the wood. (See Figure 5.) Primer dries

Figure 1. To cut the tops, temporarily tack the stock together. Scribe a 24″ arc on the top sheet from corner to corner, using a third corner as the center of the arc.

24" RADIUS

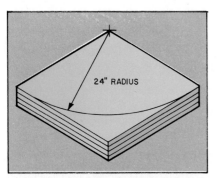

Figure 2. Pad saw the tabletops on a bandsaw. This will save a lot of time — and insure that all the tops turn out exactly the same.

Figure 3. Round over the edges of the plywood with a shaper or router. Be sure to round both sides of an edge.

Figure 4. If there are any 'voids' showing in the plywood, fill them with wood putty.

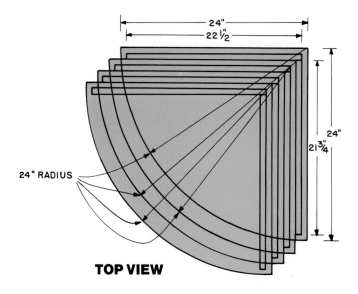

TOP VIEW

fairly thick, and it will completely cover the wood grain with no need to sand it beforehand. However, you'll need to finish sand the primer after it's dry. If you can still see any wood grain, apply a second coat of primer and sand again.

When the tables are completed, primed and sanded, cover them with several coats of epoxy paint. (See Figure 6.) You can use either a brush or a spray gun to apply this paint; if you're careful, the results should be the same. The only advantage of a spray gun is that it saves time — sometimes. But in the hands of a careful, patient woodworker, a brush can be just as effective.

Variations

You don't *have* to paint the tables, you know. This modern design looks just fine if you let the wood grain show. If you choose not to paint, I suggest you use a good cabinet-grade plywood, veneered on both sides. *Don't* shape the edges. Instead, cover the edges with 'veneer tape' to hide the plies. When you finish the project, sand carefully to avoid scraping through the thin veneers.

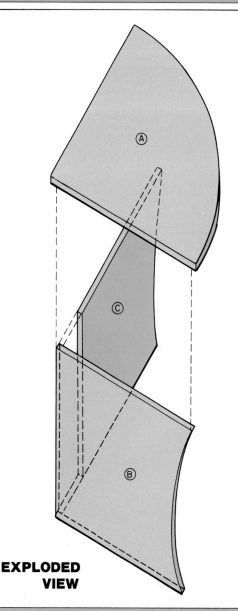

EXPLODED VIEW

Figure 5. To cover the imperfections in the wood, cover the tables with several coats of auto body primer. Sand between each coat.

Figure 6. Finally, apply a high-gloss enamel paint. If you have properly prepared the surface of the tables, a brushed-on finish should look every bit as good as one that was sprayed on.

BILL OF MATERIALS — Nesting Tables	
Finished Dimensions in Inches	
Large Table	
A. Top	3/4 x 24 x 24
B. Large Side	3/4 x 22-1/2 x 23-1/4
C. Small Side	3/4 x 21-3/4 x 23-1/4
Medium-Large Table	
A. Top	3/4 x 24 x 24
B. Large Side	3/4 x 22-1/2 x 21-3/4
C. Small Side	3/4 x 21-3/4 x 21-3/4
Medium-Small Table	
A. Top	3/4 x 24 x 24
B. Large Side	3/4 x 22-1/2 x 20-1/4
C. Small Side	3/4 x 21-3/4 x 20-1/4
Small Table	
A. Top	3/4 x 24 x 24
B. Large Side	3/4 x 22-1/2 x 18-3/4
C. Small Side	3/4 x 21-3/4 x 18-3/4

Designed and built by Dan Gabriel

Rocking Horse

It's the next best thing to a real pony!

A rocking horse holds a special fascination for a child. It's more than a toy; it's a promise: A promise of adventure, of freedom, of wonderful people and places just over the next horizon.

Dan Gabriel understands this promise more than most. When his daughter, Biddy, asked for the proverbial pony that all children desire, Dan determined to fashion one himself. The care he took in constructing Biddy's pony is evident to anyone who appreciates fine woodworking. In addition to poplar, oak, hair, and leather, you can almost sense the adventure and taste the freedom that Dan built into this project. After all, what better way is there for a

daughter to grow up than riding through her childhood on a promise hand-crafted by her father?

Dan cautions anyone who would attempt to follow his plans that this is not a simple project. It requires an enormous amount of trials and errors. "The first head I carved," recalls Dan, "looked more like a bulldog than a pony. It took me a long time to get it to look like something you'd want to ride."

Each piece hand-fitted to the next. When you consider all the odd angles in this project, this adds up to an enormous amount of work. Dan estimates that he spent the better part of every evening for almost three months making the rocking horse. But, in the end, it was worth it. "Biddy insists on kissing her pony good night every time she goes to bed," says Dan. "What better return on my time could I ask for?"

Roughing Out the Horse

The first problem that Dan grappled with when he set out to build this horse was deciding what wood he should make it from. Everyone he talked to recommended basswood.

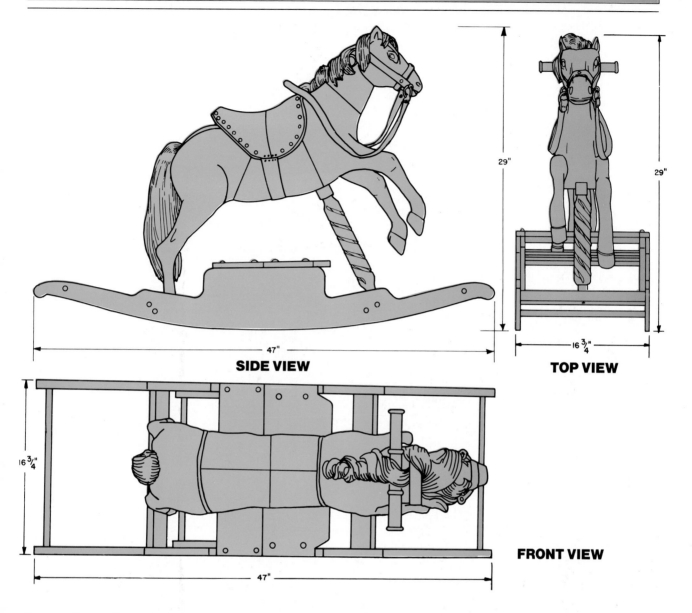

SIDE VIEW

47"

TOP VIEW

29"

16 3/4"

FRONT VIEW

16 3/4"

47"

29"

Carvers the world over prefer this wood because it's easy to work with. But, Dan wasn't convinced that basswood was right for this project. "There really isn't that much carving involved," he explains. "With the exception of the head, the horse is 'built' and the parts rounded over." Besides, it was hard to find pieces of basswood large enough to make the legs.

Dan eventually settled on poplar. It's fairly light, strong, and it has a close grain that makes it easier to carve than many other hardwoods. It's also relatively inexpensive. "When I screwed up," Dan says, " I didn't feel like I was wasting good lumber."

Making the horse from a single, solid piece of wood was out of the question. No matter how you would orient the grain, two of the legs would have been weak. Also, large, thick pieces of wood are apt to split or check as time goes by. Instead, Dan built up a hollow horse from many different pieces, always positioning the grain to give the individual piece the maximum possible strength.

Start at the top, with the head. Cut five pieces according to the head pattern. *However,* only the two outside pieces should include the ears, and only the three middle pieces should include the tenon at the base of the neck. Cut a 1″ deep notch along the neck and top of the head in the middle-most piece. When the pieces are glued together, this notch will form a dado in which to mount the mane.

Carve the shape and details on the head, as shown in the patterns. Actually, there are only three details that require any carving skill — the ears, the eyes, and the nose. The rest of the head simply requires careful rounding and shaping. What sort of tools should you use? Dan says, "I used anything that cut wood." The tools he relied on the most, however, were Surform® for rounding and shaping, and a set of *sharp* chisels for detail work.

Tip ◆ If you're an inexperienced carver, you'll find you have better control if you use a mallet with your chisels. Don't actually hit them with the mallet; just *tap* them gently until you've cut as deep or removed as much stock as you want. Hold the mallet loosely; your hand won't fatigue as quickly.

I SQUARE = 1½"

HEAD PATTERN

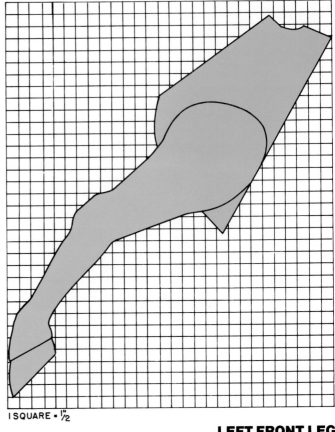

I SQUARE = 1½"

LEFT FRONT LEG PATTERN

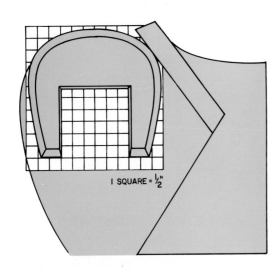

I SQUARE = ½"

SADDLE FRAME PATTERN

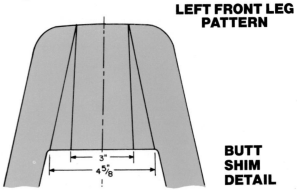

3"
4⅝"

BUTT SHIM DETAIL

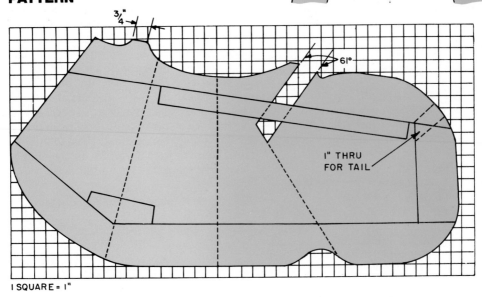

¾"

61°

I" THRU FOR TAIL

BODY PATTERN AND LAYOUT

I SQUARE = I"

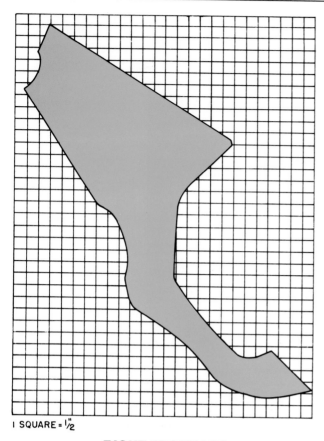

I SQUARE = 1½"

RIGHT FRONT LEG PATTERN

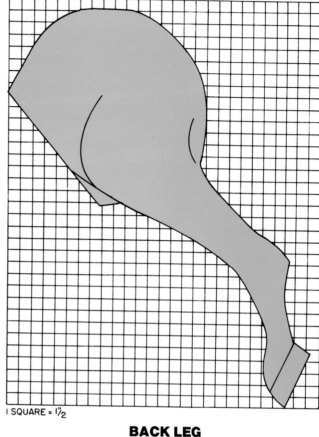

I SQUARE = 1½"

BACK LEG PATTERN

When you've got the face and neck of the horse looking like a horse, make the parts for the rest of the body. As mentioned earlier, the body is *hollow*. The left and right body parts are attached to spacers. Each side consists of a front and back leg, a 'back side', and a 'front side' — four parts in all. Holding the side parts apart are five spacers —saddle, back (or top), butt (for want of a more polite term), belly, and chest.

In addition, a 'saddle frame' rests in a slot between the back and butt, and back legs and back side. A glue block reinforces the joint between the belly and chest, and a saddle support joins the saddle and back. Finally, two 'leg shims' hold the back legs so that they are slightly splayed. These shims are tapered from the bottom of the horse to the top. Dan used a hand-held belt sander to do the tapering.

Make the side parts first, laying them out so that they all fit together properly. Then, make the spacers, glue block, and shims. Attach the sides to these parts *temporarily* with wood screws. True up any parts that don't butt properly with adjoining parts. Also, attach the head temporarily and fit it to the front legs. Lastly, make and shape the saddle frame. This one piece will require more patient handwork than all the others combined. But you'll find it's absolutely essential when it comes time to cover the saddle with leather.

Tip ◆ Countersink the screws deeply into the wood. They will soon become a permanent part of the project.

Shaping the Horse

With the horse roughed out, begin to shape the body. Work mostly with Surform® rasps, removing just a little stock at a time until the horse begins to look more and more like a horse. (See Figure 1.) If you happen to hit a screw, remove it. Drill the countersink slightly deeper, and replace the screw.

Tip ◆ Before you begin shaping the horse, you might want to visit a toy store and buy a cheap plastic toy horse. Use this as a model when you're shaping the body parts and putting in the muscle detail.

Figure 1. You'll find that a good selection of Surform® rasps are invaluable when it comes time to shape the various parts of the horse.

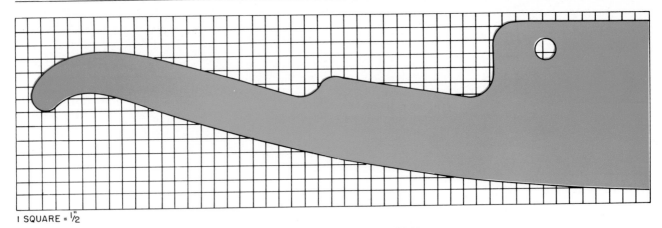

I SQUARE = $\frac{1}{2}''$

ROCKER HALF PATTERN

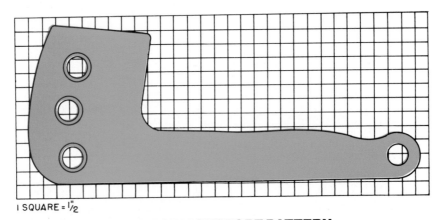

I SQUARE = $1\frac{1}{2}''$

PLATFORM SUPPORT PATTERN

Figure 2. The body of the horse is hollow. The side pieces are held apart by spacers, and the head attaches to the body via a tenon.

Only two areas on the body require any true carving — the hooves and the saddle. Both of these are extremely simple; just make a deep groove to delineate the hoof or the saddle.

When you're finished shaping the horse, disassemble the pieces. They should look something like the pieces shown in Figure 2. Then reassemble them with glue and wood screws. Cover all the screw heads with poplar plugs. Wipe off all excess glue with a damp rag.

When the glue dries, do any fine shaping that remains to be done. Then, finish sand the entire horse.

Making the Rocker Stand

Any good rocker stand for a rocking horse should include a firm platform for the child's feet. This provides a measure of safety and makes it easier for the child to set the horse in motion.

Dan wanted Biddy to have a solid place to plant her feet, but he didn't want her to outgrow the horse too soon. So he designed an *adjustable* platform that can be lowered as the child grows and his or her legs get longer.

The adjustable part of the platform is attached to two supports which are, in turn, hinged to the rockers. Each of these supports have four 13/16″ holes drilled in them. Three of these holes in the front of the supports make it possible to adjust the platform to three different heights.

A 3/4″ dowel locks this platform in each position. This dowel is passed through a 13/16″ hole in the *right* rocker (as you're looking toward the rear), through the holes in the supports, and into a slot in the left rocker. The right end of the dowel then drops down into a slot just under the hole in the right rocker, locking it in position until you raise the platform slightly. (See Figure 3.)

Cut out the parts for the platform, according to the patterns provided. Assemble the rockers, stationary platform, adjustable platform, platform supports, and dowel stretchers with glue and wood screws. Cut the flat stretchers, but don't assemble them to the rockers just yet.

Turn the support post on your lathe. The design for this post is left up to your own discretion and taste. Dan cut a spiral in his post with a Router-Crafter®, so that it resembles the traditional support post on a carousel.

Drill a hole for the upper end of the support post in the underside of the horse, between the chest and the belly spacers. Drill a hole for the lower end in one of the flat stretchers. Temporarily assemble the flat stretchers, horse, and support post, and lay this assembly in place between the rockers. Carefully mark the positions for the flat spacers. Disassemble the horse and support post, and attach the flat stretchers to the rockers with glue and wood screws. Finally, assemble the support post and horse to the rocker stand.

Finishing Touches

Finish sand all parts that still need it, then stain and finish the project. (Dan used a walnut oil stain and covered this with several coats of Deft®.) You *must* completely finish the wooden parts of this project *before* you add any hair or leather.

Add the hair before you do the leather work. The mane is just an old wig, and the tail is a 'fall'. Dan picked up both the wig and the fall at a secondhand store. A slightly curved

block of wood — the 'mane keeper' — holds the mane in place in the groove in the neck. Hide this keeper by gluing some extra hair to the top of the block. The tail is held in a 1″ hole in the butt by a wooden plug. To hide this plug, position the tail so the hair falls down over it.

Dan used the leather from an old purse to cover the saddle and to make the reins and cinch. Rivet the reins to the nose with screw eyes and rings. (See Figure 4.) The rings and eyes are available at any hardware store, and the rivets and any other leatherworking tools you may need are available at a leathercraft store. To finish the saddle, put a thin foam rubber pad down on the saddle, then stretch the leather over this. Nail the leather in place with upholstery tacks, and trim it up. Finally, edge the saddle with 1/4″ hemp rope. (See Figure 5.)

And that's it. Now all you need is a small daughter or a son to ride the rocking horse away into the sunset.

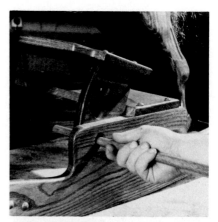

Figure 3. Once the platform is adjusted to the desired height, a 3/4″ dowel is inserted through holes in the supports. This dowel then drops into slots in the rockers, locking the platform in place.

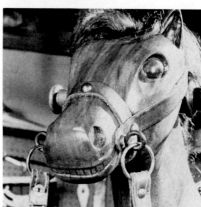

Figure 4. Rivet the reins to the nose with brass screw eyes and rings.

Figure 5. Hold the leather saddle in place with upholstery tacks, then edge it with a length of rope.

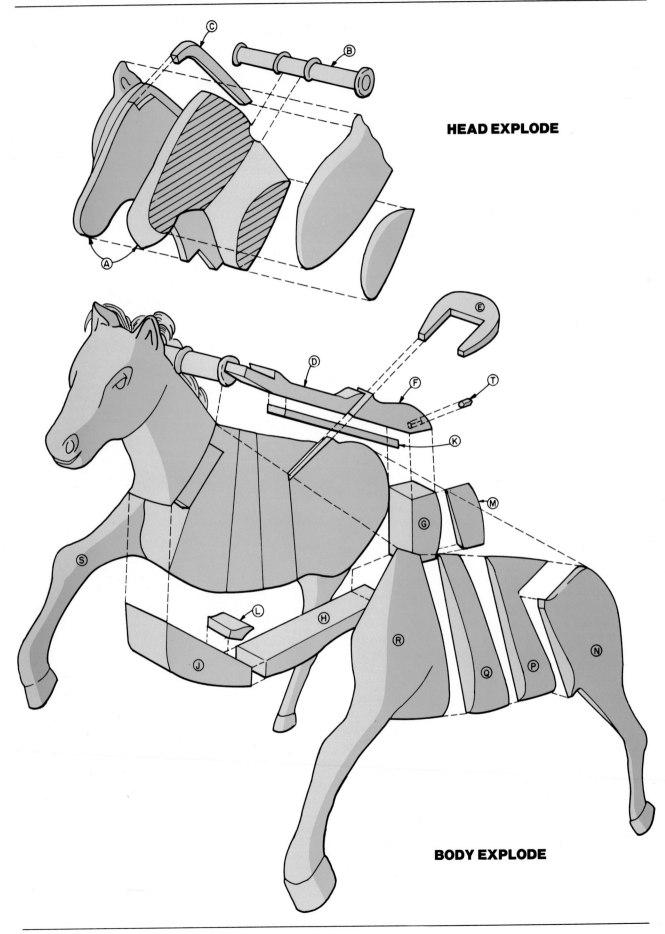

HEAD EXPLODE

BODY EXPLODE

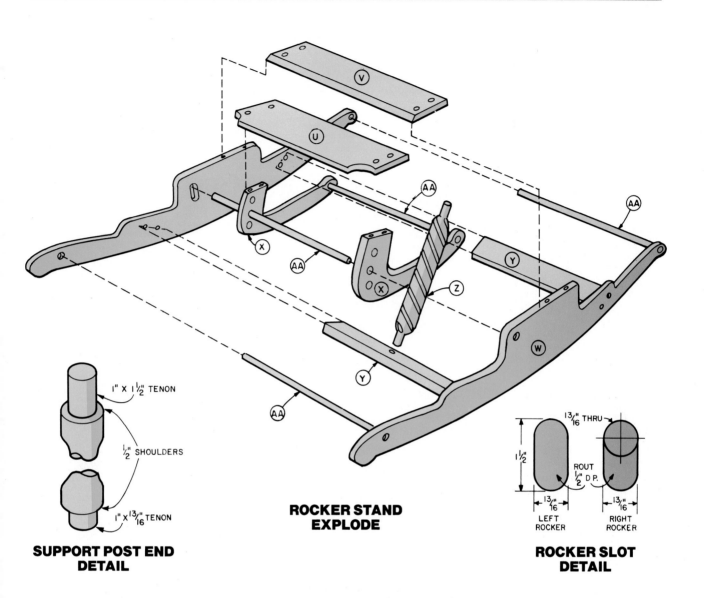

ROCKER STAND EXPLODE

SUPPORT POST END DETAIL

1" X 1½" TENON
½" SHOULDERS
1" X 13/16" TENON

ROCKER SLOT DETAIL

13/16" THRU
1½
ROUT ½" D.P.
13/16"
LEFT ROCKER
13/16"
RIGHT ROCKER

BILL OF MATERIALS — Rocking Horse

Rough Dimensions in Inches

A.	Head (5)	13/16 x 11 x 12-1/2
B.	Handgrip	1-3/8 dia. x 9-1/2
C.	Mane Keeper	5/8 x 1-1/2 x 7-1/2
D.	Saddle	1-3/4 x 3 x 10
E.	Saddle Frame	13/16 x 5-1/2 x 6
F.	Back	1-3/4 x 3 x 7
G.	Butt	1-3/4 x 3 x 4-1/4
H.	Belly	1-3/4 x 3 x 15
J.	Chest	1-3/4 x 3 x 6-1/4
K.	Saddle Support	13/16 x 3 x 10-3/4
L.	Glue Block	1-1/4 x 3 x 2-3/4
M.	Leg Shims	13/16 x 8-1/2 x 8-1/2
N.	Back Legs (2)	1-3/4 x 13 x 16-1/2
P.	Back Side (2)	1-3/4 x 5 x 8-1/2
Q.	Front Side (2)	1-3/4 x 4-3/4 x 9-1/2
R.	Left Front Leg	1-3/4 x 14
S.	Right Front Leg	1-3/4 x 12-3/4
T.	Tail Plug	3/4 dia. x 1-1/2

U.	Adjustable Platform	13/16 x 6-1/2 x 16-3/4
V.	Fixed Platform	13/16 x 4-3/4 x 16-3/4
W.	Rockers (2)	13/16 x 6-5/8 x 47
X.	Platform Supports (2)	13/16 x 5-3/4 x 15-1/4
Y.	Flat Stretchers (2)	13/16 x 2-1/4 x 15-1/8
Z.	Support Post	2 dia. x 14-1/4
AA.	Dowel Stretchers (4)	3/4 dia. x 15-3/4

Hardware

#10 x 2" Flathead Wood Screws (3-4 dozen)
Leather for Saddle (10" x 14")
Leather for Reins (3/4" x 62")
Leather for Cinch (1-1/4" x 15")
1" Rings (2)
Leather Rivets (4)
Brass Screw Eyes (2)
Upholstery Tacks (4-5 dozen)
1/4" Hemp Rope (40")

Hexagonal Picnic Table

This sturdy outdoor table seats six 'in the round'.

Yes, I know — it looks like a big spider. Actually, I built this picnic table to resemble a giant, ferocious insect for a very good reason. It scares off the ants.

The design also has several other advantages. First of all, the conversation flows better and the food gets passed quicker when people are seated in the round. And second, the table is just about tip proof. (Remember the picnic where you, Cousin Ed, and Aunt Edna all sat on the north side of the table, and Uncle Edsel sat on the south? Edsel's weight,

through some quirk of genetics, was equal to the three of you. As long as he stayed put, so did the table. But when Edsel went to fetch another side of beef, the picnic table reared up like a frightened horse and you ended up wearing the potato salad.)

Adjusting the Dimensions

As designed, the hexagonal picnic table will seat six adults in relative comfort (relative to the weather and the number of mosquitoes in the vicinity of the table). However, if you want to seat more than six people — or if long legs run in your family — you may want to increase the dimensions somewhat.

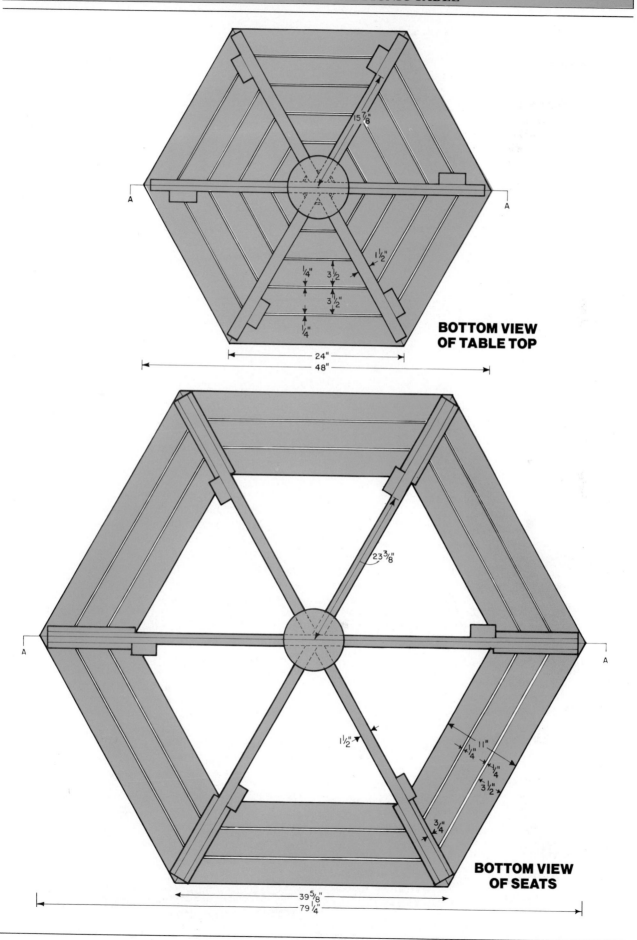

**BOTTOM VIEW
OF TABLE TOP**

**BOTTOM VIEW
OF SEATS**

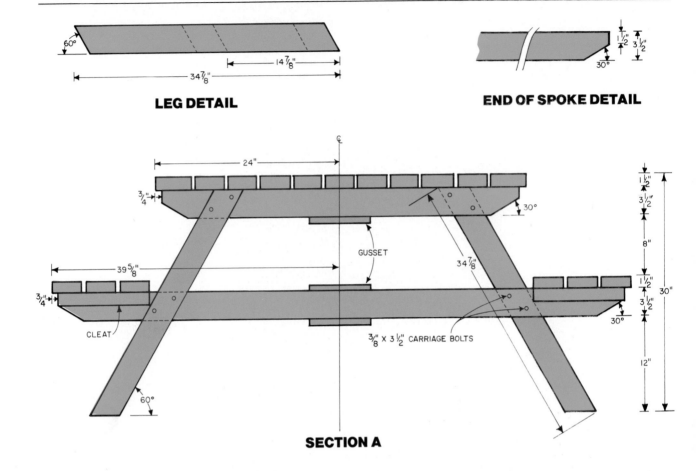

LEG DETAIL

END OF SPOKE DETAIL

SECTION A

To enlarge the seating capacity and/or the leg room, simply increase the length of the spokes, the top planks, and the seat planks. The equation is simple: If you want to increase the diameter of the table and the attached seat by 4″, add 4″ to the length of the long spokes, 2″ to the length of the short spokes, and 2″ to the length of all planks. The other parts will remain as shown in the drawings.

> **Tip ◆** If you increase the diameter of the table 4″, move the legs 2″ away from the center. Keep the legs as far to the outside as possible. Otherwise, the table may become unstable.

Of course, it goes without saying, that if you increase the diameter of the top and seats, you'll also have to increase the amount of building materials. As designed, I used 15 ten-foot construction grade redwood 2x4's. If you add 4″ to the diameter of the table, get yourself one or two more boards.

Building the Wheels

The picnic table consists of two large six-sided 'wheels'. These wheels are suspended one above the other by six legs attached to the spokes. Both wheels are built from 2x4's in exactly the same manner.

Cut all the parts to length, mitering the ends as needed. The planks are mitered at 30° across the *face* of the board, while the short spokes are mitered at 30° through the *thickness*. The shortest spokes are *double-mitered* — first cut them to the same length as the short spokes. (See Figure 1.)

Then turn them over, and make a second miter cut. (See Figure 2.) The 'point' created by this second cut should be 3/4″ from either side of the board (half the thickness).

Taper the outside ends of the spokes at 60°, using a circular saw, sabre saw, or table saw. If your table saw miter gauge will tilt to 60°, you can make a simple jig to do all the taper cuts quickly and accurately. Just attach a long wooden face to the miter gauge, and clamp a stop block to this face. Clamp the board you want to taper in the jig, and slowly feed it into the blade. (See Figure 3.)

Warning: Be extremely careful when tapering the spokes on a table saw, as this operation must be performed with the saw guard flipped up and out of the way.

Attach the cleats to the outside ends of the seat spokes, using 6d *galvanized* nails. These cleats provide extra support for the seat planks. They're not needed for the top spokes, because the tabletop shouldn't have to support Uncle Edsel's weight — very often.

Figure 1. Miter the ends of the short and the shortest spokes at 30°. Initially, make both sets of spokes the same length.

Tack the spokes together to form two 'stars', one large (for the seats) and one small (for the tabletop). Working from the outside toward the inside, attach the planks to the spokes with 16d *galvanized* nails. I'm stressing the use of galvanized nails because ordinary nails will rust and eventually ruin the project. Also, allow a 1/4" gap between the planks. If you position the planks edge to edge, the wood will swell up, trapping the moisture, and it will begin to rot.

> **Tip ◆** Don't hammer the nails all the way in until you've positioned *all* the planks on a wheel. Just tack the planks in place until you're sure they all fit. (See Figure 4.)

If you've increased the diameter of the table, you must also increase the length and the *number* of top planks. You'll also have to figure out how long each successive course of planks should be. To do this, use this rule of thumb: If your planks are 3-1/2" wide, each row of planks is 4-1/4" *shorter* than the row to the outside. For example, if the outermost row of planks is 28" long, the next row to the inside will be 23-3/4", the next will be 19-1/2", and so on. This allows for the 1/4" gap between rows.

Once you've attached the planks to the wheels, add a gusset to the bottom of the top wheel, and two gussets — one on top, one on the bottom — to the seat wheel. These gussets strengthen the union of the spokes. Orient the grain of the gussets so that it's *perpendicular* to the grain of the long spokes. (See Figure 5.)

Attaching the Legs

To attach the legs to the table, turn the top wheel upside down on a level surface — the floor of your shop or a driveway. Turn the seat wheel upside down on top of it.

Using concrete blocks or scrap wood (or both), prop the seat wheel up off the top wheel, so that the tops of the seats (facing down) are *exactly* 13" off the ground, all the way around the wheel. Also, center the seat wheel over the top wheel as best you can.

Clamp two legs to the top spokes on opposite sides of the wheel. Measure carefully to be sure that these legs are properly positioned. Then measure where they meet the seat spokes to see if the seat wheel is centered. When you're sure the spokes are positioned correctly and the wheels are centered, clamp the legs to the seat spokes. Drill holes for the carriage bolts, insert the bolts, and remove the clamps.

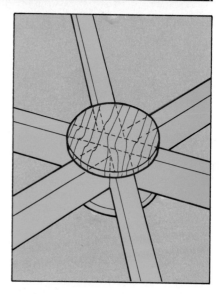

Figure 2. Turn the shortest spokes over and cut a second 30° miter. This will 'point' the spokes. That point should be equidistant from both sides of the board.

Figure 3. If your table saw miter gauge will tilt to 60°, you can make this simple jig to taper the spokes. But be extremely careful when you cut, since you must flip the saw guard up out of the way to use this jig.

Figure 4. Tack the planks in place, working from the outside toward the inside. Don't hammer the nails in all the way until you have positioned all the planks.

Figure 5. Position the gussets over the union of the spokes to strengthen the joint. The wood grain of the gusset should be perpendicular to the grain of the long spoke.

Repeat this process for each set of legs, until you have attached all six legs. (See Figure 6.) It's possible to use 16d nails to attach the legs, but carriage bolts are better. They can be tightened if the table ever becomes 'wobbly', and they let you partially disassemble the table if you want to move it or store it.

Finally, turn the table right side up. If you want, finish it with a good oil-based outdoor stain.

Figure 6. Clamp the legs in place on the spokes, measure to see that all parts are properly positioned and centered, *then* drill holes for the carriage bolts.

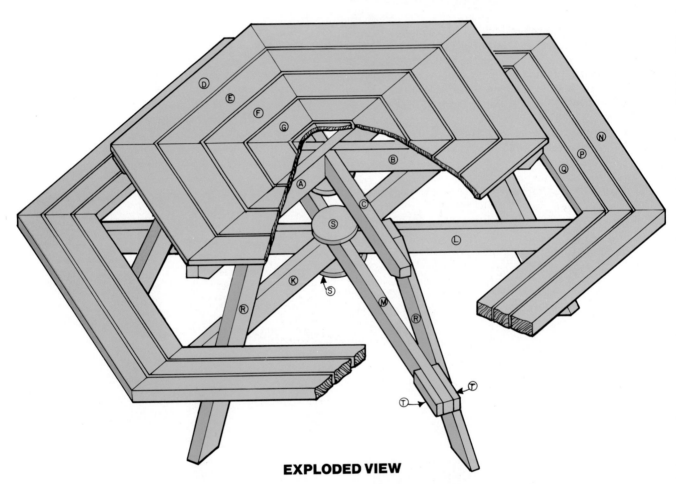

EXPLODED VIEW

BILL OF MATERIALS — Hexagonal Picnic Table

Finished Dimensions in Inches

A.	Long Top Spoke	1-1/2 x 3-1/2 x 46-1/2	**N.**	First Course Seat Planks (6)	1-1/2 x 3-1/2 x 39-5/8
B.	Short Top Spokes (2)	1-1/2 x 3-1/2 x 22-13/16	**P.**	Second Course Seat Planks (6)	1-1/2 x 3-1/2 x 35-3/8
C.	Shortest Top Spokes (2)	1-1/2 x 3-1/2 x 22-3/8	**Q.**	Third Course Seat Planks (6)	1-1/2 x 3-1/2 x 31-1/8
D.	First Course Top Planks (6)	1-1/2 x 3-1/2 x 24	**R.**	Legs (6)	1-1/2 x 3-1/2 x 34-7/8
E.	Second Course Top Planks (6)	1-1/2 x 3-1/2 x 19-3/4	**S.**	Gussets (3)	7-1/2 dia. x 3/4
F.	Third Course Top Planks (6)	1-1/2 x 3-1/2 x 15-1/2	**T.**	Cleats (12)	3/4 x 1-1/2 x 12
G.	Fourth Course Top Planks (6)	1-1/2 x 3-1/2 x 11-1/4			
H.	Fifth Course Top Planks (6)	1-1/2 x 3-1/2 x 7			
J.	Top Center Pieces (2)	1-1/2 x 2-1/2 x 5-5/8			
K.	Long Seat Spoke	1-1/2 x 3-1/2 x 77-3/4			
L.	Short Seat Spokes (2)	1-1/2 x 3-1/2 x 38-7/16			
M.	Shortest Seat Spokes (2)	1-1/2 x 3-1/2 x 38			

Hardware

16d Galvanized Common Nails (2 lb.)
6d Galvanized Common Nails (1/2 lb.)
3/8″ x 3-1/2″ Carriage Bolts, Washers, and Nuts (24)

Designed and built by Nick Engler

Making Knives

Get a handle on your knives — safely and securely.

I'm certain that manufacturers of kitchen equipment put powerful magnets in their garbage disposals just for spite. Leave a piece of silverware at the edge of the sink when you flip the switch and suddenly — GRIIIND! —your cutlery looks like you invited a convention of psychic spoon benders over for dinner.

Kitchen knives with wooden handles die a particularly horrible death in a disposal. The blades can usually be straightened and resharpened, but more often than not, the handles are ruined. At our house, we reserve the back of the silverware drawer as a makeshift morgue for these casualties — knives with handles too chewed up and splintered to use; blades too good to throw away.

After losing a favorite paring knife in this manner, I decided I had collected enough dead knives. There *must* be a way to resurrect them. Handles couldn't be too hard to replace, could they?

I was right. Knife handles *aren't* hard to replace. They require some careful work, however. But once you get the hang of it, you need never throw away another disposal-ravaged knife. Furthermore, you can make your own knives! Here's how:

Replacing a Knife Handle

A knife handle is held to the blade with two or more soft brass rivets. Sometimes the handle consists of two pieces of wood with the blade sandwiched in between. On other knives, the handle is a single piece of wood with the blade inset in a saw kerf. However your knife is put together, the first order of business is to drill out the rivets and remove the handle. (See Figure 1.)

Don't throw away the old handle yet. Instead, use it as a pattern for a new one. Rough out a new handle from a hard, dense oily wood — these will stand up to food juices and dishwater better than porous woods. The best woods are rosewood, ebony, teak, coco-bolo and similar 'exotics'. These are expensive, but it only takes a small amount to make a handle.

Tip ◆ When you saw the wood, cut a little wide of the pattern. (See Figure 2.) You can sand the handle to the proper dimensions *after* you attach it to the blade.

Using the blade as a template, mark the new handle blank(s) where you want to put the rivets. (See Figure 3.) You'll have to drill several times for each rivet. First of all, you'll have to counterbore for the rivet heads on both sides of the handle. Then you'll have to drill a hole for the shaft of the rivet. (See Figure 4.)

It's best to start out by drilling a tiny hole, 1/16″ in diameter, all the way through the blank(s) to mark the position of the rivet. (See Figure 5.) If the knife handle consists of two halves, tape them together temporarily so the rivet holes will line up exactly. Next, counterbore for the rivet heads. Drill the counterbore just a hair deeper than the thickness of the head. Finally, drill for the rivet shaft. You'll get the best results if you use brad-point bits when drilling

Figure 1. To remove an old handle from a knife, drill out the brass rivets.

Figure 2. Saw a new handle blank on your bandsaw. Cut wide of the line — you can sand off the extra stock later.

Figure 3. Use the blade as a template to mark the positions of the rivets on the handle blank.

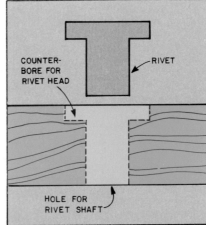

COUNTER-BORE FOR RIVET HEAD

RIVET

HOLE FOR RIVET SHAFT

Figure 4. Before you can insert a rivet in the handle, you must drill a hole for the rivet shaft and counterbore for the rivet head.

Figure 5. To mark the exact position of the rivets on both sides of the handle blank(s), drill small holes about 1/16″ in diameter all the way through the wood.

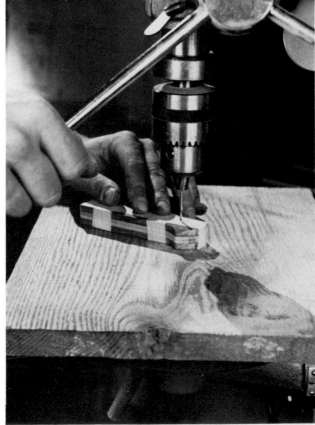

the counterbore and shaft holes. The indentation left by the brad points make it easy to center a small hole inside a large one.

> **Tip ◆** There are special drills available that drill the counterbore and shaft hole in one step. (See Figure 6.) A drill stop helps insure that the counterbore is not too deep.

When you've made all the rivet holes, rivet the handle to the blade. Knife rivets come in two parts — male and female. The male rivet looks like a small tack with a blunt pin. The female rivet has a hollow shaft. When you tap the male rivet into the female, the pin causes the hollow shaft to expand slightly, wedging the rivet in the wood. (See Figure 7.) This keeps the handle snug on the knife.

Before you pound any rivets, wrap a generous amount of masking tape around the sharp edge of the blade. (See Figure 8.) This will keep you from cutting yourself during the next few steps. Assemble the handle blank(s) and the blade, lining up the holes. Insert the female rivets first on one side of the handle. Then lay the handle on an anvil with the heads of the female rivets pointing down. Insert the male rivets from the top and tap them home with light blows from a small hammer. (See Figure 9.)

With the handle blanks securely in place, sand all excess stock from the handle so that the wood is flush with the metal. (See Figure 10.) You may also wish to do some 'shaping' on the sander, making indentations for fingers and

Figure 8. Before you rivet the handle to the blade or sand the excess stock from the handle, cover the exposed area of the blade with several layers of masking tape.

Figure 6. There are special drills available which allow you to drill the shaft hole and counterbore for the rivet head all in one step.

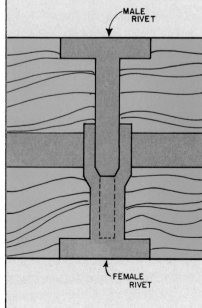

MALE RIVET

FEMALE RIVET

Figure 7. The pin of the male rivet is tapped into the female rivet, causing the shaft of the rivet to expand. This wedges the rivet in the wood and holds the handle securely to the blade.

Figure 9. Tap the male rivets home with a light hammer. Be sure the heads of the female rivets are resting on an anvil or some other hard metal surface.

Figure 10. Use a belt sander to remove excess stock from the handle and sand the wood flush with the rivets.

rounding hard edges. Finish sand and polish the handle by hand.

Warning: Taping the blade is a good idea when you're riveting the handle together, but it's essential if you intend to machine sand the handle. I cannot say that too strongly —**Taping the blade is an absolute must.**

Finally, apply a waterproof finish to the handle if you so desire. You'll find that if you used an oily wood, you really don't need to finish the wood. Just wipe it with a little linseed oil.

Making New Knives

Making a new knife is no different from the process I just described except that you need to either fashion or buy a knife blade.

If you choose to fashion a blade, start with a good piece of tool steel, about 1/16″ thick. Slowly grind it down on a bench grinder or belt sander/grinder — I prefer the latter. This is a tedious process. Use very light pressure and dip the steel in a cup of water as you work to keep it cool. If the steel becomes too hot to hold, you're working too fast.

You can also buy pre-ground knife blades from several companies. Often, these companies offer a selection of blade shapes and sizes, so that you can put together quite a set of kitchen cutlery or hunting knives, if you're so inclined. (See Figure 11.) I would suggest that you look around for carbon steel blades and avoid stainless steel. Stainless steel never

Figure 11. If you wish to make your own knives, many companies sell an assortment of kitchen and hunting blades.

tarnishes, but you can't put a really keen edge on it. Nor will it hold an edge for very long.

Here's an address for a mail order company that handles a good assortment of knife blades:

Indian Ridge Traders
P.O. Box 869
Royal Oak, MI 48068

These folks also sell knife rivets and the rivet drills shown earlier in this chapter, as well as sharpening supplies and other stuff for knife enthusiasts.

If you want to buy tool steel to grind your own blades, look in the Yellow Pages under "Steel Distributors". If you can't find this heading in the consumer pages, check the business-to-business listings.

TIPS

MAKING KNIVES

Removing Rust Blossoms

Damage to wooden handles isn't the only thing that can ruin your fine knives. Good carbon steel can be slowly eaten away by 'rust blossoms'. These flower-like blooms of rust are caused by beads of moisture drying on the steel and eating away a microscopic hole. The next time the steel gets wet, the water tends to stay in this depression, and the hole grows bigger.

◆　If you catch these blossoms in time, you can remove them with steel wool and a little oil. But if they get too big, they can be all but impossible to remove by hand.

◆　Rockwell makes a 500# brushing/cleaning belt for your 1″ belt sander/grinder that will remove even the most stubborn rust spots in no time. (See Figure A.) It also does a great job of polishing tarnished metal saws, hammers, chisels — any tool that's been damaged by water or chemicals. It's available through the mail from:

Prakto, Inc.
P.O. Box 1023
Birmingham, MI 48012

Figure A. Plagued with tarnished or rusty tools? Rockwell's Power Tool Division makes a brushing/cleaning belt (#31-476) that will help restore damaged metal surfaces.

Designed and built by Nick Engler

Custom Knife Keeper

This custom-made knife block fits your knives like a glove.

Like any fine steel blade, a good set of kitchen knives need to be sheathed. A wooden 'knife block' protects the edges of the blades — and makes your kitchen a safer place to work.

You can make a 'custom' knife block — custom fitted to your knives — by laminating alternate strips of 1/8″ and 3/4″ thick stock. Before you glue the stock together, trace the shape of the blades on the 1/8″ stock. (See Figure 1.) Cut these shapes out on the bandsaw, then clamp the block together temporarily and check the fit. You may have to widen the slots slightly for some curved blades. When you're satisfied with the fit, glue up the block.

You can hang this block on the wall or set it on your kitchen counter. If you elect to set it on the counter, you may want to cut one corner at 45°, then dowel two 'legs' to the bottom. This will keep the knives at a convenient angle so that you can get them in and out of the block easily.

Finish the block with tung oil or Danish oil.

EXPLODED VIEW

(Dimensions: 3/4″, 1/8″, 3-1/2″, 10-3/4″, 45°, 8-5/8″, 3″, 5″, 3/4″, 1/4″ × 2″ DOWEL, 5″)

Figure 1. Trace the shape of the blades on the 1/8″ stock, using the blades themselves as a template. Cut out these shapes on a bandsaw.

BILL OF MATERIALS — Custom Knife Keeper

Finished Dimensions in Inches

A.	Blocks (6)	3/4 x 3-1/2 x 10-3/4
B.	Spacers (5)	1/8 x 3-1/2 x 10-3/4
C.	Legs (2)	3/4 x 5 x 5
D.	Dowels (4)	1/4 dia. x 2

Designed and built by Nick Engler

Bible Box

A design from the past adds elegance to any twentieth-century room.

Among the first woodworking objects to be built in this country were small storage chests. These were called 'Bible boxes' because they were about the same size as a seventeenth century Bible. Indeed, they were sometimes used to protect Bibles, since printed books were so precious in the early colonies. However, more often they were used to store medicines, salt, gunpowder and bullets, and other small essentials for life in the New World.

Many Bible boxes held paper and other writing materials, and were used as 'lap desks'. These usually had a slanted lid to hold the paper at a comfortable writing angle. The Bible box you see here is patterned after just such a desk built during the Pilgrim era. It still has many uses today—as a humidor, jewelry chest, even a lap desk. Small boxes never go out of style.

Box Joints

The construction of any box is usually quite simple: Just assemble four sides, a bottom, and a lid. The construction of this Bible box is no different, but we've added a few twists to make the box stronger, more challenging, and generally just 'fancy it up'.

The sides are joined by fingerlaps or 'box joints'. (That's appropriate.) If you have a dado accessory for your table saw, these joints are simple to make:

First, select the 'inside' and 'outside' faces of the side pieces and mark the inside so that you can find it easily. Lay out the finger joints on the *inside* faces with a scratch awl or sharp knife. (See Figure 1.) This is the only way to get a

Figure 1. Lay out the fingerlaps on the *inside* face of the side pieces using a scratch awl. This will keep the dado blade from chipping the wood.

Figure 2. Cut the fingerlaps with the *inside* face of the board facing **away** from the blade. Use a miter gauge extension and spacer to accurately space the fingers.

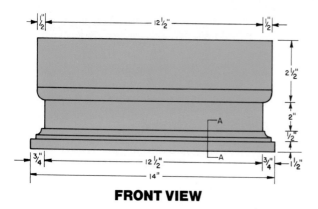

FRONT VIEW

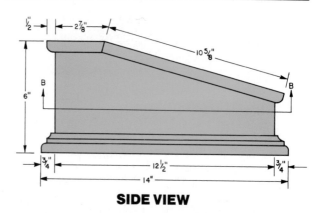

SIDE VIEW

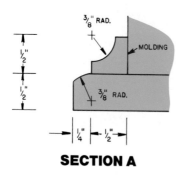

SECTION A

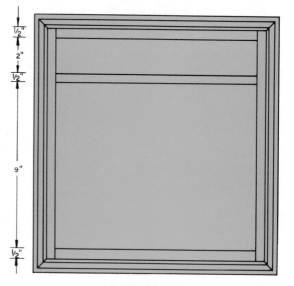

SECTION B

good, clean box joint. By 'scoring' the wood, you tear the wood grain cleanly between the fingers. This keeps the dado blade from chipping the wood when you cut.

Once you've laid out the joints, cut them on the table saw. You'll need to make an auxiliary miter gauge extension, as shown in the drawings. The extension has a small 'spacer' board the same width as the fingerlaps, to automatically space the fingers. (See Figure 2.) As you cut, *be sure* the inside face of the piece faces *away* from the blade (towards you). The scored lines must be on the back side of the cut in order to keep the wood from tearing out.

Fitting and Assembly

Dry assemble the box sides to make sure that the joints fit evenly, then decide which will be the 'front' and 'back' of the box. Cut 15° tapers in the two remaining sides, leaving a small flat towards the back end. (See Figure 3.) Once again,

a jig will help you do this job more accurately than you could do by eyeballing it. Tape the two sides together and 'pad saw' them in the jig to make sure that they are precisely the same.

Reassemble the pieces again and mark where the tapered sides meet the front. Then rip the front piece at 15°. You can do this on a table saw, but we found it was easier to get all the parts to match by ripping the front piece on a bandsaw (sawing slightly wide of the marks), then removing the millmarks on a belt sander. (See Figures 4 and 5.)

Assemble the front, back, and sides with glue. Be careful to clamp the pieces square to each other while the glue

Figure 3. Using a taper jig to taper the sides. Tape the pieces together and 'pad saw' them to make sure they are precisely the same.

Figure 4. Bevel-rip the front piece on a bandsaw at 15°, sawing just wide of the cutline.

Figure 5. Remove the millmarks and sand down to the cutline on a belt sander.

Figure 6. To make a strip molding, *first* cut the molded shape in the edge of a board with a router or shaper.

Figure 7. After you've cut the shape, rip the molding from the board. *Never try to shape a thin strip.* Thin, narrow boards may come apart in your hands.

sets up. When the glue is dry, assemble the bottom to the box with glue and brads, then add the spacer inside the box.

> **Tip ◆** The size and position of the spacer is just a suggestion. As shown, it will hold writing paper on one side, and pens and pencils on the other. You may wish to design your own spacers, trays, or even drawers for the box, depending on what you want to store in it.

Carefully measure the length of the flat and the tapered edges on the side pieces. (The measurements on the drawings are accurate for *our* Bible box, but yours may differ slightly depending on how you cut the box joints and the tapers.) Cut the 'top' and the 'lid' pieces to overhang the box on all sides by 1/2″. The two mating edges (where the top meets the lid) should be cut at 7-1/2°. Attach the top to the box with glue and brads, then hinge the lid to the top.

Fancy It Up

Now for a bit of decoration: Using a router or a shaper, cut a cove in the edge of a piece of scrap 14″ long or longer. (See Figure 6.) Rip the coved edge off this scrap on the table saw or bandsaw, and repeat until you have four pieces of strip molding. (See Figure 7.) Miter the ends of the molding and apply it around the bottom of the box, as shown in the drawings.

Warning: Never try to shape thin, narrow strips to make moldings. These break easily and may come apart in your hands while you're shaping them.

When the first colonists built their own Bible boxes, a bit of molding was the *least* amount of decoration that they would use. Most boxes were quite fancy, with intricate panel moldings, appliques, or 'chip' carvings. In later centuries, these Bible boxes and lap desks were often 'tole' painted.

If you want the decoration, use your imagination. There are many commercial carvings that you can buy from woodworking suppliers to attach to the sides or lid. Or use a woodburning tool to create designs. Or just leave the box unadorned. After all, sometimes simple is just as elegant as fancy.

EXPLODED VIEW

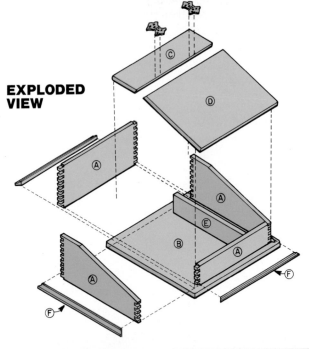

BILL OF MATERIALS — Bible Box

Finished Dimensions in Inches

A.	Sides (4)	1/2 x 5 x 12-1/2
B.	Bottom	1/2 x 14 x 14
C.	Ledge	1/2 x 3-3/8 x 13-1/2
D.	Lid	1/2 x 10-5/8 x 13-1/2
E.	Divider (optional)	1/2 x 2-1/2 x 11-1/2
F.	Molding Strips (4)	1/2 x 1/2 x 13-1/2

Hardware

3/4″ Wire Brads (1-2 dozen)
Decorative Hinges and Mounting Screws (1 pair)

Designed and built by Nick Engler

Cassette Racks

This simple shelving system provides attractive storage for your audio or stereo cassettes.

Technology has a way of getting out of hand. Just about everyone I know of who owns an audio tape player or video cassette recorder has a few dozen tape cassettes laying about in no apparent order. Try to play any given cassette, and you have to sort through your entire collection to find it.

I was no different, of course. My own living room had audio and video cassettes proliferating everywhere, like mushrooms. Once upon a time, I made a half-hearted attempt to organize them all in an old gunpowder box. But they leaked out, two or three at a time, and ended up in their same old piles by the time a week was gone. Finally, the situation became so acute that I took drastic action: I actually built several special racks to organize the cassettes!

Rack Design

Since I'm somewhat allergic to hard work, I designed the rack so that it's extremely simple to build. So simple, in fact, that I managed to produce four of them in just a few hours. Study the drawings and you'll see why they're so quick and easy — there are only three parts. Furthermore, there are only two joints. The shelves fit in dadoes in the sides, and the rails fit in holes.

As you can see by the drawings, the audio cassette rack differs from the video cassette rack only in size. The two of them are made exactly the same. However, you may wish to vary the width of the shelves or the number of shelves to suit your own particular storage problems. If the dimensions shown here for the entire project won't work for you, use the Audio Rack Detail or the Video Rack Detail to help design your own rack.

Construction and Assembly

There are only two steps in the assembly of these racks that require any finesse. The first comes when you bevel-rip the shelves. It's difficult to accurately measure the width of a bevel-rip before you do the actual cutting. For this reason, rip the first edge on all boards *plus* several scrap boards.

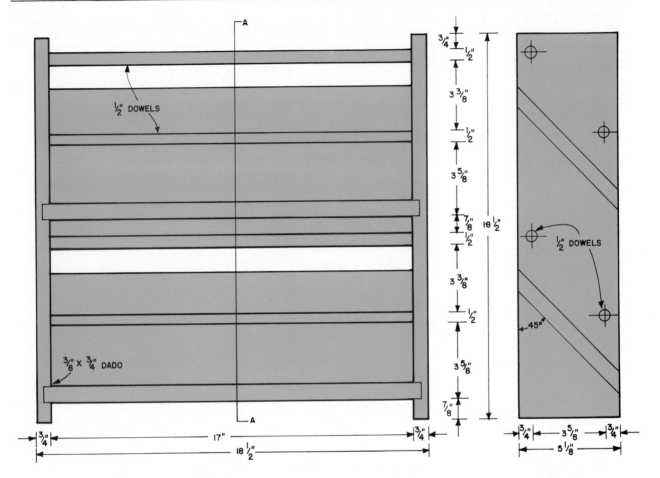

FRONT VIEW

SECTION A

AUDIO CASSETTE RACK

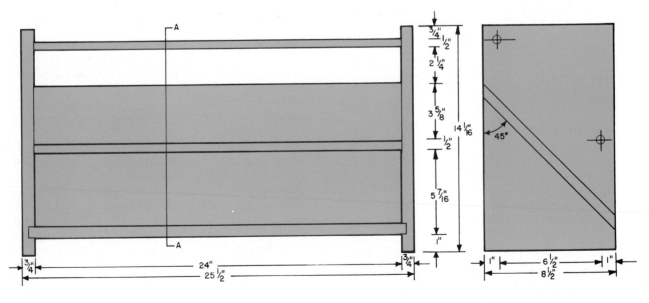

FRONT VIEW

SECTION A

VIDEO CASSETTE RACK

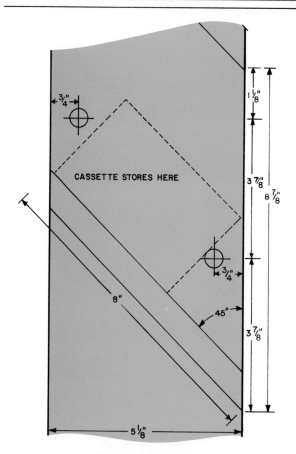

AUDIO CASSETTE RACK DETAIL

CASSETTE STORES HERE

3/4"

8"

45°

1 1/8"

3 7/8"

8 7/8"

3/4"

3 7/8"

5 1/8"

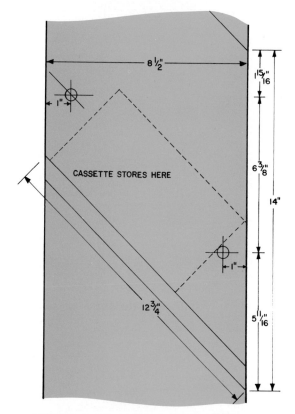

VIDEO CASSETTE RACK DETAIL

CASSETTE STORES HERE

8 1/2"

1"

8"

1"

12 3/4"

1 15/16"

6 3/8"

14"

5 1/16"

When you rip the second edge, cut the scrap wood first and measure it, in case the width of the rip needs to be adjusted.

> **Tip ◆** If you have a table saw with a tilting table (rather than the usual tilting arbor), be sure to position the rip fence on the *down* side. (See Figure 1.)

Be sure to leave a little extra stock so that you can joint the sawn edges. This will save sanding time later on. When you joint stock at an angle, always tilt the fence in toward you, if you possibly can. (See Figure 2.) An 'acute' jointer fence angle is always safer than an oblique angle. It also makes it easier to joint the stock accurately.

The second step that requires some extra care is in making the dadoes in the sides. These must be cut at a 45° angle. You can cut them on a table saw, using the miter gauge to achieve the angle; or on a radial arm saw, with the arm turned at 45°. (See Figures 3 and 4.) Either way, you

Figure 1. Bevel-rip the shelves at 45°. If you have a table saw with a tilting table, be sure to position the fence on the 'down' side.

Figure 2. After ripping, joint the edges at 45°. It's a great deal safer and much easier to be accurate if you tilt the fence in toward you.

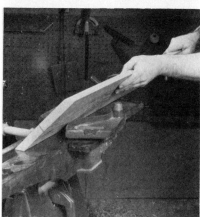

Figure 3. If you cut the dadoes on a table saw, use the miter gauge (and a miter gauge extension) to achieve the necessary 45° angle.

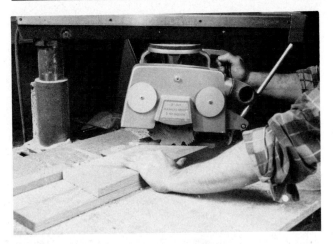

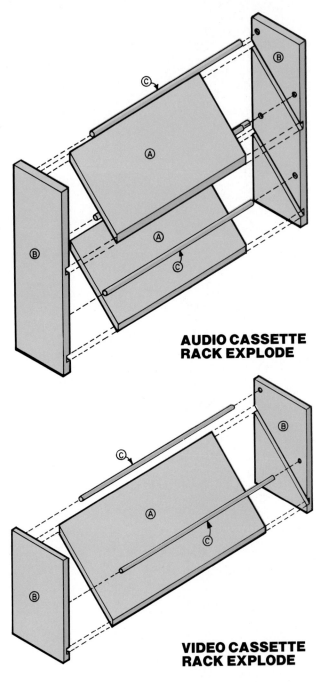

Figure 4. If you cut the dadoes on a radial arm saw, turn the arm to 45°. Cut by pushing the saw *away* from you.

Figure 5. If need be, you can join two or more cassette racks by doweling the top of one to the base of another.

AUDIO CASSETTE RACK EXPLODE

VIDEO CASSETTE RACK EXPLODE

may have trouble with the stock chipping out on one side of the dado, where the knives are cutting up *against* the grain. To prevent this, lay out the dado carefully with a scratch awl or sharp knife. If you make the scores deep enough, they will stop the chipping.

Tip ◆ If you use a radial arm saw with a dado accessory to make this joint, use this cutting technique: First, draw the saw out to the end of the arm. Position the stock, turn the machine on, and cut the dado by pushing the saw *away* from you. If you attempt to make the dado by pulling the saw toward you, the knives will try to 'climb' the stock and may jam.

Once you have cut all the parts and the necessary joints, sand all the pieces. Then assemble them with wood screws and glue. If you wish, you can make two or more cassette racks to stack on top of each other by doweling the top of one rack to the base of another. (See Figure 5.)

And that's it! Of course, these racks won't solve all your cassette storage problems. My cassettes still have a nasty tendency to jump ship and congregate in their original piles. But at least now I have an attractive place to put them all when company comes. That's progress, I guess.

BILL OF MATERIALS — Cassette Racks

Finished Dimensions in Inches

Audio Cassette Rack

A.	Shelves (2)	3/4 x 8 x 17-3/4
B.	Sides	3/4 x 5-1/8 x 18-1/2
C.	Rails	1/2 dia. x 17-3/4

Video Cassette (VHS) Rack

A.	Shelf	3/4 x 12-3/4 x 24-3/4
B.	Sides	3/4 x 8-1/2 x 14-1/16
C.	Rails	1/2 dia. x 24-3/4

Designed and built by Nick Engler

Picture Framing, Simplified

This simple method lets you frame your own pictures without a lot of special tools.

It seems we *always* have a few pictures around the house that need framing. I make frames for them on a fairly regular basis, but there always seem to be one or two more. I'm convinced that they come out of a bottomless well somewhere and make their way through secret passages to the secret corners of our closets.

I probably shouldn't complain; it used to be much worse. A few years ago, you could have opened the door to any one of our closets and a half dozen rolled up pictures would have tumbled out, demanding frames. For a long time, I toyed with the idea of buying some "professional" framing tools — a power miter saw and/or one of those racy-looking whiz-bang framing clamps. Then one day, my wife pointed out the obvious: "You'd think with a shop full of tools, you could make a few picture frames."

She was right, of course. Making picture frames is no big deal. Any woodworker with a table saw or a radial arm saw has all the equipment he or she needs. After a few hours' thought — and a few months' procrastination — I came up with this quick, simple method for framing:

Making the Framing Stock

You can buy your own picture framing stock, of course. But unless you want something really fancy, there's not much

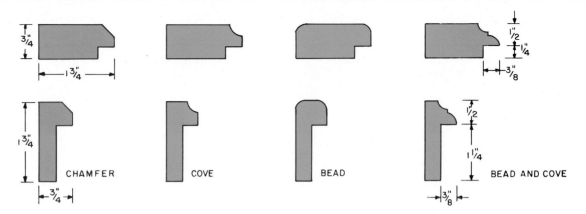

EXAMPLES OF 'FLAT' AND 'STANDING' FRAMING STOCK

point in it. If you have a saw and a molder accessory — or shaper or router — you can make some very handsome-looking stock.

Rip the stock to the desired width and joint both edges. Go ahead and rip a *lot* of stock. You might as well make a lot of framing stock while you're set up for it. Sooner or later, you'll be framing a lot of pictures.

Decide whether you want the wide 'flat' or the narrow edge of the stock to face front on the frame. The traditional arrangement is to present the flat, showing off as much wood as possible. But I prefer using a narrow edge for the front of the frame. This makes the picture stand out slightly from the wall. (Refer to the drawings.) Whatever your preference, the techniques presented here will work for you.

Once you've ripped and jointed the stock, cut a rabbet in the back side. This rabbet will hold the glass, matting, and

picture in the completed frame. You can make the rabbet in one step with a dado accessory, or in two steps with an ordinary saw blade. I prefer using the saw blade because it gives a smoother cut.

Cut the small dimension of the rabbet first. (See Figure 1.) Then turn the stock 90° and cut the large dimension. (See Figure 2.) Be careful to position the stock and the rip fence so that the waste is on the *outside* of the saw blade, *opposite* the rip fence. If the waste is pinched between the fence and the blade, it may kick back. (See Figure 3.)

Shape the front of the frame to suit yourself. If you have a molding head for your table saw, this can be used to cut any number of designs. So can a shaper, or a router mounted to a router table. (See Figure 4.) And if you want to make a very simple shape, such as a cove or chamfer, you can do these on a table saw or a jointer, respectively. Set up

Figure 1. Cut the small dimension of the rabbet first. Usually, this will allow you to rest the flat of the stock on the table.

Figure 3. Never cut a rabbet so that the waste is caught between the blade and the fence. This may cause the stock to kick back.

Figure 2. Make the second cut with the waste on the outside of the saw blade, *opposite* the rip fence. Be careful with these cuts since they must be performed without a saw guard.

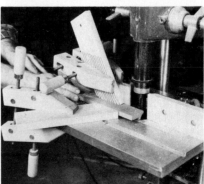

Figure 4. If you have a shaper, you can use it to cut a design in the framing stock. Notice that the featherboard helps guide the wood across the cutter.

your table saw for 'cove cuts' to hollow out coves in the framing stock. (See Figure 5.) To make a chamfer, simply tilt the fence of your jointer at the desired angle. (See Figure 6.) Use your imagination; there are probably a lot of tools around your shop you can use either by themselves or in combination to shape the stock the way you want it.

> **Tip** ◆ When you cut a chamfer on the jointer, always tip the fence in toward the blade. An 'acute' fence angle makes it much easier to cut an accurate chamfer. It's also much safer.

Completely sand the finished stock. You'll find it saves a lot of time to sand the framing stock now, *before* you cut and glue it. After the frame is assembled, all the sanding you'll have to do is a little 'touch up' sanding around the corners.

Mitering the Frames

Perhaps the most tedious chore in making picture frames is in cutting the miters — accurately. **Both** the miter angle and the length of the frame members must be right on the money, or there will be gaps in the miters. Most folks spend quite a bit of time 'shaving' the miters down until they all fit just right. And many of those folks lose their religion about the fifth time they shave a miter too close and ruin the frame member.

Fortunately, there's an easier way. A simple jig for your saw will help you accurately measure the length of each frame member as you cut it. Furthermore, this jig can be arranged to measure the *inside* dimensions of the frame, so that all you have to do is measure your picture and cut the stock, without stopping to figure in the width of the frame, the depth of the rabbet, and all that other confusing stuff. The jig takes this all into account.

First, make sure that you've adjusted your saw or miter gauge to cut at *precisely* 45°. To gauge this, use a drafting triangle to line up the saw blade with the fence (on a radial arm saw) or the saw blade with the miter gauge (on a table saw). (See Figure 7.)

Now for the jig: When I said this was a simple jig, I meant it. It's just a single board with a scale attached. If you

Figure 5. You can cut a simple cove in framing stock on your table saw by passing the wood across the blade at an angle. Make multiple passes and take small 'bites' — no more than 1/8" at a time.

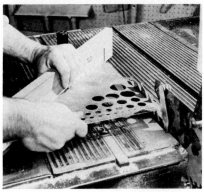

Figure 6. Use a jointer to make quick, smooth chamfers. Always tilt the fence in towards the blade. This arrangement is safer and gives better results.

Figure 7. Use a drafting triangle to set the miter angle. This will insure that the cut will be *exactly* 45°.

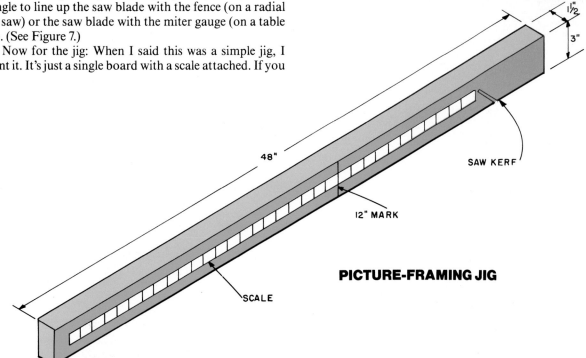

PICTURE-FRAMING JIG

SAW KERF

12" MARK

48"

SCALE

3"

1½"

Figure 8. If you use a radial arm saw to cut the miters, use the jig to replace the fence.

Figure 9. If you use a table saw, use the jig as a miter gauge extension. Drill horizontal slots where you attach the jig to the miter gauge, so that you can adjust the relationship of the jig to the blade.

cut the miters on a radial arm saw, use this board to replace the fence. (See Figure 8.) If you use a table saw, use the board as a long miter gauge extension. (See Figure 9.) Here's how to make it work for you:

The dimension that you're interested in measuring is the distance between the *inside* corners of the mitered frame member, where the cut slices through the rabbet. (See Figure 10.) This dimension will always correspond to the measurement of the picture you want to frame. To set up the jig to measure this dimension, first mount the board on your saw. Cut off a scrap of framing stock approximately 15″ long. Miter one end, then measure *exactly* 12″ from the inside corner of that miter to a point on the *inside* of the stock. (See Figure 11.) Miter the other end of the stock, carefully shaving the stock until the blade just brushes the 12″ mark. Clamp the stock in place, and put a pencil mark on the jig where the *outside* corner of the stock rests against the board. (See Figure 12.) Remove the scrap and either draw or attach a scale to the jig, lining up the 12″ mark on the scale with the pencil mark on the jig. (See Figure 13.)

> **Tip ◆** Paper scales for use with jigs like these are available from many woodworking suppliers. You can also use the tape from a broken tape measure.

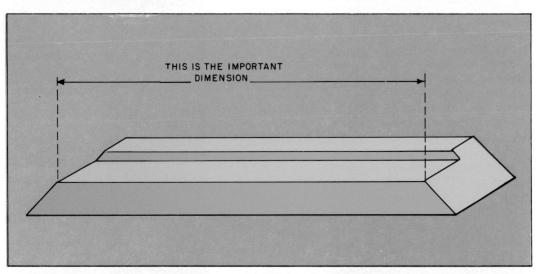

THIS IS THE IMPORTANT
DIMENSION

Figure 10. The only dimension you really need to be concerned about in picture framing is the measurement between the two *inside* corners of the miters, where the cuts intersect the rabbet.

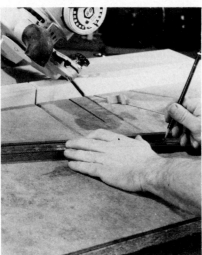

Figure 11. Miter one end of some scrap stock, then measure exactly 12″ from the inside corner of the miter to a point somewhere along the length of the rabbet.

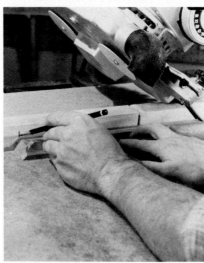

Figure 12. Miter the second end and shave the stock down until the blade just brushes the 12″ mark. Mark the jig where the outside corner of the first miter touches it.

Cut the frame pieces you need, using *only* the measurement of the picture(s) to be framed. Miter one end first; then the other, lining up the outside corner of the first miter with the proper measurement on the scale. If you have a lot of similar frame members to cut, clamp a stop block to the jig to automatically gauge the length as you cut. (See Figure 14.)

Assembling the Frames

Frames are fairly difficult animals to clamp because the mitered corners tend to slip. For this reason, the woodworking industry (and woodworking writers) have invented hundreds of special 'picture framing' clamps and clamp jigs. The manufactured clamps sometimes cost upwards of a hundred dollars, while the jigs can take hours to make. And not a one of them is as accurate or as easy to use as the simple 'band clamp'.

The Jorgensen Company of Chicago, Illinois, makes a nylon web band clamp long enough to clamp up some pretty big frames. This band clamp isn't any better or worse than other band clamps on the market, but the Jorgensen folks also throw in four metal corners to use when clamping up picture frames. (See Figure 15.) These metal corners are important: They keep the miter joints from slipping while

the glue dries *and* they allow the band to slide evenly over the stock as you tighten the clamp. This insures that the clamping pressure will be even on all four sides. This evenly distributed pressure further insures that the frame will be perfectly square when you release the clamp.

These clamps are available in most hardware stores and lumberyards. You can also buy them through the mail from most woodworking suppliers. The last time I looked, the cost was under ten dollars (1985 prices). You probably couldn't make a picture framing clamp-jig for that.

To assemble a frame, apply a generous amount of glue to the miter joints. Use a little more glue than you think is necessary because the end grain will soak it up. Assemble the frame on a flat surface, using the 'tack' of the wet glue to hold the parts together long enough to put the metal corners in place and stretch the band clamp around the frame. Slowly tighten the band clamp, adjusting the joints if necessary. When the band is completely tight, check the frame for squareness with a carpenter's square.

After the glue has dried, remove the band clamp and the metal corners. Scrape off any glue beads with a sharp chisel. If you want to reinforce the miter joints, drive two small brads in each corner at a 90° angle to each other. (See Figure 16.)

Finishing the frames is a matter of personal preference. I prefer tung oil. Like the method I've outlined here, it's simple and quick — and versatile. If you want a dull finish, just apply a single coat. If you want a gloss, apply two, three, or more coats until you get the sheen you're after.

Figure 13. Attach or apply a scale to the jig, lining up the 12″ mark on the scale with the pencil mark on the jig. The scale may have to be mounted upside down, depending on whether you prefer to work right- or left-handed.

Figure 15. The best tool for clamping up a picture frame is an inexpensive band clamp. Be sure to get a clamp that includes the metal corners you see here. These are essential.

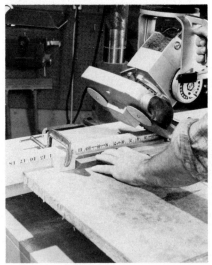

Figure 14. If you need to cut a number of framing parts all at the same length, clamp a stop block to the jig.

Figure 16. After the clamp has been glued up, reinforce the corners with a few small brads.

TIPS
FRAMING

Making a Matte-Cutting Jig

Many pictures — particularly photos — look better if they're 'matted' before they're framed. A matte is a thick piece of textured, colored cardboard that is cut to make a border for the picture.

◆ Matte board is relatively simple to cut, provided you have a 'matte knife'. This tool looks like a block plane and it holds a razor-sharp knife to cut the matte. Usually this knife is mounted at an angle so that it makes a neat bevel as it cuts.

◆ You'll get much better mattes if you use a straightedge to guide this matte knife. Here again, manufacturers have produced all sorts of expensive contraptions to help do this. But unless you're going into the matte-cutting

business, all you really need is the simple jig shown in the diagram. This jig consists of nothing more than a straightedge hinged to a cutting surface.

To use the jig, position the uncut matte under the straightedge. Clamp down the unhinged end of the straightedge; this holds the matte board in place. Run the knife along the straightedge, cutting the matte. (See Figure A.) Release the straightedge, reposition the matte for another cut. Repeat as needed, until you've cut the complete border.

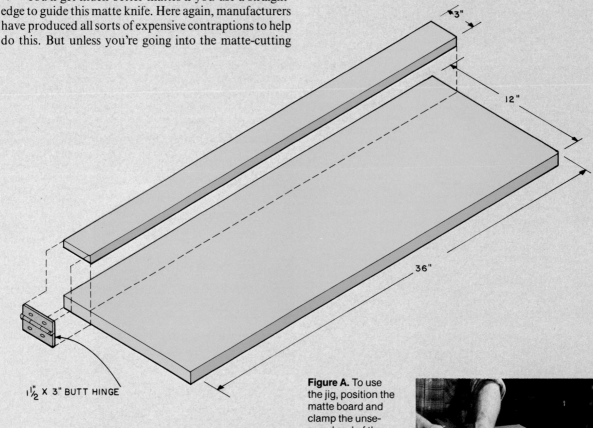

3"

12"

36"

1½" X 3" BUTT HINGE

**MATTE-CUTTING
JIG**

Figure A. To use the jig, position the matte board and clamp the unsecured end of the straightedge to the cutting surface. Run the matte knife along the straightedge, cutting the matte. Release the clamp and reposition the matte for the next cut.

Designed and built by David Wakefield

Animated Toys

A hidden cam adds action to these delightful push toys.

Think back to when you were just five years old (about a million years ago next October). Remember how a clever push toy fascinated you? The real fascination, of course, wasn't just that the toys could be pushed. You were captivated because the action of pushing created another result — a sound, another action, or both. And you spent hours trying to figure it out.

David Wakefield is one of those rare grown-ups for whom that fascination has not yet diminished — he's still trying to figure it out. Every now and then he has a burst of insight, and the results are what you see here: toys that move when you move them. Push the hippo and her mouth opens in a yawn, then snaps shut. Push the lobster and his pincers claw the air menacingly. Fascinating.

A Simple Cam

The secret to this fascinating motion is a hidden cam. Inside the front wheels of the toy is a small knob or 'cam', set off-center. As you push the toy, the cam comes around and hits a lever of some sort. In the case of the hippo, the lever is a corner of her upper jaw. As the cam pushes against the lever, it causes the jaw to open. (See Figure 1.) As the cam

Figure 1. As the cam presses against the lower corner of the hippo's jaw, it causes the mouth to open.

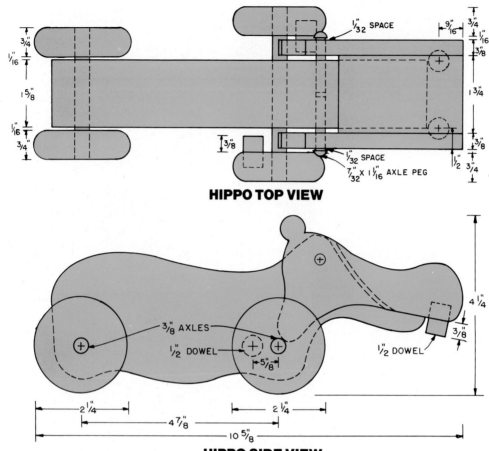

HIPPO TOP VIEW

HIPPO SIDE VIEW

HIPPO BODY AND HEAD PATTERN

1 SQUARE = 1/2"

Figure 2. When the cam moves on, the jaw drops back in place.

moves on, the lever drops back into place and the jaw closes. (See Figure 2.)

This cam-and-lever arrangement must be built carefully out of extremely hard woods. A wooden toy must absorb a lot of abuse, and the moving parts get the worst of the punishment. David works mostly in cherry, but also recommends maple, oak, or beech. Most commercial dowels, axle pegs, and toy wheels that you can buy are made from either maple or beech.

Construction

Both the hippo and the lobster are constructed in much the same manner. Cut the shaped parts out on a bandsaw, then

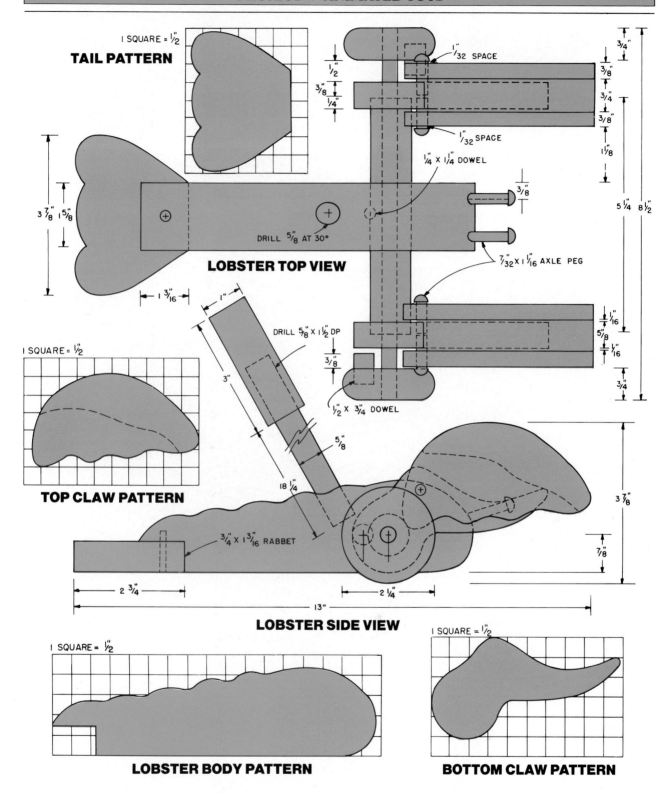

TAIL PATTERN

I SQUARE = 1/2"

1/32" SPACE

1/2"
3/8"
1/4"

3/4"
3/8"
3/4"
3/8"
1 1/8"

1/32" SPACE

1/4" X 1/4" DOWEL

3 7/8" 1 5/8"

DRILL 5/8" AT 30°

LOBSTER TOP VIEW

3/8"

5 1/4" 8 1/2"

7/32" X 1 1/16" AXLE PEG

1 3/16"

1"

DRILL 5/8" X 1 1/2 DP

1/16"
5/8"
1/16"

I SQUARE = 1/2"

3"

3/8"

3/4"

1/2" X 3/4" DOWEL

5/8"

18 1/4"

TOP CLAW PATTERN

3 7/8"

3/4" X 1 3/16" RABBET

7/8"

2 3/4"

2 1/4"

13"

LOBSTER SIDE VIEW

I SQUARE = 1/2"

LOBSTER BODY PATTERN

I SQUARE = 1/2"

BOTTOM CLAW PATTERN

assemble the moving parts — the lobster claws or hippo head. Glue the 3/8" thick sides to the spacer blocks with aliphatic resin (yellow) glue.

When the glue dries, remove the millmarks from all the bandsawn pieces and round over the edges. Two sanding tools will help make short work of these chores: A small drum sander, 1" in diameter, will reach into the curves in the patterns. (See Figure 3.) And a 'flap' sander or flutter sheets will quickly remove any hard corners. (See Figure 4.)

As you drill the holes in the pieces, bear in mind that the dowels and pegs must seat tightly in some holes, and move freely in others. For example, the axles should be snug in the wheels. But these same axles must turn inside the body of the toys. When a dowel must turn or move inside another piece, drill the hole 1/16" oversize. Drill 5/16" holes for the 1/4" pegs, and 7/16" holes for the 3/8" axles. (Hole sizes are indicated on the patterns.)

Figure 3. A small drum sander helps to remove the mill-marks from the bandsawn parts.

Figure 4. A 'flap' sander or 'flutter sheets' round hard corners quickly and easily.

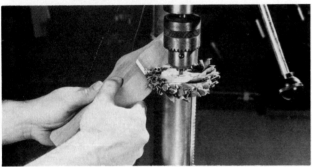

Tip ◆ To insure that all the parts work smoothly, rub the dowels or pegs with paraffin before you assemble the toys. However, be careful *not* to rub paraffin where the dowels or pegs will be glued.

The axle hole that runs through the spreader on the lobster is 5-1/4″ long. You might think this poses a problem, since most wood bits are only 3-1/2″ to 4″ long. But you can drill long holes with short bits by using this simple technique:

First, make sure that the piece you want to drill is cut so that both ends are *precisely* square. **This is important!** If the stock isn't square, this trick won't work.

After you've cut the part, clamp a scrap board to the table of your drill press. Drill a shallow hole in the scrap the same diameter as the hole you want to make in the piece. Drop the table so that you can drill the piece, but *don't move the scrap.* Keep the hole in the scrap directly under the bit.

Drill halfway through the piece. Then put a short dowel in the hole in the scrap block. Turn the part over, and use this dowel to position the part under the drill. (See Figure 5.) Drill a second hole in the piece from the other side. The two holes will meet and form one long hole. (See Figure 6.)

Tip ◆ When drilling end grain, use a very low speed and light pressure to keep the bit from overheating. When drilling long holes, back the bit out frequently to clear out the chips.

Assemble all pieces with glue. *Don't* use screws or nails for reinforcement. These sharp metal fasteners may pose a danger to the child if the toy comes apart. If you want to

Figure 5. To drill two 'mating' holes in a piece, use a short dowel set in a scrap to position the piece on the drill press. This dowel must be the same diameter as the hole you want to drill, and it should be positioned *precisely* under the drill bit.

Figure 6. Remove the dowel to drill the first hole halfway through the piece. Then turn the piece over and replace the dowel. Place the piece over the dowel (as shown) to drill the second hole. The two holes will meet in the middle, forming one long hole.

reinforce a joint, use 1/4″ dowels as pegs. David recommends that you reinforce two of the joints on the lobster in this manner: Both the tail and the spreader should be 'pegged' to the body. Drill the holes for these pegs from underneath the body, so that they are less noticeable.

When you insert the pegs, be careful that they don't interfere with any moving parts. For example: If you peg the spreader in the lobster body, be sure that the peg doesn't rub the axle. When you peg the upper claws to the lower claws, don't get the axle pegs so tight that the claws bind. The same caution applies to the hippo's head.

Finishing

Finishing a toy is always something of a problem, since most toys will eventually be chewed on and most wood finishes are toxic. But there are a few non-toxic finishes you can use.

The traditional toy finish is mineral oil. Apply a liberal coat, then sand it into the grain with very fine (180# or finer) sandpaper. Don't use vegetable oil; this will go rancid and create a breeding ground for bacteria.

Tip ◆ If you use mineral oil, the toy will have to be refinished from time to time. Mineral oil never really 'sets up' in the wood, it evaporates slowly.

There are two commercial finishes on the market that are non-toxic *after* they have dried completely. Danish oil eventually loses its toxicity, but only after it has set up for at least 30 days. If you don't want to keep the toy on the shelf for that long, use 'salad bowl dressing'. This becomes safe after just 48 hours.

If you want to color the wood, mix food dyes 1 to 1 with water and apply them with a brush or a rag. Your choice of colors is limited to red, green, blue, and yellow, but you can mix these to get other shades. For example, red and green will make brown. Red and blue make purple. And so on. Let these colors dry thoroughly, then seal them in the wood with a coat of non-toxic oil or salad bowl dressing.

David Wakefield is a professional toymaker and proprietor of 'Howling Wolf Woodworks', of Millfield, Ohio. He's currently writing a book on animated toys, which will include thirty of his ingenious designs.

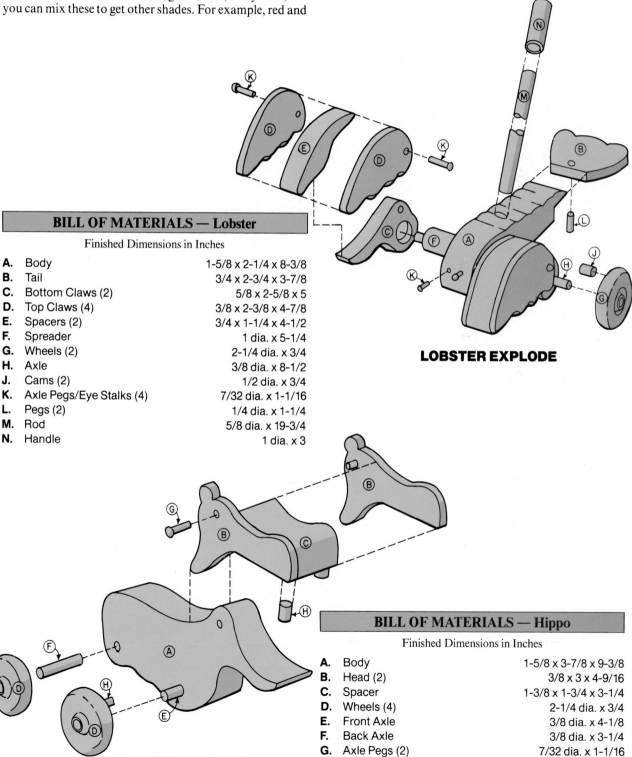

BILL OF MATERIALS — Lobster

Finished Dimensions in Inches

A.	Body	1-5/8 x 2-1/4 x 8-3/8
B.	Tail	3/4 x 2-3/4 x 3-7/8
C.	Bottom Claws (2)	5/8 x 2-5/8 x 5
D.	Top Claws (4)	3/8 x 2-3/8 x 4-7/8
E.	Spacers (2)	3/4 x 1-1/4 x 4-1/2
F.	Spreader	1 dia. x 5-1/4
G.	Wheels (2)	2-1/4 dia. x 3/4
H.	Axle	3/8 dia. x 8-1/2
J.	Cams (2)	1/2 dia. x 3/4
K.	Axle Pegs/Eye Stalks (4)	7/32 dia. x 1-1/16
L.	Pegs (2)	1/4 dia. x 1-1/4
M.	Rod	5/8 dia. x 19-3/4
N.	Handle	1 dia. x 3

LOBSTER EXPLODE

HIPPO EXPLODE

BILL OF MATERIALS — Hippo

Finished Dimensions in Inches

A.	Body	1-5/8 x 3-7/8 x 9-3/8
B.	Head (2)	3/8 x 3 x 4-9/16
C.	Spacer	1-3/8 x 1-3/4 x 3-1/4
D.	Wheels (4)	2-1/4 dia. x 3/4
E.	Front Axle	3/8 dia. x 4-1/8
F.	Back Axle	3/8 dia. x 3-1/4
G.	Axle Pegs (2)	7/32 dia. x 1-1/16
H.	Cams/Teeth (4)	1/2 dia. x 3/4

TOYS

Making Toy Wheels and Axle Pegs

Hardwood toy wheels and axle pegs are available from many commercial suppliers. If you want to purchase these parts, here are two addresses:

Woodworker's Supply   Leichtung
5604 Alameda N.E.   4944 Commerce Pkwy.
Albuquerque, NM 87113   Cleveland, OH 44128

However, you can also make your own if you have a lathe equipped with a drill chuck:

◆   Cut wheel blanks out on a drill press, using a holesaw. (See Figure A.) Keep in mind that because of the saw kerf, the blank will be 1/4″ smaller in diameter than the saw. If you need a 2-1/4″ wheel, use a 2-1/2″ holesaw.

◆   After you cut out the blanks, drill the axle holes to the proper diameter. Temporarily, 'friction fit' a short axle in a blank, then clamp this axle in the lathe chuck. Shape and finish the wheel as you would a faceplate turning. (See Figure B.)

◆   To turn the axle pegs, first make the Miniature Turning Jig shown here. Mount this jig in front of the lathe chuck. Select a dowel 1/8″-1/4″ larger in diameter than you want the finished axle peg to be. Insert this dowel through the jig and clamp it in the lathe chuck. Then turn the peg as if it were a tiny spindle turning. (See Figure C.) Measure carefully as you work and remove just the right amount of stock. Normally, an axle peg should be 1/16″ smaller than the axle hole in the wheel (to allow free movement), and *precisely* the same size as the mounting hole.

Figure B. To shape and finish the wheel, use a drill chuck mounted on your lathe. If you don't have this accessory, you can also use your drill press as a 'vertical lathe'.

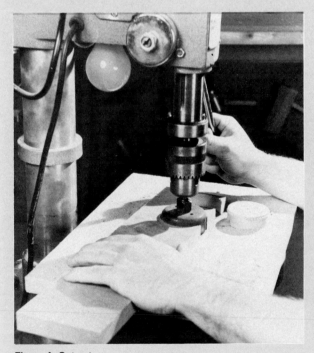

Figure A. Cut out wheel blanks with a holesaw. Remember, the blank will be 1/4″ smaller than the diameter of the saw.

Figure C. Use this simple jig to turn axle pegs. Measure frequently and carefully as you work.

Designed and built by Nick Engler

Under-the-Tool Cabinets

These simple, inexpensive cabinets make good use of the wasted space under your power tools.

Storage space is always at a premium in any woodworking shop. Why, then, do power tool manufacturers prop their tools up on metal legs, wasting the space under the machine?

With a little plywood and a little work, you can reclaim that space. These 'storage stands' or 'under-the-tool' cabinets support your power tools at the proper height *and* provide places to keep your accessories and hand tools.

Cabinet Design and Construction

As shown, these cabinets support a radial arm saw, drill press, and a variety of 'benchtop' tools. However, these same designs can be used to support other power tools. For example, the drill press cabinet also supports a jointer at the correct working height. The radial arm saw cabinet can be used to support a lathe or table saw. And once you grasp the construction techniques we've used, you can custom design your own stands for any stationary power tool in your shop.

The stands are all simple box construction, using butt joints. The top and the bottom of the boxes rest *on* the side members. (Refer to the working drawings.) *This is important!* If you attach the top and bottom so that they are held between the sides, the cabinets will not support the load of a heavy power tool.

101

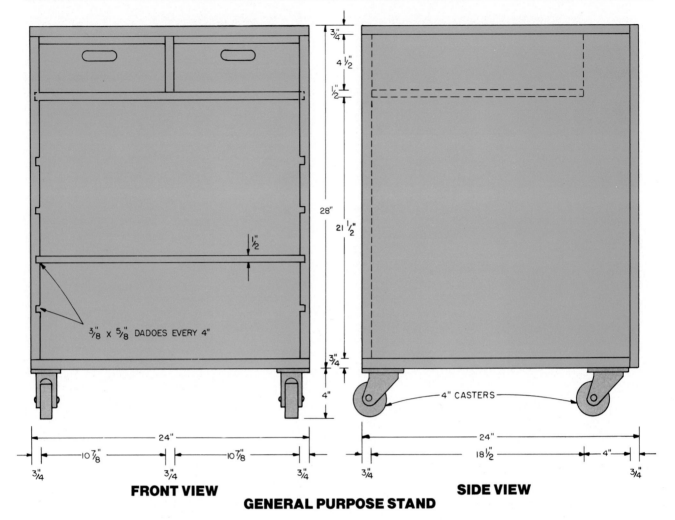

FRONT VIEW   **SIDE VIEW**

GENERAL PURPOSE STAND

The *horizontal* parts in the interior — the shelves and drawer supports — are set in dadoes. There is no need to cut dadoes for the vertical parts, since these do not need to resist any heavy sideways thrust. The supports are fastened permanently in place, while the shelves slide freely in the dadoes.

Also note that many of the interior parts are cut short so that they sit 4″ back from the doors. This gives you room to mount pegboard on the inside of the doors and hang frequently used tools within easy reach. (See Figure 1.)

The material for these cabinets is inexpensive, but strong: The outer shell (and some of the inner braces on the larger cabinets) are made from 3/4″ thick plywood. Many of these parts are cut 1/8″-1/4″ short of the measurements in the drawings, so that the visible edges can be faced with 1/8″ wood strips. (See Figure 2.) This is not necessary, but it does improve the overall appearance of the cabinets. The sliding shelves, drawers, and drawer supports are all made from 1/2″ plywood. The doors are built with a 1 x 2 frame and a 1/4″ plywood panel.

Figure 1. Pegboard mounted on the inside of the cabinet doors lets you store frequently-used accessories where you can get at them quickly.

Figure 2. Cut the outside parts of the box 1/8″-1/4″ smaller than the finished dimension, then face the visible edges with wood strips. This will hide the 'plies'.

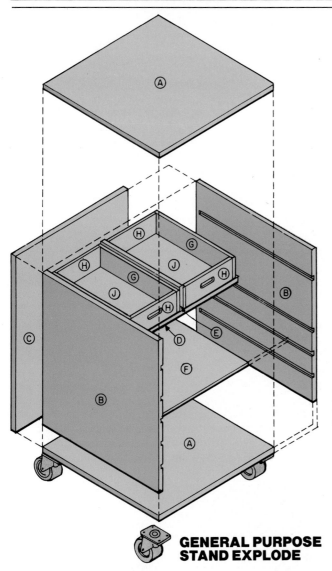

GENERAL PURPOSE STAND EXPLODE

a hand router. Make the dadoes for the shelves 1/16" over-size (9/16" wide) so that the shelves will slide in and out of the cabinets easily.

Glue facing strips to those edges that need them, then assemble the parts in this order: First, attach the sides and back to form a C-shape. Second, add the top and bottom to make a basic box. Finally, add any fixed interior parts such as dividers or shelf supports. Use plenty of glue to reinforce each joint.

We don't suggest you nail these parts together as you go; nails may let go eventually. Screws will keep the cabinet rigid for a much longer period of time. However, each cabinet requires a lot of screws, and it will take a lot of time to drill pilot holes for all of them. There's a way around this dilemma: Use *drywall screws*. These fasteners require no pilot holes and they can be driven home quickly with a screwdriver attachment on your electric drill. (See Figure 5.)

Figure 3. The floor of your shop makes a great surface to cut up large sheets of plywood. Back up the stock to be cut with a scrap sheet of Cellutex® and adjust the depth-of-cut on your circular saw so that it just barely penetrates the plywood.

Cutting and Assembly

The first step in building a plywood project is to slice up the plywood. This is always something of a pain, since the sheets are invariably too big to cut safely on a table saw.

The best method we know to whittle a 4 x 8 sheet down to manageable size is to lay it on the floor of your shop, on top of a large sheet of Cellutex® or similar soft building material. Adjust your circular saw so that it cuts just 1/16" deeper than the width of the plywood, then cut up the plywood sheets. (See Figure 3.) The scrap material under the plywood will keep the saw from biting into the floor. Incidentally, we cut the parts we needed for all three cabinets shown here from 2-1/2 sheets of 3/4" plywood, 1 sheet of 1/2" plywood, and 1/2 sheet of 1/4" plywood.

Remember to cut *some* of the 3/4" plywood parts slightly smaller than you actually need, *if* you plan to face the visible edges with wood strips. The dimensions and the edges to be faced are given in the Bill of Materials. If you do *not* wish to fool around with facing, use the dimensions in the working drawings to determine the actual measurements.

Cut the dadoes in the side members and any other parts that need them. The best tool for this chore is a table saw and a dado accessory. (See Figure 4.) However, you can also use

Figure 4. Cut the needed dadoes on a circular saw. Make the dadoes for the sliding shelves 1/16" oversize so that the shelves slide easily.

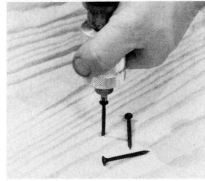

Figure 5. Use dry-wall screws to fasten the parts of the cabinets together. These fasteners require no pilot holes and can be driven easily with an electric hand drill.

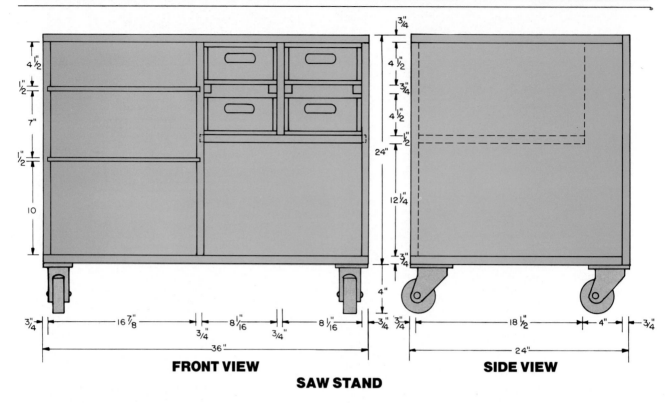

FRONT VIEW

SAW STAND

SIDE VIEW

Drawers, Shelves, and Doors

The drawers are miniature versions of the cabinets themselves: basic plywood boxes. Drill two 1″ holes in *both* the front and back of the drawers so that you can pull them out without worrying how they go back in. To make this job go a little faster, pad drill the parts. (See Figure 6.) Unlike the cabinets, the drawers can be assembled with nails since they don't have to support the weight of a heavy power tool. However, be sure to use plenty of glue between each joint.

The shelves are even simpler than the drawers — just single sheets of plywood. Like the drawers, drill holes near the front and back edges for finger pulls. If you plan to store heavy tools on these shelves, you may want to reinforce the undersides with strips of wood so the shelves won't sag. If you plan to keep a lot of little tools on them, you may want

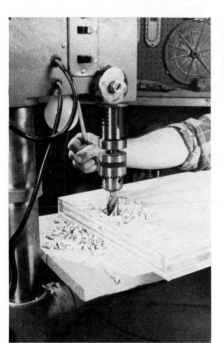

Figure 6. To make quick work of the drilling chores on this project, pad drill the finger pulls in the drawer parts and sliding shelves.

Figure 7. Use a dado set to cut 3/8″ grooves in the inside of all door frame parts.

Figure 8. Use this same dado setup to cut tenons in the ends of the door frame rails. A tenoning jig holds the rails perpendicular to the table.

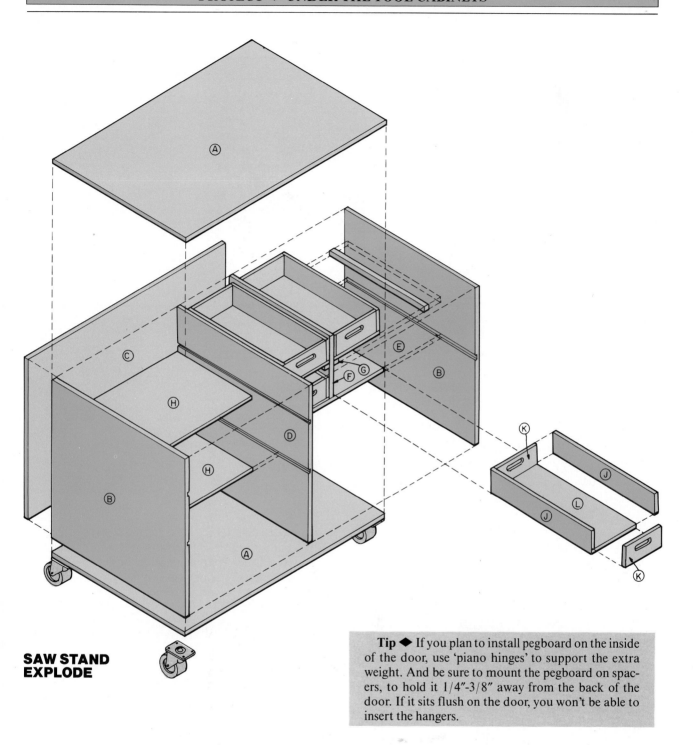

**SAW STAND
EXPLODE**

> **Tip ◆** If you plan to install pegboard on the inside of the door, use 'piano hinges' to support the extra weight. And be sure to mount the pegboard on spacers, to hold it 1/4"-3/8" away from the back of the door. If it sits flush on the door, you won't be able to insert the hangers.

to put strips all around the top edges. These strips would keep the tools from rolling off, and make the shelves into trays.

You could make the doors out of single sheets of plywood, but frame-and-panel doors save weight, materials, and add some class to the cabinets. Besides, these doors are fairly easy to make: Just cut 3/8" grooves in the inside edges of the frame parts with a dado accessory. (See Figure 7.) Then use the same dado setup to cut tenons in the ends of the rails. (See Figure 8.) Glue the rails to the stiles, but leave the panels to float free in the grooves. When the glue dries, hinge the doors to the cabinets and install magnetic catches.

Mobility

The dimensions on the working drawing assume that you want to mount a set of casters under each cabinet. Casters make a stationary power tool mobile, and this mobility has several big advantages, especially in a small shop. You can store your power tools up against a wall, and only pull them out as you need them. You don't have to keep them in the middle of the floor, taking up space. You can also rearrange your shop for each project. It saves a lot of time and steps when you can set up your tools in the order in which you need them, instead of crisscrossing the shop constantly.

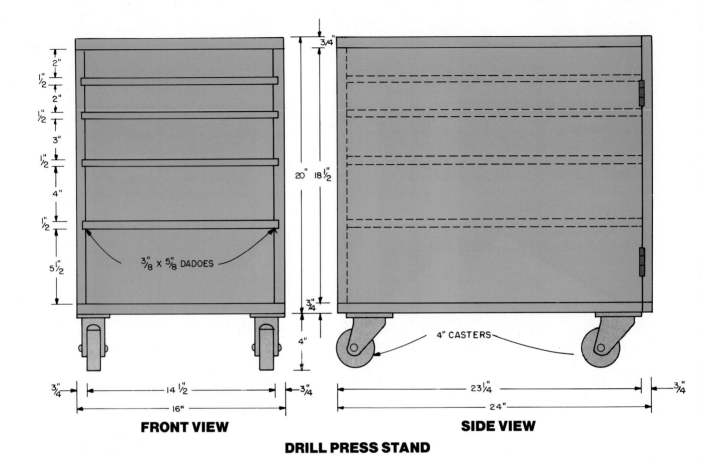

FRONT VIEW **SIDE VIEW**

DRILL PRESS STAND

We also assume that you want to install big casters — 4″ tall. Big casters roll easily across rough surfaces, power cords, sawdust, and the other impediments you'd normally find on a shop floor. Big casters are also available with 'brakes', unlike small casters. (See Figure 9.) These are nothing more than foot-activated clamps that squeeze the wheel mounts together so that the wheels won't turn. This allows you to quickly immobilize the power tool without chocking the wheels — and just as quickly, make it mobile again.

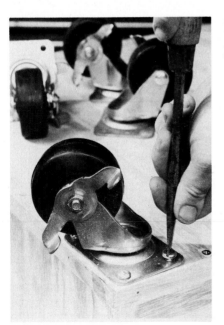

Figure 9. Several models of casters are available with foot brakes. These let you mobilize (and immobilize) your stationary power tools as needed.

BILL OF MATERIALS — Drill Press Stand

Finished Dimensions in Inches

A.	Top/Bottom* (2)	3/4 x 16 x 23-1/4
B.	Sides** (2)	3/4 x 18-1/2 x 23-1/4
C.	Back	3/4 x 14-1/2 x 18-1/2
D.	Shelves (3-4)	1/2 x 15-1/8 x 22-1/2
E.	Door Panel	1/4 x 12-5/8 x 16-5/8
F.	Door Rails (4)	3/4 x 2 x 12-3/4
G.	Door Stiles (4)	3/4 x 2 x 20

*Cut these pieces 3/4 x 15-3/4 x 23-1/8, then attach 1/8 x 3/4 strips to the side and back edges.

**Cut these pieces 3/4 x 18-1/2 x 23-1/8, then attach 1/8 x 3/4 strips to the back edges.

Hardware

20″ x 1-1/2″ Piano Hinges and Mounting Screws (2)
Cabinet Door Catch and Mounting Screws
Door Pull
4″ Casters with Brakes and Mounting Screws (4)
2″ Drywall Screws (1/4 lb.)

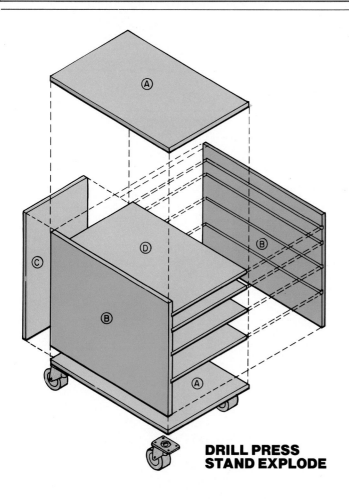

**DRILL PRESS
STAND EXPLODE**

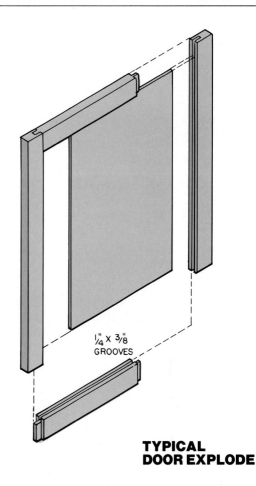

1/4" X 3/8"
GROOVES

**TYPICAL
DOOR EXPLODE**

BILL OF MATERIALS — General Purpose Stand

Finished Dimensions in Inches

A.	Top/Bottom* (2)	3/4 x 23-1/4 x 24
B.	Sides** (2)	3/4 x 23-1/4 x 26-1/2
C.	Back	3/4 x 22-1/2 x 26-1/2
D.	Drawer Support	3/4 x 18-1/2 x 23-1/4
E.	Drawer Divider	3/4 x 4-1/2 x 18-1/2
F.	Shelves (2-3)	1/2 x 18-1/2 x 23-1/8
G.	Drawer Sides (8)	1/2 x 4 x 18-1/2
H.	Drawer Fronts/Backs (8)	1/2 x 4 x 9-3/4
J.	Drawer Bottoms (4)	1/4 x 10-3/4 x 18-1/2
K.	Door Panels (2)	1/4 x 8-5/8 x 24-5/8
L.	Door Rails (4)	3/4 x 2 x 8-3/4
M.	Door Stiles (4)	3/4 x 2 x 28

* Cut these pieces 3/4 x 23-1/8 x 23-3/4, then attach 1/8 x 3/4 strips to the side and back edges.

**Cut these pieces 3/4 x 23-1/8 x 26-1/2, then attach 1/8 x 3/4 strips to the back edges.

Hardware

28" x 1-1/2" Piano Hinges and Mounting Screws (2)
Cabinet Door Catches and Mounting Screws (2)
Door Pulls (2)
4" Casters with Brakes and Mounting Screws (4)
2" Drywall Screws (1/4 lb.)

BILL OF MATERIALS — Saw Stand

Finished Dimensions in Inches

A.	Top/Bottom* (2)	3/4 x 23-1/4 x 36
B.	Sides** (2)	3/4 x 22-1/2 x 23-1/4
C.	Back	3/4 x 22-1/2 x 34-1/2
D.	Divider	3/4 x 22-1/2 x 22-1/2
E.	Drawer Support	3/4 x 17-5/8 x 18-1/2
F.	Drawer Divider	3/4 x 9-3/4 x 18-1/2
G.	Drawer Ledges (4)	3/4 x 3/4 x 18-1/2
H.	Shelves (2)	1/2 x 17-1/2 x 18-1/2
J.	Drawer Sides (8)	1/2 x 4 x 18-1/2
K.	Drawer Fronts/Backs (8)	1/2 x 4 x 7
L.	Drawer Bottoms (4)	1/4 x 8 x 18-1/2
M.	Door Panels (2)	1/4 x 14-5/8 x 20-5/8
N.	Door Rails (4)	3/4 x 2 x 14-3/4
P.	Door Stiles (4)	3/4 x 2 x 24

*Cut these pieces 3/4 x 23-1/8 x 35-3/4, then attach 1/8 x 3/4 strips to the side and back edges.

**Cut these pieces 3/4 x 22-1/2 x 23-1/8, then attach 1/8 x 3/4 strips to the back edges.

Hardware

24" x 1-1/2" Piano Hinges and Mounting Screws (2)
Cabinet Door Catches and Mounting Screws (2)
Door Pulls (2)
4" Casters with Brakes and Mounting Screws (4)
2" Drywall Screws (1/2 lb.)

TIPS

CABINETS

Semi-Mobile Cabinets

Casters with brakes are a great way to make power tools mobile, but there is a drawback. The casters swivel — even when the brakes are locked — and the tool may move slightly. For this reason, some craftsmen prefer a tool that sits on four sturdy legs.

◆ There are two good compromises between sturdiness and mobility, if you need to move your tools only occasionally. In each case, go ahead and build your cabinets with legs instead of casters. These legs can be an integral part of the cabinet framing, or they can simply be 2 x 4's screwed to the bottom of the cabinet box.

◆ If the tool is fairly light (such as a bandsaw or small drill press), attach two *non-swiveling* casters to the legs, just 1/2″ above the floor. When you need to move the tool, simply tilt it back on the wheels until all four legs lift off the floor. Roll the tool where you want it, as if the casters were a permanently-attached 'dolly'. (See Figure A.)

◆ If the tool is too big or too squat to tilt (such as a radial arm saw), mount swiveling casters to 2 x 4's. Hinge the 2 x 4's to the side of the cabinet so that when boards are pressed down all the way, the casters will lift the tool off its legs. Make braces out of scrap boards to hold the casters in the 'down' position. (See Figure B.) Mount the braces so they pivot up, out of the way. When the braces are up, the casters will flop up, and the cabinet will sit back down on its legs. (See Figure C.)

Figure A. You can attach two non-swiveling casters to the legs of a power tool, just above the floor, to make a permanently-attached 'dolly'.

Figure B. A brace holds the casters down, lifting the tool cabinet off its legs.

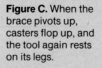

Figure C. When the brace pivots up, casters flop up, and the tool again rests on its legs.

Designed and built by Nick Engler

Trivets

A simple trick turns a solid board into a delicate lattice.

N ow and again, you run across a special woodworking technique which allows you to create a finished project in one simple step. 'Piercing' is just such a technique. The delicate trivets you see here were made from a solid block of wood using this unique method — and nothing else.

Well, almost nothing else. There is a little sanding involved. That's the trouble with woodworking: There's *always* a little sanding involved. But don't worry; we found a tool that makes sanding pierced boards a snap.

Piercing

To 'pierce' a board, first cut grooves part way through it with a saw blade, dado, or molder. Turn the board over, and cut another set of grooves at a different angle to the first. If the grooves are deep enough, there will be holes wherever the grooves on one side cross the grooves on the other. If the grooves are fairly large and cut at regular intervals, the board will become an intricate lattice, as if it were made from dozens of smaller boards carefully arranged and glued together.

The shapes of the holes that are pierced in the board are controlled by two variables — the shape of the grooves and the angle at which you cut them. For example, if you cut two

Figure 1. Two sets of square grooves, cut at 90° to one another, will produce square holes.

Figure 3. Round bottom grooves, cut at 90° to each other, pierce the board with round holes.

Figure 4. Line up the holder with the cutter, and clamp the holder's brace to the miter gauge extension. Cut the groove slowly and carefully, using a push block to hold the blank in place.

Figure 2. Reduce the angle at which the grooves are cut to 60°, and the holes will appear diamond-shaped.

sets of square grooves perpendicular (90°) to each other, the holes will be square. (See Figure 1.) Reduce the angle slightly to 60°, and the holes will appear diamond-shaped. (See Figure 2.) Change from square grooves (cut with a dado, usually) to round grooves (cut with a molder), and the holes will appear round. (See Figure 3.)

Making Trivets

To make pierced trivets, you'll first need to make a simple table saw jig, as shown in the drawings. This jig holds the trivet blanks at the correct angle to the dado or molder, and helps you to space the grooves as you cut them. You may want to make several 'holders' to use with the same miter gauge extension. These interchangeable holders can be used to hold the blanks at several different angles to the cutter, for a variety of effects.

To use the jig, secure the miter gauge extension to your miter gauge. Place a blank in the holder, line up the holder to cut the first groove, and clamp the holder's brace to the extension. Turn on the table saw, and *slowly* advance the blank over the cutter. (See Figure 4.)

Warning: Use a push block to hold the blank in place on the jig, as shown. *Do not* try to hold it in place with your bare hands. You must be very careful when cutting the grooves, since you must work without a guard.

After you've completed the groove, *turn off the table saw.* Let the cutter come to a complete stop, then release the clamp on the jig. Realign the holder for the second groove, and repeat.

You can also use a radial arm saw for piercing. (See Figure 5.) To make trivets, you won't need a miter gauge extension — you can use the saw's fence — but you will have to modify the holder slightly. Add two wooden 'clamps' on either side to secure the blanks, as shown in the drawings.

> **Tip ◆** When using a dado or molding cutter on a radial arm saw, draw the saw out past the work, *then* turn the machine on. Cut by pushing the saw *away* from you, back toward the fence. (See Figure 6.) If you cut by pulling the saw toward you — the normal sawing technique for a radial arm saw — the cutters will want to 'climb' the work and they may jam.

Sanding the Trivets

Sanding these intricate lattice-work trivets can really be a chore, since there are so many grooves. However, a set of 'flutter sheets' makes this job a breeze. These ingenious sanding tools are available from several woodworking suppliers, or you can make your own.

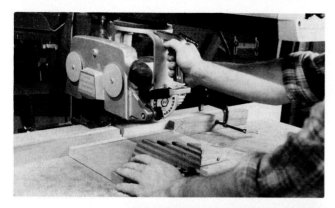

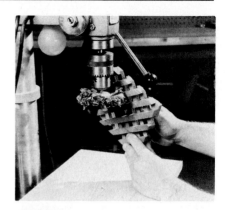

Figure 7. Use a set of flutter sheets, mounted on your drill press, to sand the grooves in the trivets.

Figure 5. You can also make trivets on a radial arm saw, using a modified jig.

Figure 6. When using a dado cutter or molding head on a radial arm saw, cut by pushing the saw *away* from you — just the opposite of how you work normally.

Figure 8. If you can somehow mount the flutter sheets on your saw, you can use your trivet jig to speed up the sanding chore. Use the same settings to sand the trivets as you used to cut the grooves.

Mount enough flutter sheets on an arbor so that the stack of sheets is just a little smaller than the width of the grooves. Then mount the arbor on your drill press. Turn the drill on and carefully run each groove across the whirling sheets. (See Figure 7.) The fingers of the flutter sheets automatically adjust to the shape of the grooves.

If you can mount your flutter sheets on your table saw or radial arm saw, you can use the trivet jig to help with the sanding. (See Figure 8.) Just let the jig run the trivets over the sandpaper, using exactly the same setting you used to cut the grooves.

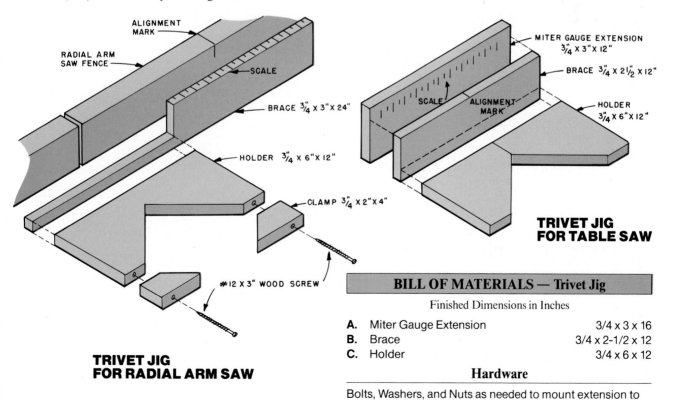

TRIVET JIG FOR RADIAL ARM SAW

TRIVET JIG FOR TABLE SAW

BILL OF MATERIALS — Trivet Jig		
Finished Dimensions in Inches		
A.	Miter Gauge Extension	3/4 x 3 x 16
B.	Brace	3/4 x 2-1/2 x 12
C.	Holder	3/4 x 6 x 12
Hardware		
Bolts, Washers, and Nuts as needed to mount extension to miter gauge.		

TRIVETS

Making and Using Flutter Sheets

Flutter sheets have been a common abrasive tool in the furniture industry for many years. However, they are still hard to find for most home woodworkers. Only a handful of mail order tool companies carry them, and we've never seen them in a hardware store.

◆ If you have trouble locating a source of flutter sheets, you can easily make your own. Simply tear several 4″ wide *cloth-backed* abrasive belts into 2″ strips to make approximately fifty 2″ x 4″ sheets. (Paper-backed abrasives won't last.) With a hole punch, make a 1/4″ hole in the center of each sheet. Then cut five or six 1″ long 'fingers' on either end of the sheets. (See Figure A.) You may want to make flutter sheets of two different grits — 100# and 180# — for coarse and fine sanding.

Saw the head off a 1/4″ x 3-1/2″ carriage bolt. Mount the flutter sheets on the threaded end of the bolt between nuts and fender washers, as shown. Chuck the unthreaded end in a drill press. Work at a slow to medium speed — 1000-2000 RPM.

◆ You'll quickly find that flutter sheets are much more versatile for contour sanding than ordinary 'flap sanders'. By varying the *number* of flutter sheets you stack on the shank, you can sand many different *types* of contours. For instance, if you need to reach into deep crevices, use just a few flutter sheets. For rounding over hard edges or sanding lightly curved contours, use as many sheets as the shank will hold.

◆ You can also control the *cutting speed* of the abrasive according to the *orientation* of each sheet on the shank — how you mount them in relation to their neighbors. To get a fast cut, stagger the flutter sheets so that on every other sheet the abrasive faces either up or down. For a slow cut, orient the sheets so that on the top half of the stack the abrasive faces up, and on the bottom half it faces down. (See Figure B.)

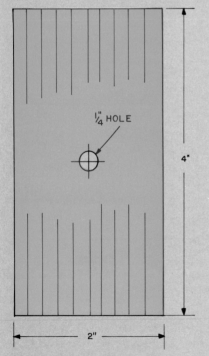

Figure A. A typical flutter sheet is 2″ wide and 4″ long. Punch a 1/4″ hole dead center, and cut 1″ fingers in the long dimension, as shown.

1/4″ HOLE

4″

2″

**FLUTTER SHEET
LAYOUT**

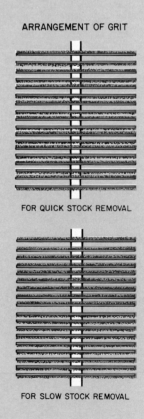

ARRANGEMENT OF GRIT

FOR QUICK STOCK REMOVAL

FOR SLOW STOCK REMOVAL

Figure B. The cutting speed of the abrasives depends on how you mount them on the shank.

Quick-and-Easy Shelves

It only takes a few hours to build these attractive shelving units.

A friend of mine, who runs a research institute, claims that one of the most puzzling mysteries in science has to do with shelves:

"Put up a shelf, and a few minutes later, it's completely full," he observes. "In less than an hour, you can't do without it. Where did you keep all that stuff *before* you built the shelf? I'm not convinced that you ever had the stuff.

"What we're dealing with here is one of the primal forces of nature: The existence of an empty shelf creates a vacuum that causes books, stereo equipment, boxes of laundry detergent, and other household objects to materialize out of thin air. They could come from another plane or universe, but most probably they're rapidly assembled from unemployed subatomic particles. I've requested a grant from the AASS (Association for the Advancement of Shelving Science) to study the phenomenon."

Well, it's a good hypothesis, but cause and effect seem to travel in the opposite direction around my home. The

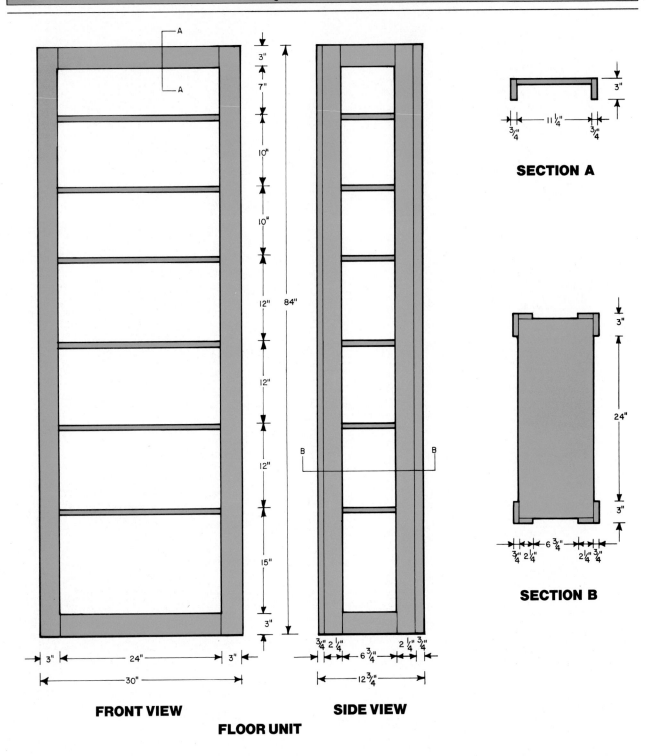

SECTION A

SECTION B

FRONT VIEW   **SIDE VIEW**

FLOOR UNIT

accumulation of too much stuff and no place to put it elicits a number of pointed comments from my better half. This in turn creates an overwhelming sense of guilt that sooner or later causes me to build some shelves. (As hard as I try, I can't seem to procrastinate long enough to cause the shelves to assemble themselves from subatomic particles. It usually takes a few boards, and quite a bit of assistance from me.)

My own contribution to shelving science, however, has little to do with the causal relationship between shelves and the stuff that sits on them. What I would like to share with you is a simple *design* to help you build more shelving in less

time. The units you see here can all be built in a few hours. The design is modern, good looking, and inexpensive to execute — the shelves you see in the lead photo were built from #3 common pine. Furthermore, the design can be easily adapted to your own needs. The lead photo shows several floor-to-ceiling units, but you can also build smaller units, hanging shelves, even a bookcase headboard using the very same construction techniques. (See Figures 1 and 2.)

Quick and Easy Construction

As you look over the drawings, notice that all the joints are

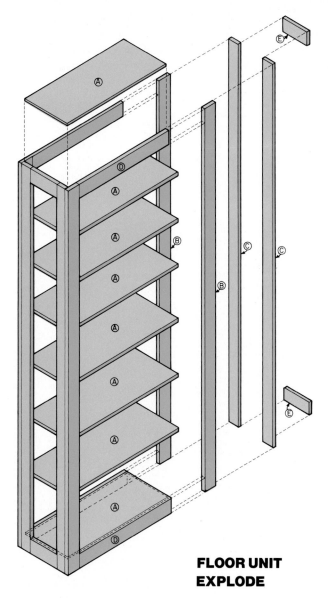

**FLOOR UNIT
EXPLODE**

Figure 1. These hanging shelves are built just like the large units. The only difference is that the front rails have been left out to make room for glass doors. The shelves are hung by holes in the back stiles.

Figure 2. This headboard bookcase is another variation on the same design. The only difference here is that the upper shelf is enlarged slightly to 'cap' the piece.

Figure 3. If you want a country look, use cut nails to assemble the shelving units. When set flush to the surface, these fasteners appear to have a square head, like old-timey nails.

Figure 4. If you don't want to dowel the rails to the stiles, you can 'toenail' them, as shown.

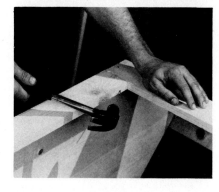

simple butt joints. There are no dadoes, grooves, or rabbets to cut anywhere. To make the shelves, you simply rip the parts to the proper width, cut them to the proper length, and assemble them.

> **Tip** ◆ It's not *quite* that simple. There is a lot of sanding to do, unless you plan to use these shelves in the shop or utility room. You'll find it much easier to surface sand all parts *before* you assemble them. Then all you have to do is touch up sanding before applying a finish.

If there is little or no joinery, what gives the shelves their strength? Glue, mostly. There is a good deal of long-grain-to-long-grain gluing surface where the front and back stiles are attached to sides and shelves. When glued in place with a high-quality aliphatic resin (yellow glue), these stiles add enough horizontal and vertical stability to keep the shelving units perfectly rigid.

It's important to reinforce all the butt joints with screws or nails while the glue dries. Screws, of course, add some strength even after the glue sets up, but they aren't essential. If you don't want to take the time to countersink and plug a lot of screw holes, use nails. I used 'cut nails' to put together the shelves in the lead shot. These have square heads and give the finished project a country look, particularly if you build it out of knotty pine. (See Figure 3.)

Traditionally, the top and bottom rails are doweled to the stiles. But even this simple joinery is not necessary. The top edges of the rails can be nailed or screwed to the shelves, then the bottom corners are 'toenailed' to the stiles. (See Figure 4.)

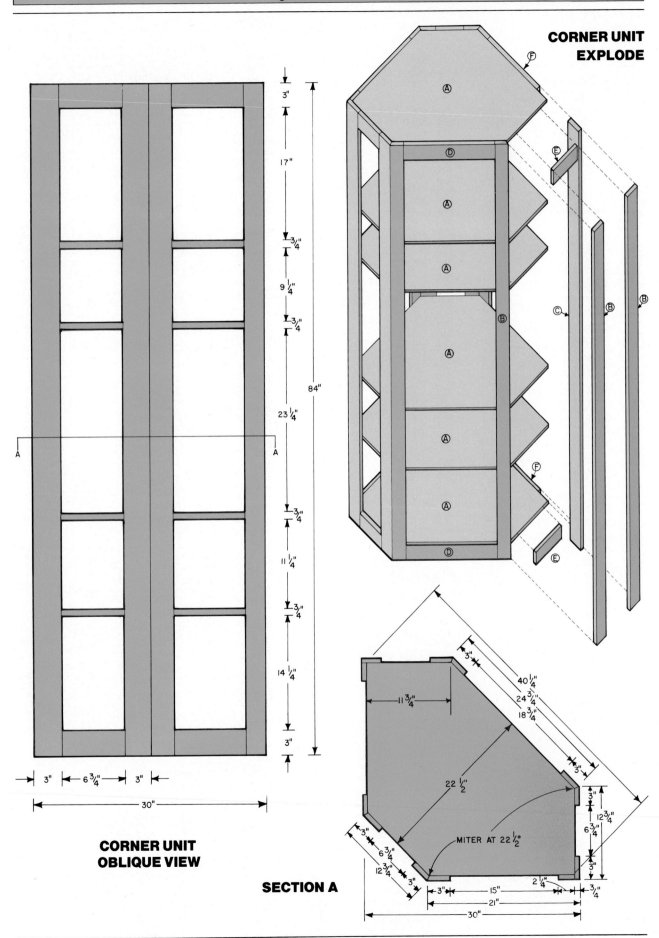

**CORNER UNIT
EXPLODE**

**CORNER UNIT
OBLIQUE VIEW**

SECTION A

Variations

The side pieces can either be two narrow stiles, as shown on the floor-to-ceiling units, or solid boards, as shown on the hanging shelves and headboard. The top of the unit can be treated as another shelf (floor-to-ceiling units), or it can be a 'cap' (headboard).

The configuration and the dimensions can be changed to fit your needs. As shown, the headboard will fit a standard double bed. But it can be made longer or shorter for other mattresses. A unit can also be as tall (or as short) as you want to make it. You can build stand-alone shelves, or several units can be made to work together. As shown in the lead shot and drawings, units can even be modified to turn a corner.

Some, like the headboard, may attach to other pieces of furniture. This may require additional reinforcement. The front stiles of the headboard are laminated to provide double strength where the bed frame bolts to them. And the lower rail is reinforced where the mattress will bump up against it. (See Figure 5.)

You may also wish to dress the shelves up a bit, depending on the decor in your home and your own preferences. I put a couple of simple frame doors on the hanging shelves mainly because I like glass doors. I shaped the edges of the headboard because the other furniture in the room has shaped edges. I could have also put some molding around the top, but I didn't feel like making molding that day.

Figure 5. Certain variations on this shelving design will require reinforcement. Here, the headboard has been reinforced where it bolts to the bed frame and where the mattress bumps up against it.

The one design element that you will almost be sure to change is the spacing of the shelves. This is up to you completely. It will be controlled primarily by what you want to store on them. The spacing shown on the floor-to-ceiling units leaves room for records, video and stereo equipment, books, plants, and other stuff that you'd normally find lying about a living room. The one drawback to this design is that once the shelves are glued and nailed in place, they stay in place. So plan carefully.

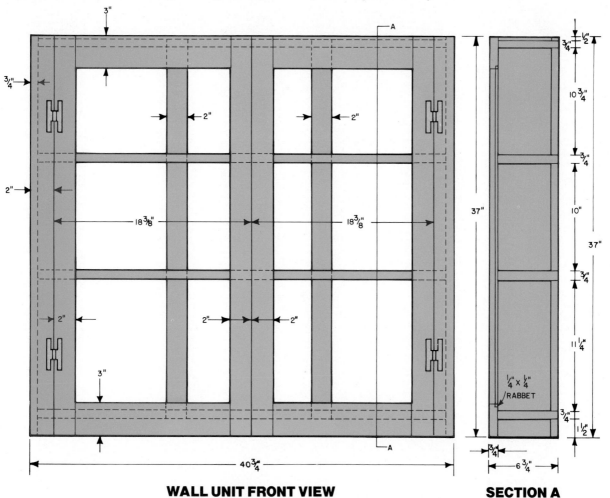

WALL UNIT FRONT VIEW

SECTION A

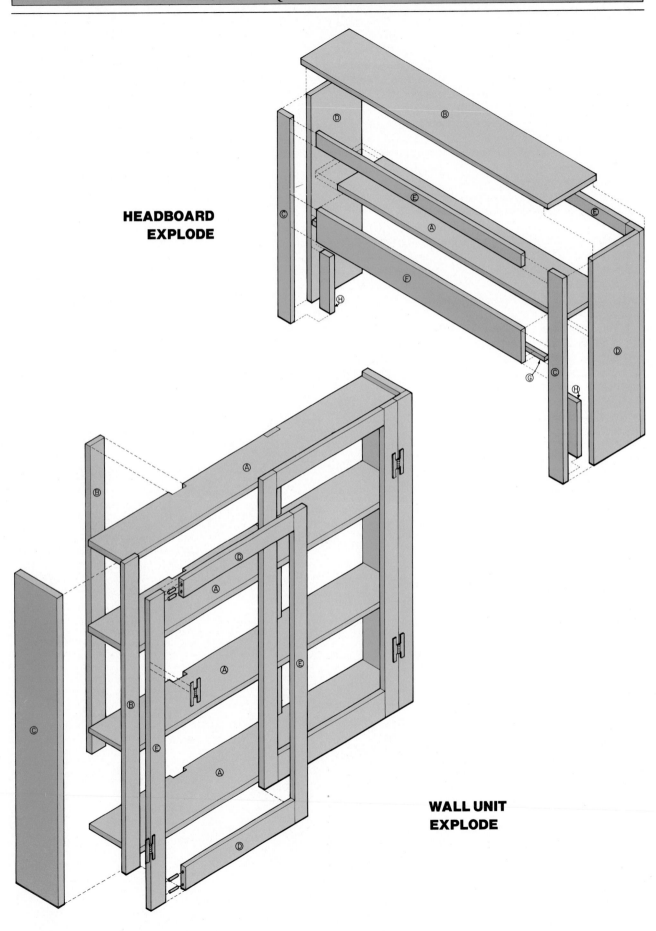

HEADBOARD EXPLODE

WALL UNIT EXPLODE

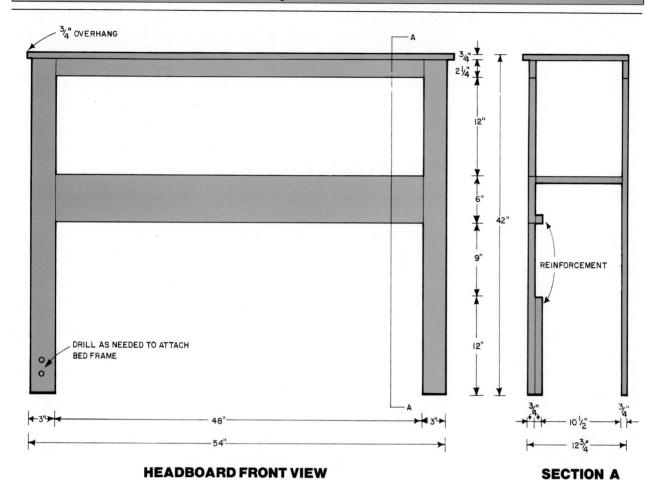

HEADBOARD FRONT VIEW

SECTION A

BILL OF MATERIALS — Quick-and-Easy Shelves

Finished Dimensions in Inches

Floor Unit

A.	Shelves (8)	3/4 x 11-1/4 x 28-1/2
B.	Front/Back Stiles (4)	3/4 x 3 x 84
C.	Side Stiles (4)	3/4 x 2-1/4 x 84
D.	Front/Back Rails (4)	3/4 x 3 x 24
E.	Side Rails (4)	3/4 x 3 x 6-3/4

Hardware

#6 Finishing or Cut Nails (1/4 lb.)
Or #8 x 1-1/4″ Flathead Wood Screws (6-7 dozen)

Corner Unit

A.	Shelves (6)	3/4 x 22-1/2 x 40-1/4
B.	Wide Stiles (10)	3/4 x 3 x 84
C.	Slender Stiles (2)	3/4 x 2-1/4 x 84
D.	Front Rails (2)	3/4 x 3 x 18-1/4
E.	Side Rails (6)	3/4 x 3 x 6-3/4
F.	Back Rails (4)	3/4 x 3 x 15

Hardware

#6 Finishing or Cut Nails (1/4 lb.)
Or #8 x 1-1/4″ Flathead Wood Screws (9-10 dozen)

Wall Unit

A.	Shelves (8)	3/4 x 6 x 39-1/4
B.	Front/Back Stiles (6)	3/4 x 2 x 37
C.	Sides (2)	3/4 x 6 x 37
D.	Door Rails (8)	3/4 x 3 x 14-3/8
E.	Door Stiles (8)	3/4 x 2 x 37

Hardware

#6 Finishing or Cut Nails (1/4 lb.)
Or #8 x 1-1/4″ Flathead Wood Screws (4-5 dozen)
1-1/2″ x 2″ Hinges (2 pair)
17-1/4″ x 35-1/2″ Glass (2 pieces)

Headboard Unit

A.	Shelf	3/4 x 11-1/4 x 52-1/2
B.	Top	3/4 x 13-1/2 x 55-1/2
C.	Front/Back Stiles (4)	3/4 x 3 x 41-1/4
D.	Sides (2)	3/4 x 11-1/4 x 41-1/4
E.	Top Rails (2)	3/4 x 2-1/4 x 48
F.	Middle Rail	3/4 x 6 x 48
G.	Rail Reinforcement	3/4 x 3/4 x 52-1/2
H.	Stile Reinforcements (2)	3/4 x 2-1/4 x 12

Hardware

#6 Finishing or Cut Nails (1/4 lb.)
Or #8 x 1-1/4″ Flathead Wood Screws (3-4 dozen)

Designed and built by Nick Engler

Colonial Tavern Sign

This traditional sign board adds a touch of class to your home, farm, or business.

Getting ready to hang out your shingle? Well, here's a classy-looking shingle ripe for hanging.
    This Colonial 'tavern sign' looks good as a business sign, a sign at the entrance to your farm or ranch, or just a sign at the beginning of your driveway announcing your name and street number. You can use the dimensions shown here, or make the sign bigger or smaller depending on your needs.

Since this is an outdoor project, use pressure-treated lumber for the sign. It's designed so that you can make the entire thing from standard builder's stock from a local lumberyard. The 3/4" stock can be ripped from a single 1x12, 8' long. And the stock for the turned end posts can be sawn from a 2x4.

Warning: The chemicals used to pressure treat lumber are poisonous, especially if you breathe or swallow them. Wear a dust mask when working the wood. And don't burn the scraps; just throw them away.

Start this project by making the crossbraces — cut them an inch or so longer than called for in the Bill of Materials. Then make the end posts. Cut the dadoes in the posts *before* you turn them, making sure that the crossbraces will fit

120

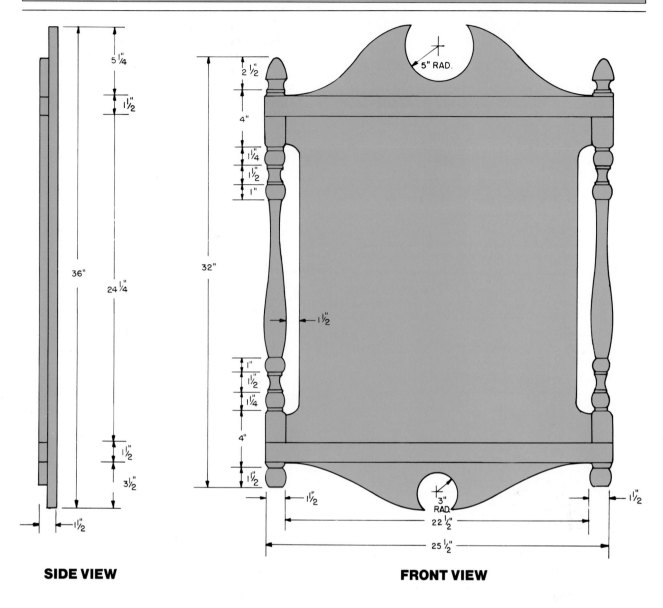

SIDE VIEW   **FRONT VIEW**

snugly in the dadoes. These dadoes will make the spindles slightly out of balance when you turn them, but if you keep the lathe below 1300 RPM, you shouldn't have any problem. (See Figure 1.)

To make the sign board, cut two 36" lengths of 1x12 — the actual dimensions will be 3/4" x 11-1/4". Enlarge the half-pattern and trace it on one board only. Temporarily tack the two boards together and pad saw them on a bandsaw. (See Figure 2.) Then pry the boards apart and attach

Figure 1. Cut the dadoes in the post stock *before* you turn the posts, then turn them at a low speed.

Figure 2. Pad saw the two halves of the sign board so that both sides are exactly the same.

them to the crossbraces with wood screws. Be sure that the braces are positioned so that they will fit in the end posts, with a little extra stock hanging over each side. Don't bother jointing and edge-gluing the boards — they'll just delaminate after a few seasons in the weather. Besides, the crack down the middle gives the sign an aura of authenticity.

Tip ◆ Use either brass, stainless steel, or galvanized screws and screw eyes on this project, so that the hardware won't rust and stain the wood.

Finally, attach the end posts to the sign board, fitting the crossbraces in the dadoes and securing them with wood screws. Cut the ends of the braces flush with the posts and sand the cut ends smooth.

Before you paint the sign, test the paint on a scrap of pressure-treated lumber. Depending on the chemical used to treat the wood, the paint may discolor. If this happens, use a paint with a different base — oil, enamel, lacquer, latex —whatever works on your sign.

There are dozens of ways you can hang the sign. You can suspend it from eye screws in the tops of the end posts or top crossbrace, or attach it to the side of a building with bolts through the crossbraces. The method will depend on how and where you want to use the sign. Rest assured, it will look classy no matter how you hang it.

BILL OF MATERIALS — Colonial Tavern Sign

Finished Dimensions In Inches

A.	Sign Board	3/4 x 22-1/2 x 36
B.	Crossbraces (2)	3/4 x 1-1/2 x 25-1/2
C.	End Posts (2)	1-1/2 x 1-1/2 x 32

Hardware

#10 x 1-1/4″ Flathead Wood Screws (12)
#10 x 2-1/2″ Flathead Wood Screws (4)
Hanging Hardware (to suit)

I SQUARE = 1"

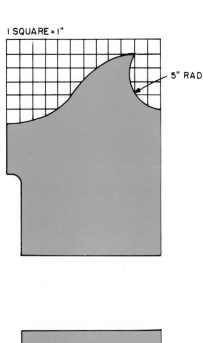

5" RAD

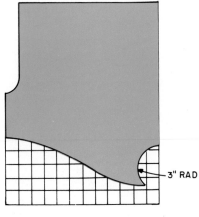

3" RAD

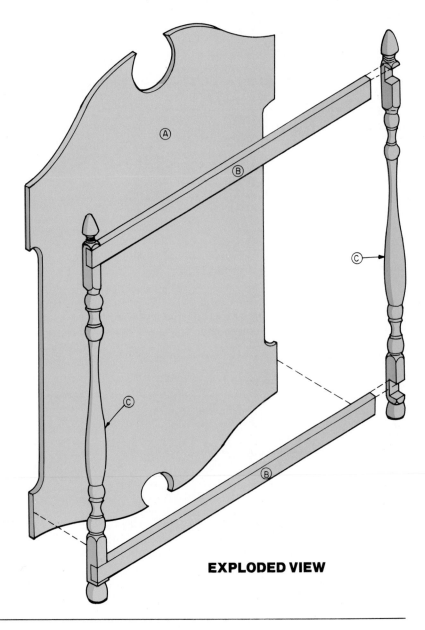

EXPLODED VIEW

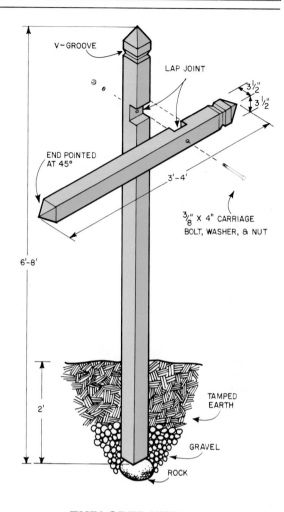

V-GROOVE

LAP JOINT

3 1/2"

3 1/2"

END POINTED
AT 45°

3'-4'

3/8" X 4" CARRIAGE
BOLT, WASHER, & NUT

6'-8'

2'

TAMPED
EARTH

GRAVEL

ROCK

EXPLODED VIEW

Colonial Signpost

What good is a sign without a post?

I f you elected to make the "Colonial Sign", you might be needing a Colonial signpost. A signpost isn't a difficult project, but it does require some special considerations and techniques.

First of all, consider the stock. The best all-around wood to use for an outdoor post is wood that has been pressure-treated with a wood preservative such as Penta®. Independent research on these preservatives indicates that treated posts will last fifty years in the ground. The next runner-up is cedar, followed closely by redwood and locust. All of these woods have natural oils that act as a preservative.

Use a sabre saw with a 5″ 'deep-cut' blade to saw a design in the top of the post, if you want one. Make a

compound cut — trace the pattern on one side, cut the pattern, then tape the waste back to the post. Turn the post 90°, trace and cut the pattern again. (See Figure 1.) When you remove the waste and the tape, you'll have a three-dimensional shape.

Setting the post is not a simple matter of setting it in concrete. In fact, that's one of the worst ways to set a post. The concrete forms a cup that holds water, and the bottom begins to rot away. Instead, dig a deep hole and put a rock or gravel in the bottom. Put the post in place, and shovel in a little more gravel. Finally, pack dirt around the sides of the post.

Figure 1. Saw a shape in the top of the post with a compound cut. Use a sabre saw and a deep-cut blade.

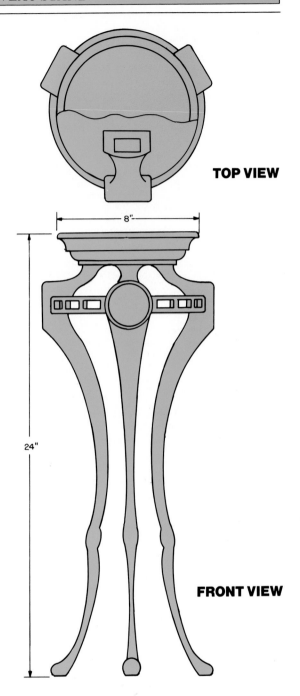

TOP VIEW

FRONT VIEW

Designed and built by Jim McCann

Art Nouveau Stand

Soft, flowing contours make this stand as much a sculpture as a piece of furniture.

During the late nineteenth century, European crafts-men began to design furniture with flowing lines and intertwining curves patterned after the 'Art Nouveau' movement. This school of design had a brief life — just ten years — but, it continues to influence many contemporary woodworkers.

One such woodworker is Jim McCann. Jim designed and made the piece pictured here several years ago as a "challenge". He fully expected the intricate contours to be a real stretch of his talents. But, once he got into the project, he was surprised how the problems began to work them-selves out. "I made a lot of things out to be more difficult than they actually were," admits Jim.

Even though the piece appears to be the product of a master carver, most of it can be cut and shaped on ordinary

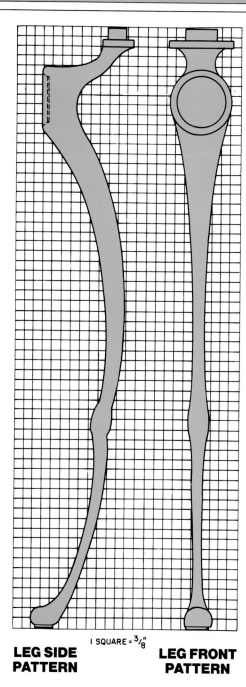

I SQUARE = 3/8"

LEG SIDE PATTERN   **LEG FRONT PATTERN**

1.) Notice that these mortises are made at two separate angles and that they are stepped to accept the ends of the rails, as shown in the drawings. To make the first step, counterbore a shallow mortise 3/8" wide, 7/8" long, and 1/8" deep (on the shallow edge). Then, drill a deeper mortise smack-dab in the middle of the first, 3/16" wide, 5/8" long, and 5/8" deep. Remember to change angles for the second mortise.

Also, cut round recesses in the fronts of the leg stock. The bottoms of these recesses will later be covered with a veneer that contrasts with the wood in the legs. There are two ways to make the recesses. The first way is to simply drill a 1/4" deep hole with a 2" multi-spur bit. The second way is to cut the sides of the recess with a 2" holesaw, then rout out the waste stock. (See Figures 2 and 3.)

Figure 1. Drill or rout the mortises in the sides of the legs at a 77° angle. This mortise should be 'stepped' to accept the tenons *and* a small part of the rails.

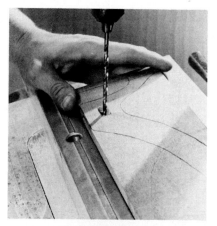

Figure 2. To make the recesses in the legs, first cut the sides with a holesaw.

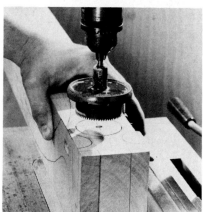

Figure 3. Finish the leg recesses by routing out the waste stock.

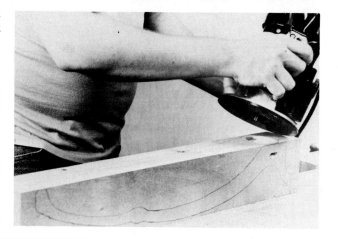

home workshop tools. With careful planning — and a good deal of patience — you can reproduce Jim's exercise in Art Nouveau in your own shop.

Making the Legs

The most striking thing about this project are the delicate legs. They are also the hardest pieces to make. The joinery is fairly simple, but it takes some time and precision to get them all alike. "I strongly suggest you make four legs, the first one as a 'trial leg'," says Jim.

Square the leg stock and lay out the leg patterns. Using these patterns as a guide, cut the joinery — it would be almost impossible to make accurate joints after the legs are shaped. Cut the tenons on top of the legs on a bandsaw, then rout or drill the mortises in the sides of the legs. (See Figure

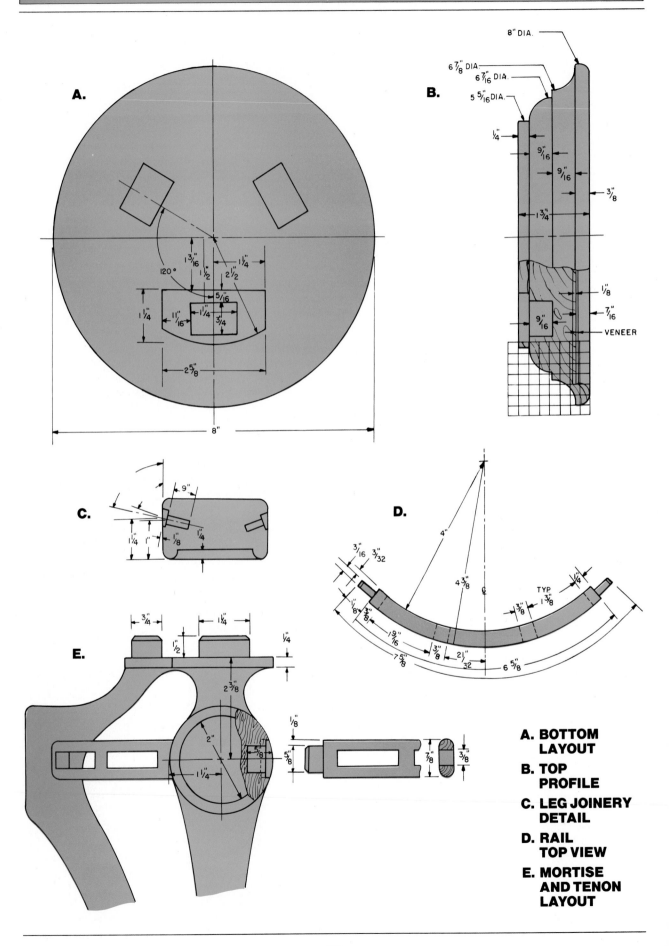

A. BOTTOM LAYOUT

B. TOP PROFILE

C. LEG JOINERY DETAIL

D. RAIL TOP VIEW

E. MORTISE AND TENON LAYOUT

To contour the legs, start on the bandsaw. Cut the general shape in the front and side using a 'compound cutting' technique. Cut the front contour, then tape the waste stock back to the board. Turn the stock 90°, and cut the second contour. (See Figure 4.) When you remove the tape and the waste stock, you'll have a rough-shaped leg.

Smooth out the contours on the leg using whatever abrasive tools are available to you. Jim rounded the legs on a drum sander, then rasped the contours around the knees. Finally, he hand-sanded the three final legs down to 120#. (Later, he polished them further.)

Making the Top

The top of the stand is made in two pieces. The top piece accepts the tenons on top of the legs, and the bottom piece hides part of the shoulders at the tops of the legs, so the legs blend smoothly in to the top.

Jim suggests that you make both pieces out of four smaller pieces, mitered and joined as shown in Figure 5. "If you make the top from one solid piece, the end grain will show on two sides of the stand, and the coloring will be uneven," Jim explains. "But if you glue up four smaller pieces in a diamond pattern, the end grains won't show — the project is totally symmetrical."

As you did when you made the legs, cut the joinery *before* you turn the pieces and before you glue the top and bottom plates together. The mortises in the tops can either be routed or drilled then the edges and corners cleaned up

with a hand chisel. Make the mortises in the bottom plate with a piercing cut, using either a jigsaw or sabre saw.

> **Tip ◆** Cut the tenons on the legs slightly larger than need be, then hand-fit each individual leg to the mortises by shaving stock from the faces of the tenons until the legs fit snugly.

Glue the top and the bottom plates together. Use the legs to properly position these pieces, but be careful *not* to glue the legs to the tabletop at this time. It would be best to remove the legs after you've secured the clamps and **before** the glue dries. Allow the glue to set up for *at least* 24 hours. Then, attach the top assembly to a faceplate and turn the top on a lathe. (See Figure 6.) Remember to turn the recess in the top 7/16" deep — deep enough to accept *both* the top veneer and its hardboard base.

Making the Rails

Cut the curved rails from solid blocks on a bandsaw. (See Figure 7.) Then, continuing to use the bandsaw, carefully cut tenons in the ends of the rails.

Make the openings in the rails on a jigsaw, using a piercing cut — just as you did when you cut the mortises in the bottom plate. (See Figure 8.) Lay out the pattern on the *insides* of the rails, then set the stock on the jigsaw with the inside *up*. Use a fine-tooth blade, and take the cut very slow. This will cut down on the amount of sanding you'll need to

Figure 4. Rough out the shape of the legs on a bandsaw with a compound cut. Cut the front profile, tape the waste stock back to the board, and cut the side profile.

Figure 5. To keep the end grains from showing, glue up four small boards in a diamond pattern to make the top and bottom plates.

Figure 6. Attach the top assembly to a faceplate and shape it on a lathe. Remember to make the recess in the top deep enough to accept both the veneer and its hard-board base.

Figure 7. Cut the curved rails out of thick stock on a bandsaw. After you cut the curves, cut the tenons.

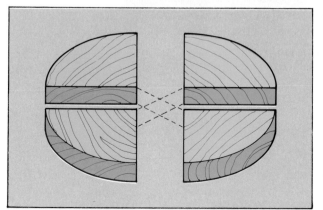

do later.

Carefully round the edges of the rails with a rasp and sandpaper, fitting them to the mortises in the legs. When you use sandpaper for shaping, be careful not to use anything coarser than 80#, and finish up with 120# — for now. If you sand with 50#, you'll never get the scratches out.

Veneering the Top and Legs

Select the veneer you want to use on the top and in the legs. As mentioned earlier, this veneer should contrast with the hardwood in the project. Jim made the stand out of cherry and selected Carpathian elm burl to cover the top and the recesses in the legs.

Cut a piece of hardboard 1/4"-3/8" larger in diameter than the recess in the top of the stand. Apply veneer to this hardboard — this hardboard keeps the veneer from checking or buckling. The hardwood top will swell and shrink with changes in humidity. If you applied veneer directly to the top, it wouldn't stay flat for long.

Attach the hardboard and the veneer to a faceplate and turn it down to its exact diameter. Make sure it fits in the top without gaps. Also, be sure your chisels are very sharp and that the glue joint between the veneer and the hardboard is complete and fully cured.

Sandwich the veneer patches for the legs between two blocks of wood, and 'pressure turn' these on the lathe to their exact diameter. In a pressure turning, several pieces of wood are held together between the lathe spindle centers with nothing but the pressure of centers. (See Figure 9.)

Apply the veneers to their respective recesses, using contact cement. You'll need some small 'veneer presses' to get the side veneers flat in the legs. The blocks that you used to sandwich the veneers on the lathe are ready-made presses for this step. You can also use the scraps from bandsawing the legs as 'cauls', so that you can attach clamps to the legs without marring the wood.

Finally, it's time to assemble the pieces. The trouble, you'll find, is that they all have to go together all at once. "Assembly requires about thirty-seven hands," Jim warns, "plus the patience of a saint — or the vocabulary of a drill sergeant."

'Dry' assemble the project first. Assemble the legs and rails, then hold them together with a web clamp. Insert the legs through the bottom plate and into the top. Put a piece of plywood over the top and another under the legs. The plywood should have three notches, spaced 120° apart, to evenly position the bar clamps. Use three bar clamps arranged around the circumference of these pieces of plywood to clamp the legs in the top. (See Figure 10.)

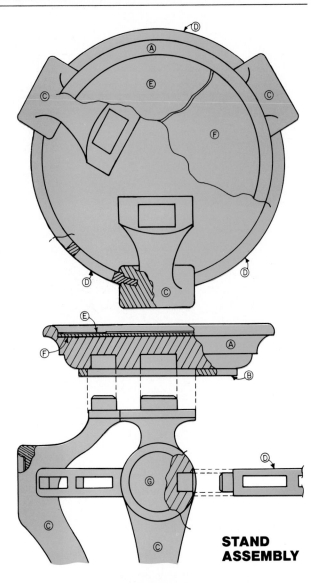

STAND ASSEMBLY

Figure 9. Turn the side veneers to their proper diameter on a lathe. Press them between two scrap blocks, held between the spindle centers.

Figure 8. Make the openings in the rails on a jigsaw, using a 'piercing cut'. Drill a small hole, insert the jigsaw blade through the hole, then clamp the blade in the chucks.

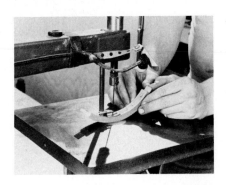

Figure 10. Wrap a web clamp around the legs and rails to hold these pieces together, then clamp the legs to the top with bar clamps. Use two plywood discs as cauls to protect the top and hold the legs in place.

128

Tip ◆ Drill holes in the bottom piece of plywood to hold the pad feet. This will keep the legs from splaying out when you tighten the bar clamps. Also: Don't tighten the bar clamps overmuch. Remember, the legs are fragile.

If everything fits correctly, mark the foot positions on the plywood. Disassemble the stand and reassemble it with glue. During the glue-up procedure, keep a wet rag handy to wipe off any excess glue.

After the glue has cured, remove the clamps. Using a rasp and hand chisels, 'blend' the tops of the legs into the bottom of the tabletop. Remove the glue beads with a chisel and finish sand to 220#.

Jim finished his table with three coats of sanding sealer and five coats of lacquer. Sand with 400# sandpaper in-between each coat of sanding sealer. Polish the last coat of lacquer with rottenstone, then pumice.

The design for the Art Nouveau Stand is the copyrighted property of Jim McCann. You may reproduce this stand for your own use or as a gift, but reproduction for sale or profit is forbidden by law.

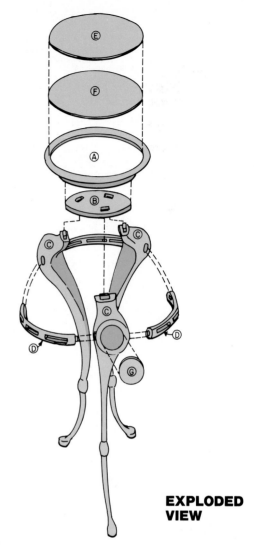

EXPLODED VIEW

BILL OF MATERIALS — Art Nouveau Stand

Finished Dimensions in Inches

A.	Top	8 dia. x 1-1/2
B.	Bottom Plate	8 dia. x 1/4
C.	Legs (3)	2-5/8 x 3-3/4 x 23-1/4
D.	Rails (3)*	3/8 x 7/8 x 7-5/8
E.	Top Veneer	7 dia.
F.	Top Veneer Base	7 dia. x 1/8
G.	Side Veneers (3)	2 dia.

* Cut the rails from stock 7/8" x 1-3/4" x 6-1/2".

TIPS

STAND

Hand-Rubbed Varnish Finish

Projects like this stand have many intricate surfaces, and consequently, traditional 'building' finishes require an enormous amount of time to apply. You have to sand between each coat to get rid of the brush strokes and other imperfections. By the time you're done, the finish may have taken you longer to apply than it took to build the project in the first place.

◆ In cases like these, consider using a hand-rubbed varnish finish. The process is simple. First, seal the wood with a single coat of sanding sealer. Allow the sealer to dry, then polish it down with #00 steel wool. Rub the project with a tack rag, carefully removing the dust, then apply a coat of clear varnish — don't worry about the brush strokes, just slap it on. Allow the varnish to get

slightly tacky — just tacky enough to feel sticky. Soak a rag in tung oil and rub the entire project down, dissolving the varnish.

◆ Some of the varnish will remain, of course. But, what remains will have been rubbed to a soft lustre, completely smooth. You shouldn't have to sand the finish down or polish it with rottenstone. Just apply a coat of paste wax, and use all the time you saved to admire your handiwork.

◆ One word of warning: This is a messy way to finish a project. Your hands get awfully sticky with varnish and tung oil. But, when you consider the time and elbow grease you save, the mess is worth it.

Designed and built by John Shoup

Sewing Notions

Delicate, precise joinery makes these two small chests elegant examples of woodworking at its finest.

I had a hard time convincing Marilyn to let me borrow the boxes that her husband, John Shoup, made for her, long enough to take their photographs. I can understand her concern. It wasn't just that she had nowhere to put her sewing notions for a few days; these boxes are treasures.

John Shoup knows small case construction with an intimacy that few craftsmen ever achieve. For years, he built fine hardwood tool boxes for a living — every tiny piece of every drawer joined with elegant precision. During that time, he gleaned more than a few secrets on how to build boxes so they stay built. He shared some of those secrets as he explained how to make the two small chests you see here.

Check Your Tools!

Before you start to make either chest, check your tools. Proper adjustment and alignment are important when you build large pieces, but they become even more critical on these small chests. Take the time to check *all* the alignments, especially on your table saw and jointer.

Also, be sure that your blades and knives are very sharp. Dull blades may wander slightly during a cut, making it impossible to cut an accurate joint. They may also tear out the wood, particularly when trying to make delicate cuts in small pieces.

Finally, as you work, double-check all your setups with a square or protractor that you're sure you can trust. Don't just rely on the stops or scales on the tools.

Making the Chest of Drawers

Plane down the stock you'll need. The sides, partitions, and drawer parts are 3/8″ thick, the drawer bottoms are 1/8″ thick, and all the remaining parts are 1/4″ thick. If you're shaving down 3/4″ stock, resaw it first on the bandsaw. You can get a 3/8″ *and* 1/4″ stock from a single 3/4″ thick board, with very little waste.

Figure 1. Cut the dadoes in the small chest of drawers with a router bit chucked in your drill press. Adjust the drill press to run at its highest speed, and cut slowly, using very little pressure.

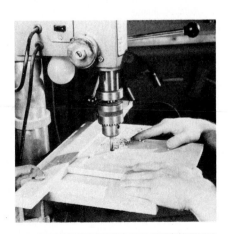

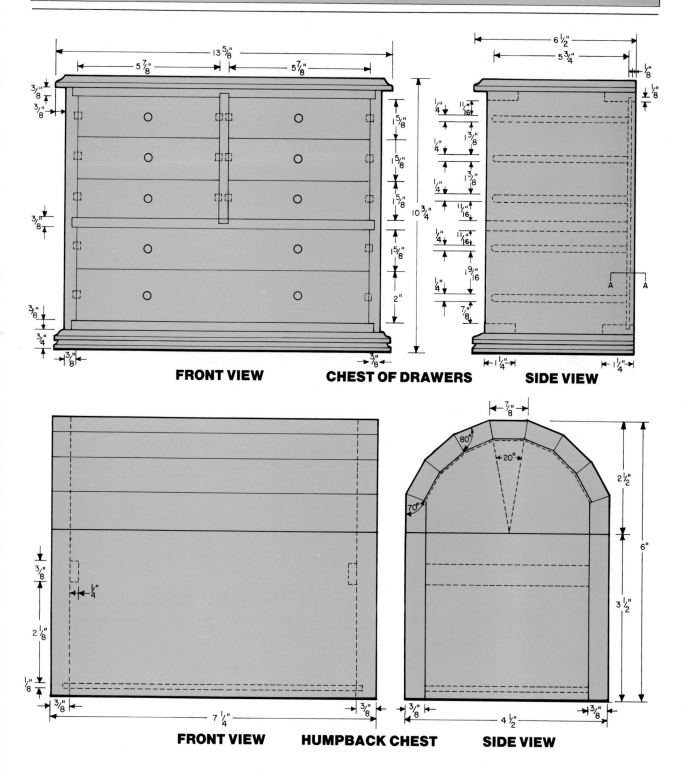

FRONT VIEW   **CHEST OF DRAWERS**   **SIDE VIEW**

FRONT VIEW   **HUMPBACK CHEST**   **SIDE VIEW**

Cut the sides, stretchers, back, and partitions to size, then cut the dadoes and rabbets in these parts. Note that the dadoes for the drawer guides are blind in front. The easiest way to make these dadoes is with an overarm router. If you don't have one, use a 1/4″ straight router bit chucked in your drill press. (See Figure 1.) Take your time with this setup; router bits in drill presses cut very slowly, even when the press is adjusted to run at the highest possible speed.

Also note that the rabbets for the stretchers in the sides are blind. Cut these as far as you can with a router, then

square off the blind ends with a carving chisel. *Don't* square off the blind dadoes; the rounded fronts serve a purpose. When the drawer guides are rounded to match the dadoes, the drawers slide easier.

Cut the drawer guides and round the front ends, fitting them to the dadoes. Then, dry assemble the case, holding it together with clamps. *Do not* glue any pieces together at this time.

Make the drawer sides, and cut the grooves in them. These grooves should be 1/64″-1/32″ wider than the drawer

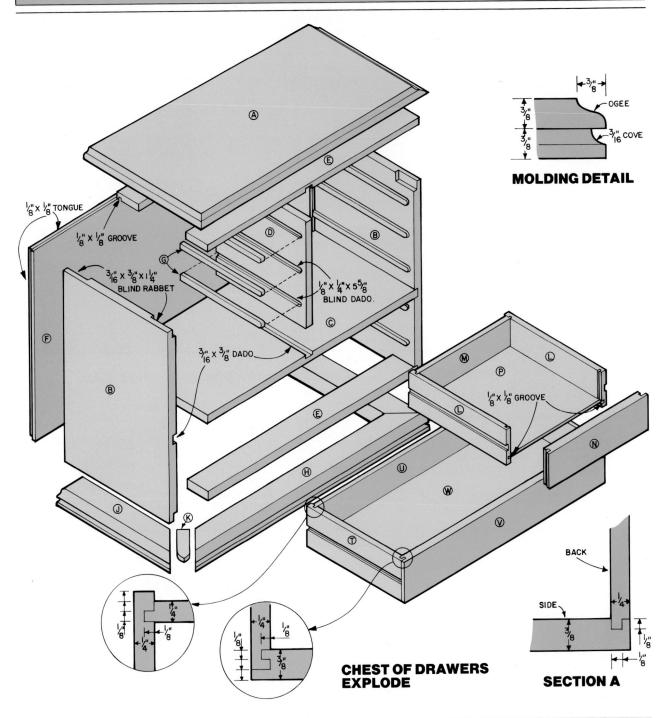

MOLDING DETAIL

CHEST OF DRAWERS EXPLODE

SECTION A

guides. But don't cut them too wide — too much slop and the drawers will rub against each other. Slide the drawer sides in the cabinet, custom fitting each one so that they all slide easily. Make sure there's the proper clearance (1/16″, no more) between each drawer. Mark the locations.

Cut the drawer fronts and backs, and join them to the sides. The fronts are attached to the sides with a 'lock' joint. To make this joint, first cut a 1/8″ groove with your table saw blade in the edges of the drawer fronts and the inside faces of the drawer sides. Then, cut the 'tongues' on the drawer fronts to length. The backs are joined to the sides with a dado and rabbet. The procedure for making this joint is similar, but it takes one less step. Make small, shallow cuts with your table saw blade to form the dadoes and rabbets.

Tip ◆ John uses a 40-tooth carbide-tipped blade. This gives a much smoother cut than ordinary saw blades.

Dry assemble the drawers and fit them in the case. Once again, you may have to do a little 'fiddling' to get them all to fit properly and slide smoothly. When you're satisfied with the fit, disassemble the drawers and make the drawer bottoms. Reassemble the drawers with glue, and when the glue has cured, check the fit of the drawers one more time. If everything still fits properly (it should), disassemble the case and reassemble it with glue.

Make the bottom molding in two passes with your router. On the first pass, cut the half-cove with a 1/2″

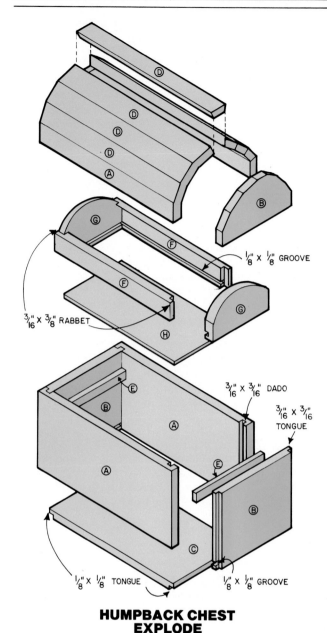

HUMPBACK CHEST EXPLODE

Labels on diagram:
⅛" × ⅛" GROOVE
3/16" × 3/8" RABBET
3/16" × 3/16" DADO
3/16" × 3/16" TONGUE
⅛" × ⅛" TONGUE
⅛" × ⅛" GROOVE

Tip ◆ Drill the screw holes in the upper stretchers slightly larger than the screw shanks. This will allow the top to expand and contract without stressing the other joints in the case.

Finish the case with a penetrating finish, such as tung oil or Danish oil. Avoid building finishes; these may interfere with the sliding action of the drawers. Be sure to apply just as many coats of finish to the inside of the case as the outside. That way, both sides of the wood will absorb moisture evenly and the case will remain square longer.

You may want to line the drawer bottoms. John uses Aleene's "Tacky Glue" to stick felt down. Both the glue and the felt are available at craft stores. You'll also want to attach drawer pulls to the drawer fronts. The tiny brass pulls that John used on this project are available from:

The Woodworker's Store
21801 Industrial Blvd.
Rogers, MN 55374

Making the Humpback Chest

While this project looks simpler than the chest of drawers, it is actually a good deal more complex. The joinery in the lid is a true test of your skill and patience.

Make the ends, front, and back first. Cut the parts approximately 1" long (or high). You'll need the extra stock; it gives you some 'fiddling' room to cut and fit the top pieces. Cut matching tongues and dadoes in the proper parts, then set the front and back aside.

Scribe an arc on the top side of the ends, and mark the center or 'pivot point' of the arc. The diameter of this arc should be the same diameter as the width of the parts. Cut the arcs out on a bandsaw, cutting slightly wide of the lines.

Insert the ends in the jig shown in Figure 3 and the working drawings. The pivot point of the arcs must be

Figure 2. To cut blind grooves for splines in mitered pieces, clamp the pieces to the rip fence of your table saw, then raise the blade.

Figure 3. To cut the top edges of the ends of the humpback chest, make a jig to hold the parts. Use the rip fence on your table saw as a guide.

core-box bit. On the second pass, shape the top edge with a 3/16" ogee bit. While you've got the ogee bit mounted in your router, also shape the top edge of the top.

Tip ◆ These shapes are just suggestions. You may have other preferences. If so, shape the bottom molding and the top according to your own lights.

Miter the bottom molding and reinforce the joints with blind splines. To make the groove for the spline, John first lowers the table saw blade all the way. He then clamps the mitered board to the rip fence and positions it over the blade. The saw is turned on and the blade carefully raised until the groove is cut to the proper depth. (See Figure 2.)

Attach the bottom molding and the top to the stretchers with small wood screws. When assembling the top, pass the screws up through the stretchers into the underside of the top. That way, the heads will be hidden.

placed over the pivot on the jig. Using a protractor, carefully rotate the ends until the front and back edges are *exactly* 90° to the front of the jig. Screw the clamp bar tight, and cut a flat on the top of the ends. Use the rip fence on your table saw as a guide. (See Figure 3.)

Loosen the clamp bar, and, measuring the protractor, rotate the ends 10° to the right. Without moving the rip fence, make a second cut on your table saw. Rotate the ends again 10° to the left and repeat. Continue until you have cut seven flats, each flat exactly 10° from its neighbors, as shown in the working drawings.

Make the top strips on the table saw, cutting several extra strips — you'll need them for checking setups. Rip one edge at 10°, then rip the second edge 1/16"-1/8" wider than needed. Cut a tiny 1/32" rabbet in the underside of both ends of the strips. This rabbet is not necessary, but it does help when it comes time for assembly.

Move the rip fence just a shade closer to the blade than it was when you ripped the second edge. Pass all the strips over the blade once again, and check the fit. They'll probably still be just a little too wide, so move the rip fence another hair closer and repeat. Continue shaving the strips in this manner until they fit the ends perfectly.

When all the 10° angles are cut properly, cut the 20° angles where the top strips join the sides. Once again, cut a little wide and shave the strips down until they fit properly.

When you're satisfied that the strips fit the ends properly, cut the ends, front, and back to the proper lengths. (Remember to allow for the saw kerf you'll make when you cut the top free of the rest of the box.) Fit the bottom to the box, and glue up the ends, front, back, and bottom. Wipe any excess glue out of the inside of the box. Let the glue cure, cut the top free of the box, then glue the top strips to the top. Once again, wipe out any excess glue from inside the box.

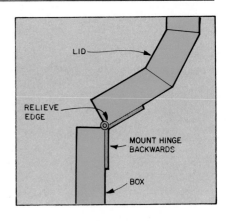

Figure 4. If you install the hinge backwards, it will automatically stop the lid when it's two-thirds open. However, you'll have to slightly relieve the back edge of the lid so that it doesn't rub the box.

Tip ◆ John decided not to glue up the whole box at once so that he could wipe the glue from the *inside* before it set up. Otherwise, he found, it's almost impossible to get all the glue out of the inside of the box. When the glue is still wet, you can clean it up easily with a damp rag.

Glue the ledges to the inside of the box, and make a small tray to sit on these ledges. Hinge the top to the box, then disassemble the hinge for finishing. When the finish is dry, cover the bottom of the tray and the bottom of the box with felt. You might also want to add a pin cushion to the inside of the top.

Tip ◆ If you put the hinges on *backwards*, cutting a small blind rabbet for the pins, the top will automatically stop when it's about two-thirds open. (See Figure 4.) You won't need to add a strap to keep the top from flopping all the way back.

BILL OF MATERIALS — Sewing Notions

Finished Dimensions in Inches

Chest of Drawers

A.	Top	3/8 x 6-1/2 x 13-5/8
B.	Sides (2)	3/8 x 6-1/8 x 9-5/8
C.	Horizontal Partition	3/8 x 5-7/8 x 12-1/2
D.	Vertical Partition	3/8 x 5-1/4 x 5-7/8
E.	Stretchers	3/8 x 1-1/4 x 12-1/2
F.	Back	1/4 x 9-1/8 x 12-3/8
G.	Drawer Guides (16)	1/4 x 1/4 x 5-3/4
H.	Front Base Molding	3/4 x 1-5/8 x 13-5/8
J.	Side Moldings (2)	3/4 x 1-5/8 x 6-1/2
K.	Splines (2)	1/8 x 3/4 x 1-1/4
L.	Upper Drawer Sides (12)	1/4 x 1-19/32 x 5-3/4
M.	Upper Drawer Backs (6)	1/4 x 1-19/32 x 5-9/16
N.	Upper Drawer Fronts (6)	3/8 x 1-19/32 x 5-13/16
P.	Upper Drawer Bottoms (6)	1/8 x 5-3/8 x 5-9/16
Q.	Middle Drawer Sides (2)	1/4 x 1-19/32 x 5-3/4
R.	Middle Drawer Back	1/4 x 1-19/32 x 11-13/16
S.	Middle Drawer Front	3/8 x 1-19/32 x 12-1/6
T.	Bottom Drawer Sides	1/4 x 1-31/32 x 5-3/4
U.	Bottom Drawer Back	1/4 x 1-31/32 x 11-13/16
V.	Bottom Drawer Front	3/8 x 1-31/32 x 12-1/16
W.	Middle/Bottom Dr. Bottom	1/8 x 5-3/8 x 11-13/16

Hardware

Brass Drawer Pulls (10)
#4 x 5/8" Flathead Wood Screws (8)
#8 x 1" Flathead Wood Screws (6)

Humpback Chest

A.	Sides (2)	3/8 x 4-1/2 x 7-1/4
B.	Ends (2)	3/8 x 4-1/4 x 5-3/4
C.	Bottom	1/4 x 3-3/4 x 6-3/4
D.	Top Strips (7)	3/8 x 7/8 x 7-1/4
E.	Tray Supports (2)	1/4 x 3/8 x 3-3/4
F.	Tray Sides (2)	1/4 x 3/4 x 6-7/16
G.	Tray Ends (2)	3/8 x 2 x 3-5/16
H.	Tray Bottom	1/8 x 2-13/16 x 5-15/16

Hardware

Clasp
Small Hinges and Mounting Screws (1 pair)

Designed and built by Nick Engler

Hanging Cupboard

A classic country design makes good use of wasted space.

What's the most frequently wasted space in your house? The attic? Under the sinks? No, it's probably the *corners*.

Think about it: There's plenty of furniture you can set in the middle of the room or up against a wall. But there are very few pieces that make good use of corners. This hanging corner cupboard is one of the few. It turns any corner into an attractive storage or display area.

Modifying the Design

As shown, the cupboard is patterned after a traditional country design. The wood is knotty pine, the latch is wood, and there is a decorative 'scroll shelf' underneath the case. (The scroll shelf was often used to hold a salt dish or other frequently-used item, so that the owner of the cupboard wasn't constantly opening and closing the door.) However, you may want to modify the design depending on the decor in your home and how you intend to use the cabinet.

For instance, if you want to give the cabinet a contemporary appearance, build it from a light, close-grain wood (such as beech or maple), substitute a flat panel in the door, and eliminate the scroll shelf. To use the cupboard as a display cabinet, use a piece of glass in the door. There are many things you can do to change the appearance and the purpose — put a piece of punched tin or stained glass in the door, attach legs to the case so that it sits on the floor — but the basic construction remains the same.

Building the Case

Start by gluing up the wide stock you'll need for the top, bottom, and shelves. I glued up a board 8' long and 20" wide for this project. Set it aside while the glue dries.

Cut all the other pieces to size, except for the back stiles. Instead, rip two boards, one 2-1/4" wide, the other 3" wide. Later — *after* you've cut the joinery — you can add stock to the bottom of these boards for the scroll shelf.

Rip one edge of the front stiles at 22-1/2°, as shown in the drawings. Without changing the saw blade angle, cut a 1/8" wide, 3/8" deep groove in the mitered edge of the front pieces. (See Figure 1.) These grooves will later be fitted with splines to reinforce the miter joint between the front stiles.

Make dadoes in the back, side and front stiles to position and support the shelves. Notice that only the two outermost front stiles get dadoes. The two innermost don't require them.

> **Tip ◆** When making dadoes on the radial arm saw, draw the saw towards the front of the machine, position the wood, and cut the dado by pushing the saw *away* from you, *toward* the fence. (See Figure 2.) Otherwise, the dado cutter will want to 'climb' the board.

After you've cut all the dadoes, glue extra stock on the back stiles to make the scroll shelf. This stock should be at least 9" wide and exactly 12" long. When the glue sets up, tack the back stiles together with the front edges flush, and pad saw the curve for the scroll shelf. (See Figure 3.)

Cut the top, bottom, and shelves from the wide board you glued up with a hand-held circular saw. (See Figure 4.) Be very careful when you lay out the pieces on this board; be certain to leave room for the saw kerfs. Don't try to cut the notches with the circular saw; do that on a bandsaw *after* you've cut the general shape of the pieces.

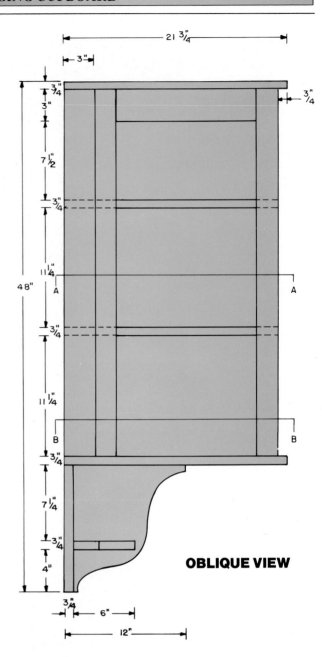

OBLIQUE VIEW

Figure 1. Leave that saw blade set at the same angle you used to rip the mitered edge of the front stiles, and cut a spline groove in those stiles.

Figure 2. When you cut dadoes on a radial arm saw, push the saw away from you, toward the fence. If you draw the saw toward you, the cutter will want to climb the board.

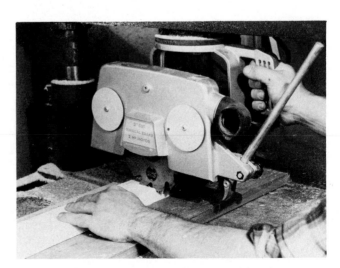

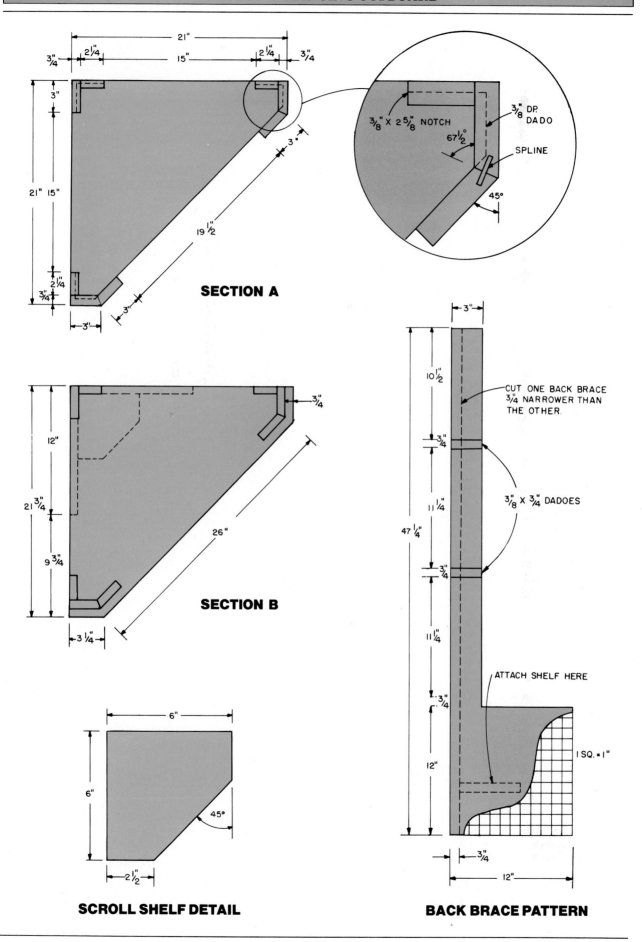

SECTION A

SECTION B

SCROLL SHELF DETAIL

BACK BRACE PATTERN

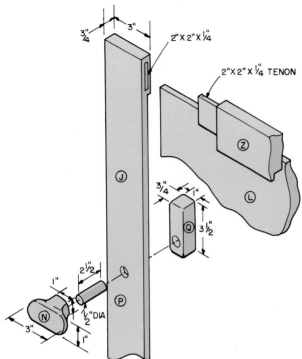

DOOR FRAME AND LATCH EXPLODE

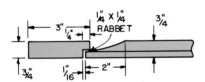

DOOR FRAME AND PANEL DETAIL

Figure 3. Tack the back stiles together, aligning the front edges. Pad saw the curve for the scroll shelf on a bandsaw.

Figure 4. Cut the top, bottom, and shelves from a wide board with a circular saw. A scrap of plywood or fiberboard under the wood protects your saw blade and the top of your workbench.

Figure 5. To make a mortise on your drill press, first drill a series of holes in the board. A milling attachment helps to line up the holes precisely.

Dry assemble the case first with wood screws to make sure that all the pieces fit. With all the miters, dadoes, and splines, you'll probably have to do a good deal of hand-fitting. When you're satisfied with the way all the pieces hang together, disassemble the case and reassemble it with glue.

Making and Hanging the Door

The cupboard door is put together with traditional frame-and-panel joinery. Cut a 1/4″ thick, 2″ long, 2″ wide tenon on either end of the door rails. Then make matching mortises in the door stiles. If you don't have a mortising accessory for your drill press, drill a series of 1/4″ holes to rough out the mortises, then clean up the inside edge with a chisel. (See Figures 5 and 6.)

> **Tip ◆** A milling accessory for your drill press does a great job of positioning the holes for a mortise. (See Figure 5.)

Cut a rabbet on the inside edge of the door frame parts to accept the panel. Remember, the rabbets in the stiles are 'blind' at both ends — they don't go all the way to the top or the bottom of the pieces. The easiest way to make blind rabbets is to use a router, then square off the blind ends with a hand chisel. After you've cut the rabbets, assemble the door frame pieces with glue, and pin each joint with 1/4″ dowels.

Cut the panel for the door to size, then make a cove cut in all four edges to 'raise' the panel. To make this cove cut, pass the panel over the blade of your table saw at 50°. (See Figure 7.) Take small bites, raising the blade just 1/8″ with each pass until the cove is as deep as you want it. (If you try too much stock in one pass, the wood will burn.) Attach the panel to the door frame with small metal 'dogs'. (See Figure 8.) *Do not* glue the panel in place; leave it free to expand and contract with the humidity.

If you want, you can also glue 'cock beading' to the outside edge of the door. This beading was a traditional decoration for furniture doors and drawers during the late eighteenth century. To make the cock beading, cut a bead in the face of a board with a molder or shaper, then slice the bead from the board on a table saw. (See Figures 9 and 10.) Fit the beading to the door, mitering the corners as if you were framing a picture.

Figure 6. Finish the mortise by cleaning up the edges with a chisel.

Figure 7. 'Raise' the panel by cove cutting the edges on your table saw. Make several passes, raising the blade just 1/8″ with each pass.

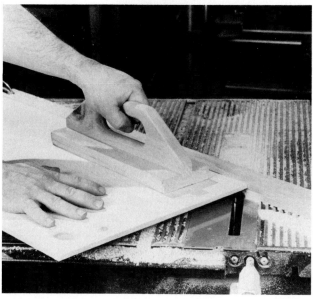

Figure 8. Use small metal tabs or 'dogs' to hold the panel in place in the frame. **Don't** glue the panel to the frame.

Figure 9. To make the cock beading for the door, first cut a bead in the face of a board using a molder or shaper.

Figure 10. Then, using your table saw, rip that bead from the board. *Never* try to shape or mold a thin board. Always do your shaping first on a thicker board, then rip a thin board from it.

Mount the door flush in the cabinet on flat hinges. As you can see, I used decorative cast iron hinges, available at most hardware stores. You can also order ornate cast iron hardware from mail order suppliers such as:

The Renovator's Supply
Renovator's Old Mill
Millers Falls, MA 01349

The catch on the door is another traditional country design. A wooden handle on the outside turns a cam on the inside. When the door is closed, the cam catches on the front stile to hold the door closed.

Finishing the Cupboard

The finish you put on the completed cupboard is, of course, up to you. But if you followed my plans pretty much as drawn and made a country piece, you may want to go a step further and apply a traditional country finish — milk paint.

Milk paint was a common washable indoor paint used in the early history of this country. The beauty of milk paint is that it covers the wood without completely hiding the grain. The first coat penetrates the wood slightly so that the color remains fast over the years, and succeeding coats build on top of the wood, giving the finish depth. But unless you apply many, many coats, knots, burls, birds-eyes and characteristics of the wood are visible through the paint.

As the name implies, one of the major ingredients in milk paint was milk — sometimes cottage cheese. The paint was usually mixed on the spot from old milk, linseed oil, and other household ingredients. Today, several paint companies make reproduction or 'imitation' milk paint for furniture. You'll find these at most paint stores.

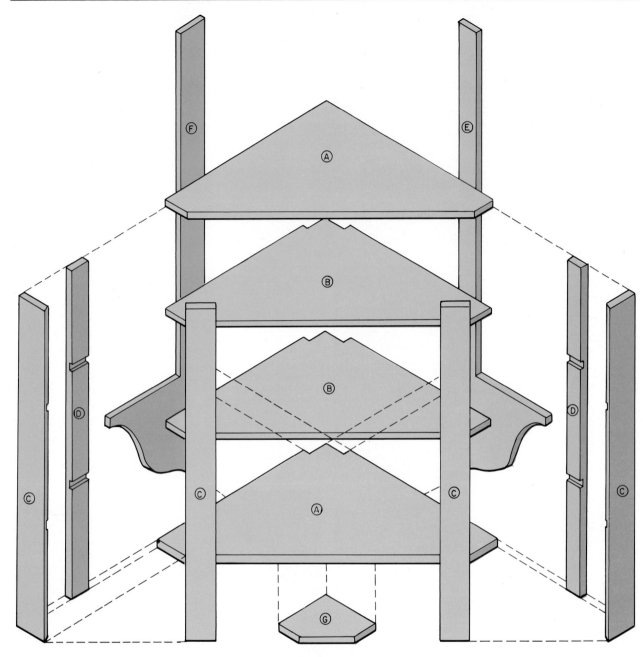

EXPLODED VIEW

BILL OF MATERIALS — Hanging Cupboard

Finished Dimensions in Inches

A.	Top/Bottom (2)	3/4 x 21-3/4 x 21-3/4	**M.**	Dowels (8)	1/4 dia. x 3/4
B.	Shelves (2)	3/4 x 20-5/8 x 20-5/8	**N.**	Handle	1 x 1-1/2 x 3
C.	Front Stiles (4)	3/4 x 3 x 34-1/2	**P.**	Cam Dowel	1/2 dia. x 2-1/2
D.	Side Stiles (2)	3/4 x 2-1/4 x 34-1/2	**Q.**	Cam	3/4 x 1 x 3-1/2
E.	Right Back Stile	3/4 x 11-1/4 x 48	**R.**	Cock Beading* (total)	3/16 x 3/4 x 102
F.	Left Back Stile	3/4 x 12 x 48			
G.	Scroll Shelf	3/4 x 6 x 6			
H.	Splines (2)	1/8 x 3/4 x 34-1/2			
J.	Door Stiles* (2)	3/4 x 2-13/16 x 31-7/16			
K.	Door Rails* (2)	3/4 x 2-13/16 x 17-7/16			
L.	Door Panel	3/4 x 13-13/16 x 25-13/16			

*If you don't use cock beading, make the door stiles and rails 3" wide.

Hardware

#8 x 1-1/4" Flathead Wood Screws (3-4 dozen)
3" Hinges (1 pair)

I SQUARE = $\frac{1}{2}$"

LARGE BOX PATTERN

I SQUARE = $\frac{1}{2}$"

SMALL BOX PATTERN

Designed and built by Nick Engler

One-Piece Box

Saw these clever boxes from a single block of wood.

Some of the most intriguing woodworking projects you can make are those that can be fashioned from a single block of wood. This egg-shaped box is just such a project. If executed properly, the grain will match all around and the box will retain the appearance of a single lump of wood. But open the drawer and people will ask, "How did you do that?"

The how of it is fairly simple. Start by sawing out an egg shape on the bandsaw. You can use the pattern provided, or make up your own. Frequently, the project will look better if you just follow the grain pattern, knots, burls, or other distinguishing parts of the wood.

Once you've cut the shape, make a second bandsaw cut all around the stock, 1/4"-1/2" in from the outside edge. This will create the 'drawer'. (See Figure 1.) Clamp the drawer in a wood clamp right side up, and hollow out a rough cavity on your drill press. If the box is fairly large, you may have to drill several holes to enlarge the cavity to the proper size. Clean up the walls of the cavity with a Surform® rasp. (See Figure 2.)

Finally, sand the millmarks from both the drawer and the 'box', and round over all edges. Finish with a penetrating finish such as Danish oil or tung oil, and cover the bottom of the drawer cavity with felt.

Figure 1. Cut the 'drawer' from the 'box' on a bandsaw. Depending on the size of the project, the walls of the box should be 1/4" to 1/2" thick.

Figure 2. Clean up the sides of large drawer cavities with a Surform® wood rasp mounted on your drill press. Hold the drawer steady in a wood clamp.

BILL OF MATERIALS — One-Piece Box

Finished Dimensions in Inches

A.	Large Box	3 x 3-1/2 x 4-3/4
B.	Small Box	1-1/2 x 1-7/8 x 2-3/8

Designed and built by Nick Engler

The Reorganized Closet

Afraid to open your closets? Here's a suggestion to help tame those monsters of misorganization.

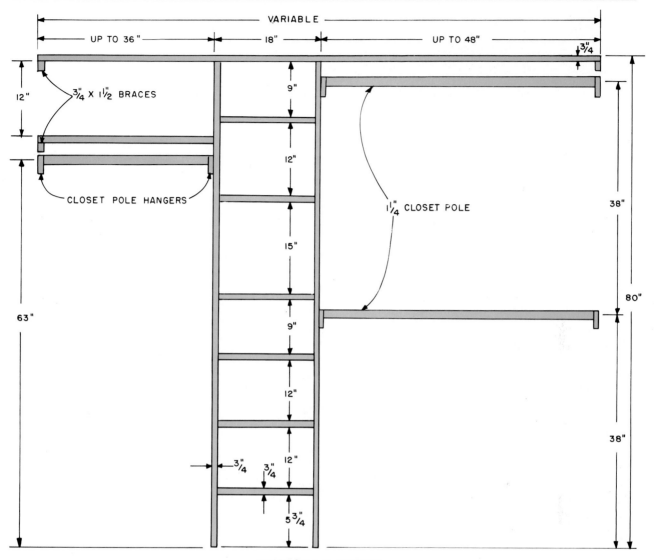

TYPICAL LAYOUT

The apparition you see in Figure 1 is an actual unre-touched photograph of the closet in our master bed-room. (Uh, a little parental guidance is suggested here. I tried to spare you the horror of opening both closet doors at once, but even one open door is pretty strong stuff for the young and impressionable.)

I guess I'd be even more embarrassed than I already am to show this mess to you if I didn't know there are a good many readers out there who have closets that look exactly like this — or worse. Feel your cheeks burning? Well, there's really no need for any of us to feel too bad. Sure, our closets look like an explosion in a clothing factory, but the reason lies more with the way the average closet is designed than it does with the average closet-keeper. (How's *that* for a neat rationalization? Heck, we're not slobs — it's the danged *closet's* fault.)

Better Space Utilization

The problem with the traditional closet design is that it ignores what people usually keep in them. Certain areas are overcrowded; the space in other areas is mostly wasted.

Let's take a critical look: Most closets have a single rod

running down the middle of them, about 66″ off the floor, and a single shelf above that. The clothes, no matter what

Figure 1. The Great American Closet is a sight to behold — poor planning and design converts innocent storage spaces into perpetual disaster areas.

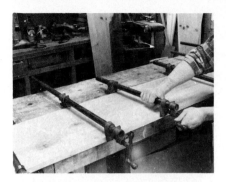

Figure 2. The shelves in my plan for a reorganized closet are 14″ wide — you'll most probably have to glue up the stock.

Figure 4. If the floor of your closet is carpeted, attach the bottom of the shelving unit to the back wall with metal brackets.

Figure 3. While you've got everything out of your closet, you might want to take this opportunity to line it with cedar chipboard. Use industrial adhesive to glue the sheets to the closet walls.

Figure 5. The hanger rods slip into their brackets from above — and they come out the same way.

their length, are hung on the rod; the shoes are piled on the floor; and everything else is precariously balanced on the shelf. The result is usually that the shelf and the floor are cluttered, and there's a lot of dead air in between.

Closets might work better if there were more shelf space and a place to keep shoes. But if you installed more shelves in a closet, wouldn't you have to sacrifice hanger space for clothes? Not necessarily.

Consider how clothes are designed and how they hang up: Most of the clothes you store in your closet — shirts, skirts, pants, sweaters — take up less than 36″ of vertical space on a hanger. A few types of clothes require more vertical space. But the rod in your closet has been installed as if all you owned were full-length dresses and overcoats. The result is that there's a lot of wasted space underneath most of your clothes when you hang them up. By wisely using *all* the space in your closet, you can increase the shelf space without sacrificing hanger space.

To do this, first make a sketch of your closet as it exists, without any shelves or hangers. Draw a single shelf running the length of the closet, 80″ above the floor. This is probably a good 10″-12″ above where your present closet shelves are installed. Next, draw a simple vertical shelving unit with 6-7 shelves, 18″-24″ wide. This unit should fit under the long shelf, dividing the closet in two parts. It should also be offset from the center, so that you can reach all the shelves easily when you open one door. In the larger of the two sections, put *two* hanger rods, 38″ and 76″ off the floor, respectively. Both these hangers will hold 'short' clothes — skirts, sweaters, etc. In the other section, draw a single hanger rod 63″ off the floor for 'tall' clothes. If you wish, put another shelf immediately above this rod.

What you've just sketched will look something like the working drawing we've included here. If you do some measuring and comparing, you will also find that this arrangement increases the shelf space in your closet by 250% or better, and the hanger space by at least 130%. Clearly, this is a better use of the available space.

Rearranging Your Closet

Experiment with this design for a bit, rearranging the elements to suit your own needs. Depending on the types of clothes you own, you might want to make one side of the closet longer or narrower. You may need more or less shelf space than we suggest. And perhaps you have a few of your own ideas that you'd like to include — a clothes hamper, a shoe rack, a barbecue pit — whatever you can squeeze in.

When you've settled on the design, don't tear your closet apart right away. First, build the shelving unit. This will take some time; all the pieces are 14″ wide, so you'll most probably have to glue up some wide stock. (See Figure 2.) You can also make the closet pole hangers and cut many of the parts to size. Have as many of these pieces as possible ready to go when you finally tear your old closet apart, so that you can put it all back together in just a few hours.

When I took my old closet apart, I decided to line the sides with cedar 'closet liner'. This material is an inexpensive chipboard made from cedar chips. I've found that a little bit goes a long way. If you have a small closet, just three or four feet wide, you can get away with lining the whole closet. But if you line an entire eight-foot closet, the smell can be overpowering. So I elected to put it on the ends only. I stuck it to the existing walls with industrial adhesive, then tacked it to the studs. (See Figure 3.)

The closet goes back together quickly, once you've got the inside cleaned out and lined like you want it. First, put the shelving unit in position and balance the upper shelf on top of it. Mark the position for the shelving braces on the closet walls and screw them in place — make sure the screws bite into the studs. Then nail the upper shelf to the braces.

Recheck the position of the shelving unit, and attach it to the upper shelf by nailing down through the shelf. Check the shelves for squareness, then 'toe-nail' the bottom of the unit to the closet floor. If the bottom of the closet is carpeted, you may want to fasten the unit to the back wall with metal brackets, instead. (See Figure 4.) If you've elected to add a shelf above the hanger rod for 'tall' clothes, nail it in place at this time. Paint the shelves or cover them with shelf paper — whichever you prefer.

Install the closet pole hangers on the closet's sides and the sides of the shelving units, and slide the hanger rods into them. (See Figure 5.) Then put your clothes, shoes, and other stuff back into the closet.

Tip ◆ If the closet pole hangers that mount to the closet walls don't line up with any studs, use molly anchors or 'butterfly' nuts and bolts to attach them.

That's all there is to it. You'll find, as I do, that this arrangement is much easier to keep straight. Of course, you'll also find that there are still plenty of excuses for letting your reorganized closet get disorganized again. But even then, you'll have the satisfaction of knowing that even though your closet may be messy, the space this mess occupies is better utilized.

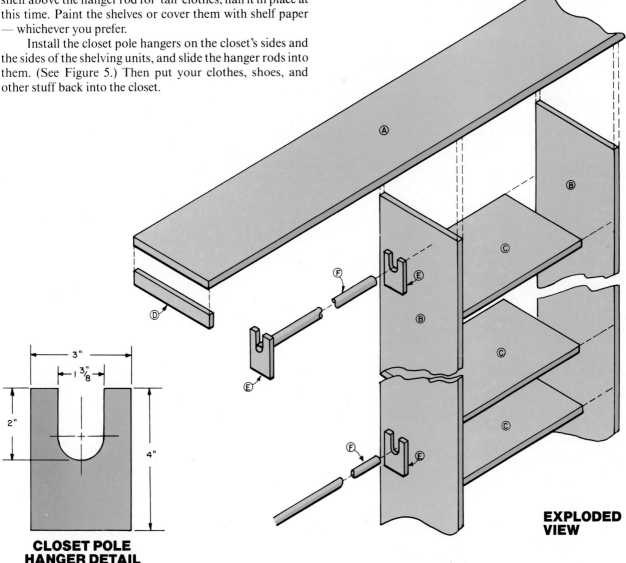

EXPLODED VIEW

CLOSET POLE HANGER DETAIL

BILL OF MATERIALS — Reorganized Closet		
Finished Dimension in Inches		

			Hardware
A.	Upper Shelf	3/4 x 14 x (Variable)	
B.	Shelving Unit Sides (2)	3/4 x 14 x 79-1/4	#8 Finishing Nails (1/4 lb.)
C.	Shelves (6-7)	3/4 x 14 x (Variable)	#10 x 2-1/2 Flathead Wood Screws (6-12)
D.	Shelving Braces (2-4)	3/4 x 1-1/2 x 14	Metal Brackets and Mounting Screws (optional)
E.	Closet Pole Hangers	3/4 x 3 x 4	3/16" Molly Anchors or 1/4" Butterfly Nuts and Bolts (as
F.	Hanger Rods (2-3)	1-3/8" dia. x (Variable)	needed)

Federal Period Sideboard

Delicate inlay work makes this project more than just a piece of furniture; it's a true treasure.

If you could go back in time and attend a harvest banquet in the home of one of the early American colonists, chances are you'd find an extra table beside the regular everyday table. It wouldn't be anything fancy; just a board stretched across two sawbucks to accommodate the abundance of guests and food.

This impromptu table was called a 'sideboard' — an appropriate term. As time went on and the country became more sophisticated, sideboards evolved into more substantial pieces of furniture. By the eighteenth century, they had become low cupboards from which the lady of the house — or her servants — served those seated around the dining table.

The sideboard pictured here, built in Baltimore, Maryland around 1800, bears little resemblance to its early namesake. It's wonderfully crafted, and covered with rich veneers. Sideboards such as this, from the height of the Federal Period, are considered by many scholars to represent the pinnacle of American cabinetry and craftsmanship. If you'd like to stretch your own talents and reach for that pinnacle, here's how our forefathers built it.

A Short Explanation

Let me qualify that last statement. This isn't *exactly* how a Federal Period cabinetmaker would have made a sideboard. Craftsmen from that period had no power tools; they had to saw their own veneer; and they didn't send off to a mail-order house for the hardware. However, this is how to reproduce a sideboard with the tools commonly found in a well-equipped home workshop. If you're careful and take your time, the result will be indistinguishable from the real McCoy.

Also, let me explain that while projects such as these are a true test of a craftsman, it is not beyond the talents of a moderately skilled woodworker. Fine furniture — or any furniture, for that matter — is built joint by joint. And there is no joint in this piece that you can't accomplish with a little care and patience. Select your woods carefully, take time to set up your tools properly, and cut each joint as accurately as you can. The end result will be something you (and your heirs) will treasure.

> **Tip ◆** Before you begin this project, take the time to adjust and align all your tools. Make sure that everything that should be square *is* square. Also, sharpen all the blades and knives you'll be using.

Selecting the Wood

When choosing the wood for this project, keep in mind that the solid stock should be absolutely clear with no knots or defects. This is particularly important as you gather lumber for the legs. These pieces are fairly delicate considering the weight they have to support, and they could easily snap if the

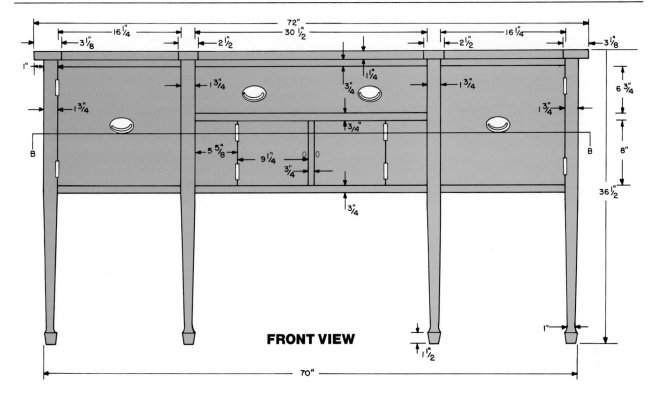

FRONT VIEW

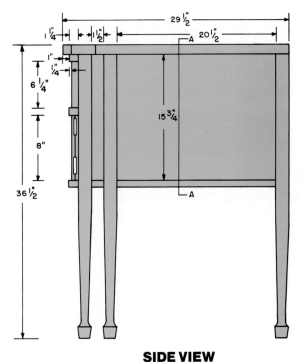

SIDE VIEW

grain isn't straight and clear.

Also make sure that the lumber is properly dried. If the wood is too green, it may change shape after you cut and join it. This will make the pieces hard to fit together, and the case will not be square. If the wood is too dry, it will be brittle and weak. Clear wood with 7%-8% moisture content rarely changes shape after you cut it, and it retains the best part of its inherent strength.

For the wide panels and other boards in this project, use cabinet-grade plywood. This may go against your grain (no pun intended), since you probably share the prejudice that all fine craftsmen work with solid wood. Well, that's not quite true, particularly when a craftsman has to cover a project with fine veneers. Solid wood makes a very unstable base for veneer — a wide board will expand and contract as much as 1/4″ for every 12″ of width with even modest fluctuations in temperature and humidity. Veneer glued to solid wood will soon crack and delaminate. Plywood solves this problem nicely.

Plywood also simplifies the project somewhat. Instead of building up elaborate web frames for the horizontal cupboard parts, you can simply cut them from a sheet of plywood. Just cut these parts so that you can easily add strips of solid wood where needed to the front edges to hide the plies.

By the way, the most popular wood that craftsmen of the period would have used to build this project was mahogany. Some pretty fancy sideboards have been built out of walnut and cherry, but these are the exception, not the rule.

Making the Legs

Begin this project by making the legs. Cut the joinery *before* you cut the tapers. This will make it easier to be accurate. Lay out the six legs in the positions that you will use them and mark which is which — back right, front middle, and so

on. Also mark the sides — back, front, right, left. You'll need to refer to these marks often as you cut the joints, to make sure that each leg gets the proper joinery in the proper side.

The top rails are dovetailed into the tops of the legs. To cut the slots for these dovetails, first drill a stopped hole in the end of the leg that opens to the side. (See Figure 1.) To keep the drill from wandering as you make the hole, you'll have to clamp a scrap piece to the leg stock. Then widen this hole to make a dovetail slot with a hand chisel. (See Figure 2.)

Figure 1. To make the dovetail slots in the tops of the legs, first drill a stopped hole. Clamp a scrap block to the side of the leg to keep the drill bit from wandering.

Figure 2. Widen the stopped hole with a hand chisel to make the dovetail shape.

Figure 3. Cut the slots in the legs with a hand-held router. A simple jig stops the router from cutting too far in either direction, so the slots are exactly the same length.

Figure 4. Cut the tenons in the panels with a dado blade on your table saw.

Cut long slots for the tenons of the panels with a router. To get all these slots exactly the same length, you may find it useful to build a jig that automatically stops the router at both ends. (See Figure 3.) Square off the ends of the slots with a chisel.

Lastly, cut dadoes in the backs of the front middle legs for the cupboard bottom. Then cut the tapers. The safest (and perhaps the easiest) way to do this is to make a compound cut on your bandsaw. Trace the pattern on the front of the legs, make the cuts, then tape the waste stock back to the legs. Turn the stock 90°, trace the pattern again, and make a second set of cuts. When you remove the tape and the waste stock, the legs will be tapered and the feet shaped.

Some Notes on Inlay

While the large, flat areas of this project are veneered, the legs are inlaid. You'll find it much easier to do this inlay after you've cut and shaped the legs, but *before* you assemble them to the case.

Inlay is a complex subject, and there isn't room to completely explain it; it needs a chapter all by itself. So we've included just such a chapter in the **Techniques** section of this book. Refer to it for the information you need to inlay the legs. And before you start your inlay work, consider these brief notes:

◆ The wood you use to inlay the legs should contrast with the wood the legs are made from. As we mentioned earlier, the traditional hardwood for this project is mahogany. The traditional inlay wood is satinwood.

◆ If possible, buy the inlay wood in 1/16″-1/8″ thicknesses. Veneers are used just 1/28″ thick, and this barely leaves you enough room to sand off the face of the inlay after you've glued it in place.

◆ If you can't get anything but veneers, *don't* glue them together to make thicker stock. The glue will saturate the thin laminations, and the inlays won't accept a finish properly. Just work very carefully with the thin stock.

Making the Case

Cut all the panels to size, then make the tenons on the ends. Use a dado cutter to cut the sides of the tenons, then notch the top and the bottom on a bandsaw. (See Figure 4.)

> **Tip** ◆ Make the side and back panels from plywood that's already been covered with a hardwood veneer that matches the wood you've chosen for this project. That will save you some time.

Add a solid strip of wood to the front edges of the cupboard bottom and dividers. Cut the front edges of the cupboard bottom and horizontal divider to the serpent shape shown in the working drawings. You can do this on a bandsaw, but you might find it easier to use a sabre saw when cutting the cupboard bottom, as it's such a large piece. Remember to cut the notches in the cupboard bottom where it fits around the front middle legs.

Make the dadoes and rabbets in the panels where other panels join them. You can use a dado blade mounted on your table saw to cut the smaller panels, but you'll find it easier to be accurate if you use a hand-held router to cut the joinery in the large parts. (See Figure 5.) Just clamp a *straight* scrap of hardwood to the pieces to use this as a guide fence.

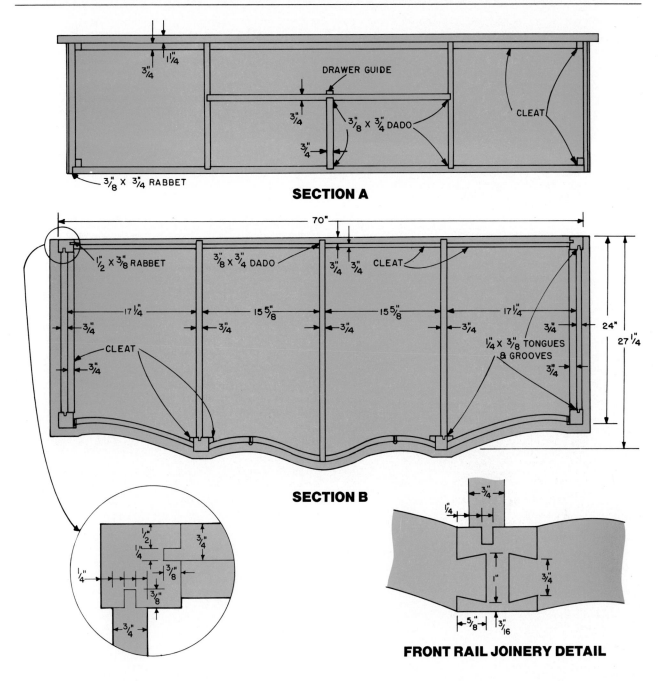

SECTION A

SECTION B

FRONT RAIL JOINERY DETAIL

Cut the shapes and the dovetail in the front rails on a bandsaw. Saw the dovetails just a little wider than the dovetail slots, then carefully custom fit them to each slot by rasping off the excess stock, bit by bit.

Assemble the case parts *temporarily* to check the fit. Hold the case together with web clamps while you're fiddling. When you're satisfied, disassemble the case, then reassemble it with wood screws and glue. (Note that the working drawings show several joints should be reinforced with cleats. This is done so that you won't have to use screws anywhere on the *outside* of the project.) Before the glue sets up, check all joints for squareness and adjust the clamps if necessary. It is extremely important that the completed case be as square as possible.

While the glue on the case dries, make the top. The top is 1-1/4″ thick, and can be built up from two sheets of

plywood — 1/2″ and 3/4″ thick. Like the side and back panels, use a sheet that's already been covered with hardwood veneer for the top sheet. Laminate the two sheets together with glue, then lay it in place and carefully mark the

Figure 5. You can cut the dadoes in the smaller parts with a dado blade, but you'll find it easier to dado the larger parts with a router. A long, straight board serves as a guide.

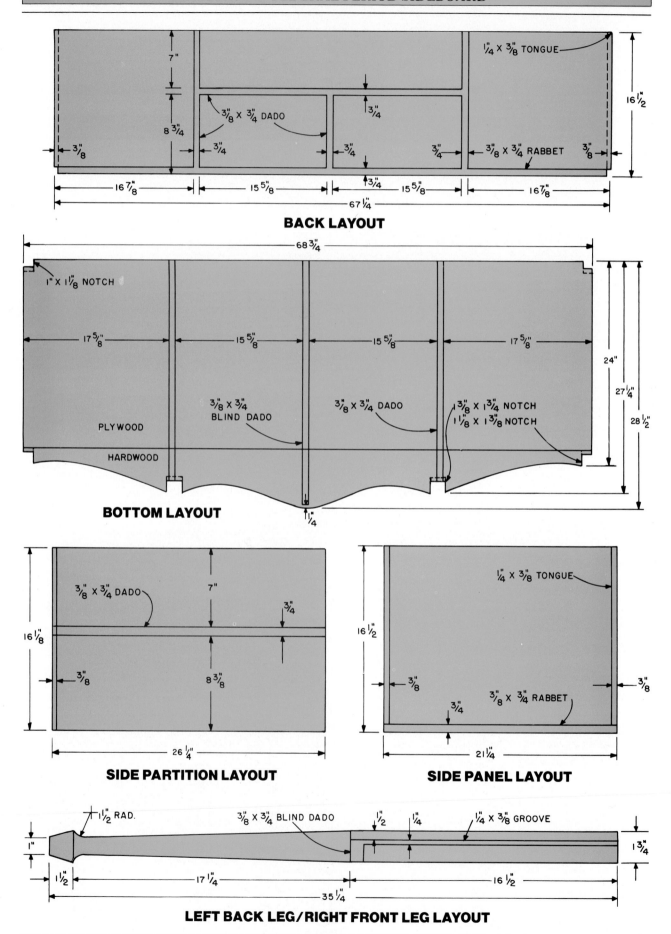

BACK LAYOUT

BOTTOM LAYOUT

SIDE PARTITION LAYOUT

SIDE PANEL LAYOUT

LEFT BACK LEG/RIGHT FRONT LEG LAYOUT

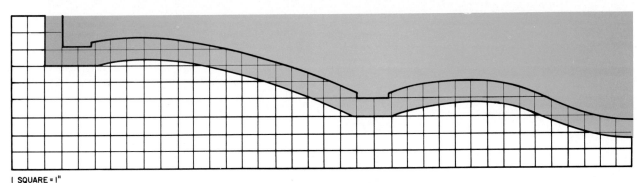

I SQUARE = 1"

SERPENT PATTERN

contours of the front, allowing for the overhang. Cut the contour with a sabre saw, then attach the top to the case with wood screws. Pass these screws up through the top cleats and front rail into the *underside* of the top. Once again, no screws should show on the outside.

Making and Fitting the Doors and Drawer

Most Federal period craftsmen would have made the curved doors by gluing strips of solid wood together edge to edge at different angles, then scraping down the joints to make a smooth contour. However, as we mentioned before, solid wood is not a good foundation for veneer. For this reason, the veneer on the doors of many beautiful old serpentine-front sideboards is cracked. There is an easy way to make a more stable door — bending by lamination.

Make two plywood forms, as shown in the working drawings. The contour of one form should match the contour of the large doors on either side of the cupboard, while the other form should echo the contour of the small middle doors *and* front panels.

Plane down an adequate amount of 1/8" thick stock from utility wood. Pine is a good choice because of its flexibility. Glue this stock edge to edge to make the necessary widths. You'll need twelve sheets as wide as the large doors, and twelve more as wide as the small doors and panels. The grain of half of these sheets should run vertically, while the other half should run horizontally.

> **Tip** ◆ The edge-to-edge bonds in these 1/8" thick sheets do not have to be particularly strong. Simply rub the stock together with a light pressure, then set the sheets on a flat surface to dry.

Remove any glue beads with a chisel, then stack six sheets together, alternating the grain direction, to make a single board 3/4" thick. Spread glue *evenly* between each sheet, and clamp them in the proper form. (See Figure 6.) After the glue dries, trim each of the parts to the proper size and fit them carefully in the cupboard. Cut the small doors from their panels on a bandsaw or radial arm saw.

> **Tip** ◆ Make the sheets an inch or so bigger than necessary, both horizontally and vertically, so that you have plenty of room to trim. This will also make alignment less critical when you clamp the sheets in the forms.

Install the small front panels in the cupboard *temporarily* with screws only. The stiffener behind these panels attaches to the cupboard bottom and horizontal divider. Mortise the doors and their adjoining parts for hinges and install the doors temporarily.

The drawer construction is standard. The front joins the sides with dovetails, and the back joins the side with dadoes. The drawer bottom rests in a groove in the front, back, and sides. A drawer guide, glued to the horizontal divider, keeps the drawer properly aligned as you pull it in and out. Only the thickness and the shape of the drawer front are non-standard — this part is made from 1-1/2" thick stock, and the serpent shape is cut with a bandsaw. (See Figure 7.)

> **Tip** ◆ Like the other veneered surfaces in this project, the drawer front should be made from plywood. Glue four 3/4" pieces together to make the required thickness.

Figure 6. To make the bent doors and panels for the serpentine front, first make two plywood bending forms. Glue up thin sheets of wood and clamp them in these forms while the glue dries.

Figure 7. Cut the serpent shape in the drawer front on a bandsaw.

Cut out and assemble the drawer parts temporarily, fitting them to the cupboard. However, don't glue them together just yet.

Some Notes on Veneering

As with inlay, veneering is a complex subject. So we've included a chapter on "Veneering" in the **Techniques** section of this book. This chapter will get you started, and many of you will find that it has all the information you need to complete this project. However, others of you will want more information. For this, we suggest your local library.

Before you start with the veneering, there are a few things you should consider:

◆ Unhinge the doors from the cupboard and disassemble the front panels and drawer front. You'll find it much easier to apply veneer to these pieces when they are removed from the case.

◆ Leave the top attached to the case when veneering the edges. Note that the grain of the edge veneer runs up and down.

◆ Federal Period craftsmen would traditionally choose a *figured* board of the major project wood, and slice veneers from it to cover these front pieces. If they were working in mahogany, they would probably search for a piece of mahogany crotch. Crotch veneer is available today from many suppliers.

◆ Make the banding from a contrasting veneer that matches the inlay. If you're working in mahogany, the traditional choice is satinwood.

◆ The decorative oval pieces of veneer marquetry and parquetry can also be purchased from veneer suppliers.

There are many, many sources for veneers in this country, but here are two mail order houses that carry all the types of wood and supplies mentioned here:

The Woodworker's Store
21801 Industrial Blvd.
Rogers, MN 55374

Constantine
2044 Eastchester Road
Bronx, NY 10461

Finishing Touches

The working drawings show that one large cupboard space is fitted with a sliding shelf, while the other is fitted with a tray for liquor bottles. This is how the original sideboard was outfitted, but it doesn't mean you have to do the same thing. What gets stored in the sideboard — and how it gets stored — is up to you.

When choosing hardware for this project, make sure you stick to the proper period. Ornate Chippendale 'cloud forms' will look out of place on the doors and drawer. The traditional pull has an oval escutcheon, with a half-oval bail. These are available from:

The Wise Company
6503 St.Claude Avenue
Arabi, LA 70032

You can also purchase door locks, drawer locks, and keyhole escutcheons from the same source.

When finish sanding the project, be careful not to remove too much stock. You don't want to dig through the veneers. Start with 120#, and work your way up to 220#. Fill the grain of the wood with a *dark* wood filler, put a sanding sealer over this, then apply a good building finish.

SIDEBOARD

Routing Jig for Long Stock

When routing long, slender stock (such as the legs in the Federal Period Sideboard), you may find it difficult to balance the router on the wood and make an accurate cut. The face of the stock is wide enough to make a stable base for the router. In this case, you may want to make a simple routing jig to give your router the proper support.

◆ Make two simple 'tables' of scrap stock, as shown in Figure A. Each table should be approximately 4" wide, and slightly longer and taller than the stock you want to rout. Clamp the stock between the tables so that the face to be routed is flush with table surfaces. Make sure the clamps don't interfere with the movement of the router!

◆ You can also nail or clamp router guides and stops to the tables. If you need to rout duplicate pieces, mark

the position of the first piece when you clamp it in place. Line up the rest of the pieces with the marks, and you won't have to readjust the guides and stops for each piece.

Figure A. To rout long, slender stock accurately and safely, clamp it between two small routing tables.

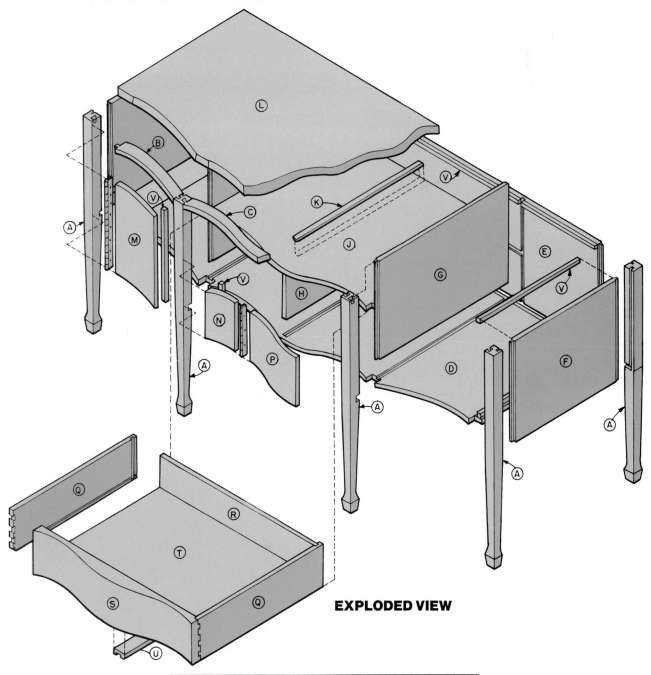

EXPLODED VIEW

BILL OF MATERIALS—Federal Period Sideboard

Finished Dimensions in Inches

A.	Legs (6)	1-3/4 x 1-3/4 x 35-1/4
B.	Front Side Rails (2)	3/4 x 1-3/4 x 17-1/2
C.	Front Middle Rail	3/4 x 1-3/4 x 31-3/4
D.	Bottom	3/4 x 28-1/2 x 68-3/4
E.	Back	3/4 x 16-1/2 x 67-1/4
F.	Side Panels (2)	3/4 x 16-1/2 x 21-1/4
G.	Side Partitions (2)	3/4 x 16-1/8 x 26-1/4
H.	Middle Partition	3/4 x 8-3/4 x 28
J.	Drawer Support	3/4 x 28-5/8 x 32-3/4
K.	Drawer Guide	1/2 x 1 x 24-3/4
L.	Top	1-1/4 x 29-1/2 x 72
M.	Side Doors (2)	3/4 x 15-5/8 x 16-1/8
N.	Middle Panels (2)	3/4 x 5-5/8 x 8

P.	Middle Doors (2)	3/4 x 7-7/8 x 9-1/8
Q.	Drawer Sides (2)	3/4 x 6-1/8 x 24-3/8
R.	Drawer Back	3/4 x 6-1/8 x 29-5/8
S.	Drawer Front	2-3/4 x 6-1/8 x 30-3/8
T.	Drawer Bottom	1/4 x 23-1/2 x 29-5/8
U.	Drawer Glide	1/2 x 2 x 22-3/4
V.	Cleats (total)	3/4 x 3/4 x 256

Hardware

#8 x 1-1/4" Flathead Wood Screws (4-5 dozen)
1-1/2" x 2" Hinges and Mounting Screws (4 pair)
Cam Locks (4)
Door/Drawer Pulls (4)

TECHNIQUES

Fundamentals of Veneering

Veneering isn't a simple art, but with a little patience and practice, even a beginner can achieve striking results.

In the late 1700's, craftsmen in Europe and America developed the first 'veneer' saws — the word comes from the French "fournir", meaning "to furnish". These ingenious tools were more accurate than previous furniture saws. They allowed the cabinetmaker to slice extremely thin boards — called 'veneers' — just 1/16"-1/8" thick.

Veneering was a boon to woodworkers of the time. This was one of the golden eras in furniture design — the end of the Chippendale Period, and the beginning of the Federal Period. Some of the most famous American cabinetmakers, such as Hepplewhite, Sheraton, and Phyfe, were just hanging out their shingles. The Industrial Revolution was making fine furniture affordable to more and more Americans, and there was an explosion in the furniture trade — particularly in the large eastern cities of Philadelphia, New York, and Newport.

The preferred furniture wood of the day was mahogany. But there were no native American sources for mahogany; it had to be imported. And because of the sudden demand, it was in extremely short supply. Veneering offered a way to stretch this material. A single 1" board of mahogany could be sliced into veneers and used to cover ten or more boards of relatively cheap native oak or pine. American cabinetmakers began to turn out 'veneered' furniture.

A few of the more imaginative craftsmen of the era recognized that veneering offered other possibilities beyond conserving valuable woods. With a little patience, a veneering artist could cut and join sheets of veneer to create patterns that were almost impossible to make with thick stock. The arts of marquetry and parquetry were born. (See Figures 1 and 2.)

As time passed, tools and materials improved. Today's veneer saws can slice sheets as thin as 1/128". Contact cement has eliminated the need for huge veneer presses to hold the veneer to the wood while the glue cures. Veneering still requires patience and careful work — moreso than many other woodworking techniques — but you can easily achieve exquisite results with only modest tools in your own homeshop.

Veneering Materials and Tools

Veneers — Veneers are now available in two forms — 'solid' and 'flexible'. Solid veneer is a thin sheet of wood, usually 1/28" to 1/36" thick. Flexible veneer is an *extremely* thin sheet of wood, sometimes just 1/128" thick, laminated to a paper backing. (See Figure 3.)

Solid veneer is usually less expensive than flexible veneer, but it can try your patience. When you first buy them, some solid veneers may be too wrinkled or buckled to work with. To fix this, sprinkle the sheets with water and clamp them between two scraps of plywood for a week or two. Use them shortly thereafter. If you let them sit too long, they'll buckle again.

Flexible veneer lays flat and rarely buckles. It also has several other advantages: It can be applied to surfaces other than wood; it can be applied to tightly curved surfaces; and it's easier to cut and join. But there are also some disadvantages. Because it's extremely thin, it's more susceptible to damage. If you ever need to sand or refinish a portion of the project, you can scrape right through the wood to the paper in short order.

Glues — Contact cement is the universal adhesive for both types of veneer. This cement is a pressure-sensitive adhesive; just position the veneer where you want it and press down on the surface. However, this is easier said than done. It takes some practice to get the veneer *exactly* where you want it. And once the veneer is pressed in place, it's down for good.

Recently, glue companies have developed a 'hot melt adhesive' for veneers. This glue comes in thin sheets. To use it, you stick it between the veneer and the surface to be veneered, then iron the veneer down with an ordinary household iron. (See Figure 4.) The drawback to this method is mostly the expense; hot melt adhesive comes in 24" wide rolls and sells for $.10 to $.15 an *inch*. It can cost as much as $18 for enough glue to veneer a standard tabletop.

Tools — The tools needed for veneering are minimal. The only special tools that are necessary are a veneer saw and a veneer roller. (See Figure 5.) In a pinch, you can use a sharp utility knife instead of a veneer saw and a rolling pin instead of a veneer roller.

Figure 1. There are several elegant ways to use veneers decoratively. By assembling small pieces of contrasting veneers, you can create a mosaic picture. This is called marquetry.

Figure 2. You can also assemble contrasting veneers to create a geometric pattern. This is parquetry.

Figure 3. 'Flexible' veneer is an extremely thin slice of wood bonded to a special paper backing. Unlike solid veneers, it won't buckle.

Figure 4. 'Hot melt adhesive' comes in thin sheets. Insert the glue sheets between the veneer and the surface to be veneered, then heat the veneer with an iron.

Figure 5. You don't need many special tools for veneering. However, here are two that you'll find particularly useful — a veneer saw and a veneer roller.

Figure 8. To true the edges, clamp the veneer between two scrap boards and run the board over a jointer.

Figure 9. Assemble the sheets on the surface to be veneered, keeping each sheet flat with push pins. Tape the seams to hold the sheets together.

Figure 6. Shown here are four common ways to match sheets of veneer to create a decorative pattern: (Clockwise, from top left) A book match, diamond match, herringbone match, and a banding.

Figure 7. To match and join veneers, first cut the sheets to size with a veneer saw. Use a straight-edge to guide the saw.

You'll also need some push pins, gummed paper tape or masking tape, a 36″ (or longer) metal straightedge, and an old brush to apply the cement or an old iron to heat it. You'll see how to use all of these tools and materials as we go along.

Matching and Joining Veneer

Unless you are covering very small areas, you'll rarely find a single sheet of veneer that will completely cover your project. Solid veneers are rarely more than 12″ wide, and while a few companies make flexible veneers in 36″ widths, most are 24″ wide. Consequently, you'll probably have to match and join two or more sheets.

This joining presents an interesting opportunity. Since the veneers don't contribute any structural strength to the project, you don't have to join them long grain to long grain. You can cut the sheets end-to-end, side-to-side, or diagonally for a variety of effects. By paying careful attention to the wood grain and carefully planning how you'll match this grain, you can create a book match, diamond, or herringbone pattern. You might even choose to run a different grain

pattern — or an entire different wood, around the edge of a sheet as a border or 'banding'. (See Figure 6.)

To match and join veneers, first cut them to size. Lay a straightedge along the cutline and saw it with a veneer saw or utility knife. (See Figure 7.) Don't press too hard; use very light strokes. Otherwise, the saw will have a tendency to follow the wood grain instead of the straightedge.

Clamp the veneers between two scrap boards so that the edges to be joined are flush with the boards. Carefully run a hand plane along the edges of the boards, or run the boards across a jointer. (See Figure 8.) This will true the edge of the veneers.

Position the veneers on the surface to be veneered and tack them in place with push pins. Make sure that all edges match, and all veneers are right side up. Then tape the seams with gummed paper tape — you could use masking tape to hold the seams together, but this tends to stretch slightly. (See Figure 9.) When you remove the push pins, you'll have one single sheet, assembled from handsomely matched veneers.

Figure 10. You may wish to reinforce each seam with glue. Remember to wipe off the excess and tape the underside of the seams while the glue dries.

Figure 11. If you wish to apply veneer to solid wood, you may want to 'crossband' the wood with inexpensive veneers first. This keeps the wood from distorting and ruining the expensive veneer.

Figure 12. Don't continue to brush the contact cement out after it becomes tacky. It just balls up in lumps.

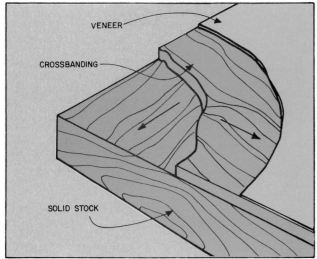

Tip ◆ Some craftsmen prefer to reinforce these seams with glue. Turn the sheet over so the tape is down, bend the edges back, and apply a thin line of glue. (See Figure 10.) Flatten the seam again, wipe away any excess glue, and put some *masking* tape on the other side of the seam while the glue dries.

Preparing the Surface

It stands to reason that you should sand and clean the surface to be veneered. But, depending on the material, there may be some other things you must do to prepare the surface.

If you're about to apply veneer to plywood, you must fill any voids or gaps with wood putty. These voids create weak spots under the veneer. If the veneer is hit or poked on a weak spot, it may split or break. This same precaution applies to deep dents, checks in the wood, or gaps in the wood joints. Make sure the surface is perfectly smooth before applying the veneer.

If you're applying veneer over solid wood, you may want to put down a layer of 'crossbanding' on both the top *and* the bottom of the lumber. This crossbanding is a cheap grade of veneer that's applied so the grain of the crossbanding runs at right angles to the grain of the wood. (See Figure 11.) This adds stability to the lumber so that it doesn't expand or contract too much with changes in the weather. This, in turn, keeps the veneer from splitting or coming loose.

Tip ◆ As you can see, crossbanding effectively turns solid lumber into plywood. It may save you some time to build your project out of plywood in the first place.

When you've properly prepared the surface, wipe it with a tack cloth, then wash it down with alcohol. This will remove any sawdust, dirt, or grease and help insure a good glue bond between the surface and the veneer.

Applying the Veneer

Before applying the veneer, first remove any tape from the *underside* of the matched sheets. Don't remove the tape from the top; you'll need it to hold the sheets together while you apply the veneer.

With an old brush, spread contact cement on the underside of the veneer and the surface to be veneered. *Both* surfaces must be evenly coated with cement in order to get a good glue bond. If the wood is porous, you may have to apply two coats. Some craftsmen like to apply three coats to the edges.

Tip ◆ Brush the cement on quickly and move on. *Don't* try to keep brushing it out once it becomes tacky. The cement will just ball up. (See Figure 12.) This creates lumps under the veneer when you try to apply it.

Let the glue dry for at least an hour, or until it's lost all its tack. If the glue has not dried properly before you apply the veneer, the bond will be weak. How do you know when it's dry enough? Look at it — properly dried cement will appear dull and clear. Then touch it in several spots with a piece of paper. If the paper sticks at any spot, it's not dry enough.

When you're satisfied that the contact cement is dry, cover the surface to be veneered with wax paper. Position

Figure 13. To help get the veneer where you want it, lay dowels over the surface to be veneered, then position the veneer on top of the dowels. When you've got the veneer properly positioned, remove the dowels one at a time.

Figure 14. To properly bond the veneer to the surface, apply hard pressure all over the sheet with a roller. Start in the middle and work out toward the edges.

Figure 15. Trim off any excess veneer with a veneer saw or utility knife, then sand the edges flush.

Figure 16. To remove the paper tape, wet it slightly with a sponge and scrape it off. Take care not to damage the veneer.

the veneer however you want it, and remove the wax paper one strip at a time. Stick the veneer down as you go, pressing lightly on the surface. Take care that you leave no air bubbles.

As an alternative method, you can lay 1/4″ dowels on the surface to be veneered, every 6″. Then lay the veneer on top of the dowels and position it where you want it. Remove the dowels one at a time, sticking the veneer down as you go. (See Figure 13.) Whether you use the wax paper or the dowels, it's wise to start sticking the veneer down in the middle and work toward the edges.

> **Tip ◆** If you develop an air bubble in one area of the veneer, stick the bubble with a push pin and press down to 'deflate' the hump.

Once you have the veneer stuck down where you want it, go over the entire surface with a roller. (See Figure 14.) Start at the middle and work out toward the edges. Press *hard*. Remember, contact cement is pressure sensitive. The more pressure you apply, the better the veneer will bond to the surface.

> **Tip ◆** If you have a stubborn area that won't bond, try ironing it with a hot household iron. Put a cloth over the area to keep the veneer from being scorched.

After the sheet of veneer is properly bonded, trim the edges with a veneer saw or utility knife. Then 'clean up' the edges so they're perfectly flush with a wood block and a sheet of 100# sandpaper. (See Figure 15.) The sandpaper will trim off any tiny overhangs neater and with less trouble than any wood plane.

Finally, remove the seam tape. Wet it slightly with a damp sponge, then scrape it off with a paint scraper or wide chisel. (See Figure 16.) Use as little water as possible to avoid damaging the veneer.

Is That All?

That's not all there is to veneering, of course. There are dozens of other decorative techniques that you may want to try, depending on your project. But these are the fundamentals. No matter how far you delve into the art, you'll find yourself coming back to these basic methods again and again.

Wood Inlay

Modern tools make this ancient technique simpler than it looks!

We've all admired the technique before and wondered how it was done — delicate shapes of contrasting wood inlaid in a larger board, looking as if the woods had grown together and the woodworker had simply sliced the tree open to reveal the design. Those designs, however, were the results of painstaking work. The old masters who perfected the technique of wood inlay worked for hours with special chisels to mate the inlays to the 'beds'.

Today, the technique has been greatly simplified by the invention of the router. Inlay still requires some skill and some patience, of course. What woodworking technique doesn't? But, with a little practice, even a modestly experienced woodworker can achieve good results.

Cutting the Shapes

The first step is to cut the shapes you want to inlay. Usually, an inlaid design consists of several smaller parts that work together to form a geometric pattern, an animal or plant, or on rare occasions, a scene.

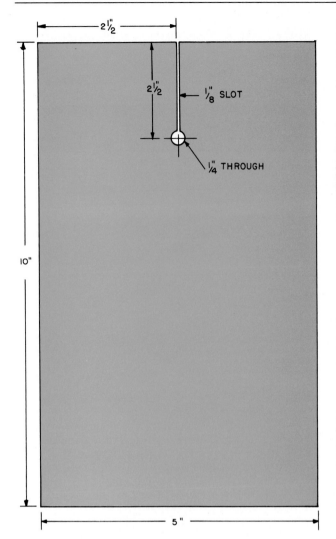

2½"

2½"

⅛" SLOT

¼" THROUGH

10"

5"

WORKTABLE FOR CUTTING INLAY

Figure 1. Saw the design with a coping saw, using a special table. If the design is tiny, use a jeweler's saw. If it's large, use a jigsaw.

Figure 2. Temporarily glue the inlay shapes to the bed where you want to inlay them, and trace their outlines with a sharp pencil.

Figure 3. Rout out the shape with a router and a small straight router bit. Cut up to, but don't remove, the pencil lines.

These individual inlays are cut from a wood — or several types of wood — that contrast with the major project wood, or the 'bed'. For instance, if the project is made from mahogany, then you'd want to cut your inlays from maple, satinwood, ebony, or rosewood, to name just a few possibilities. Maple and satinwood are lighter than mahogany, while ebony and rosewood are darker.

Plane and/or sand your inlay wood down to a thickness of 1/16″-1/8″. If the wood is too thick, you'll have to do a lot of unnecessary work to set it in the bed. If it's too thin, it may break, or you could easily sand away part of the design during the last steps in this technique.

When you've chosen the woods and reduced them to the proper thickness, cut the inlay shapes with a coping saw on a special table that looks like a miniature bandsaw table. Follow the working drawing to fashion this small worktable from 1/4″ hardwood stock. Clamp this to your workbench so that the cut-out in the table overhangs the bench top by a good 5″-6″. If it's too close, you'll bang your knuckles. Arrange a good light to shine on the worktable, and pull up a chair. Inlay is a painstaking process. You'll want to save your eyes and your back as much as possible.

Draw the design on the material with a very sharp pencil. Place the material on the worktable. Begin moving the saw up and down like an old beam saw, moving the material to cut the design. (See Figure 1.) There is some argument about whether you should cut on the downstroke or the upstroke. Tradition tells us to cut on the downstroke — this helps hold the material to the table. But I find I have better control on the upstroke. The saw stroke is so light, that it doesn't take much muscle to hold the stock down while I cut.

Tip ◆ If the design is very small, use a jeweler's saw instead of a coping saw. If the design is large, you can use a jigsaw.

Inlaying the Shapes

Once you have the shapes, *temporarily* glue them down on the wood where you want to inlay them. Use a dab of *rubber cement* on the back of each piece and let it dry for a few minutes. Then, trace around each piece several times with a very sharp pencil. (See Figure 2.)

Figure 4. Clean up the edges and the sharp corners of the routed hole with a small carving chisel.

Figure 5. The shapes should fit snugly in their holes, but you shouldn't have to use a lot of pressure to seat them.

Figure 6. Fill the holes with epoxy glue, then press the inlay shapes in place. Leave some of the excess glue around the edges of the inlays to fill in small imperfections.

Figure 7. Sand the inlays to remove the extra glue and make the surface of the inlays perfectly flush with the bed.

Figure 8. To inlay long strips of wood, make a guide for your router. If the strips are very narrow, you may have to use a Moto-Tool® to rout the groove.

Tip ◆ On dark woods, such as rosewood or ebony, use a white pencil to trace the shapes.

When you are satisfied that you have traced a sharp, visible image of the shape on the wood, remove the shapes by simply peeling them up. Clean the rubber cement residue off the shapes with acetone.

Using a hand-held router with a 1/8″ straight bit, rout out the wood to receive the shape. (See Figure 3.) Set the depth of cut so that the router makes a groove *slightly* shallower than the thickness of the inlay wood. Rout up to the pencil lines, but *do not* remove the lines.

This routing set-up won't reach everywhere. You have to remove the stock from some of the tighter corners with a carving chisel, after you've routed out as much stock as possible. (See Figure 4.) After you've cleaned up the corners, check to see if the shape will fit. If it doesn't, use the carving chisel to shave down the sides of the hole bit by bit until the shape can be pressed in. (See Figure 5.) Don't worry if there are a few little gaps here and there; these will get filled in by what you're about to do next.

Mix up a small amount of clear epoxy glue and fill each hole with it. Then, press the inlay shapes into their respective holes, squeezing out the glue. Wipe away *some* of the excess glue, but not all of it. You want to leave little pools of glue around the edges of the shapes to fill in any gaps. (See Figure 6.) Let this glue set up *at least* 24 hours.

After the epoxy has cured, sand off the excess glue. Then, sand the surface of the wood and the inlay shapes flush. (See Figure 7.) Work slowly, and don't remove any more wood than you have to.

Inlaying Strips

Sometimes, an inlay design calls for very thin strips of wood, just 1/16″-1/8″ wide. The technique for inlaying these strips in a bed is similar to the technique outlined previously, but not quite the same.

Choose a straight router bit whose diameter matches the inlay strip and mount it in the router. If the strip is very fine, you may want to use a Moto-Tool® in a router base to cut the groove. This tool uses very small bits, 1/16″ wide and less.

If the strips are to be laid out in straight lines, or large arcs, take the extra time to build a guide for the router. A guide can be as simple as a board clamped to the bed. (See Figure 8.) If you're cutting arcs, saw the shape in a piece of scrap plywood and clamp that to the bed. Don't forget to allow for the radius of the router; the arc of the guide must be smaller than the arc you want to cut.

Once you've cut the groove, fill it with glue and press the strips in place. There's no need to pre-bend the inlay strip or cut it to the proper arc. Narrow strips can bend around some very tight corners.

Designed by Rude Osolnik

Turning Green

A veteran craftsman on the lathe shares some professional secrets.

Rude Olsolnik's wood storage bin looks like an ordinary pile of firewood — if that good. There are some logs here that I wouldn't even bother to burn: wood shot through with worms and dryrot and fungus, burled and knotted wood impossible to split or saw.

But on the other end of his shop are stacks of beautiful bowls and weedpots; delicate lathe turnings that take your breath away. It's hard to conceive that these creations were once part of that homely wood pile. But the imperfect wood is perfect for Rude's purposes. Like a master diamond cutter, he scrapes away at the most ordinary of materials until there's nothing left but the extraordinary. Rude sells his turnings in galleries throughout America for hundreds, even thousands of dollars.

Rude (pronounced Roo-dee) Osolnik is one of the world's most skilled, most prolific turners. For years, he taught wood arts at Kentucky's Berea College. Today, he's 'retired', living on a mountain top not far from the college, still teaching seminars for woodworkers, still turning most every day.

Rude is a virtuoso on the lathe, a master of all lathe techniques, but he is particularly fond of green turnings. 'Found' wood, straight off the forest floor, holds a special excitement for him. "You never know what you're going to find until you wade in with a chisel," he says. "Each turning is an adventure."

PEG or No PEG?

Since Rude likes to turn lots of green wood, I right away presumed that somewhere he'd have a big vat of PEG —polyethylene glycol. But not so. "PEG is good for some applications," explains Rude. "But it has its drawbacks. If you plan carefully, you can turn green wood without it."

The 'textbook' procedure is to soak green wood in PEG prior to turning — and sometimes during the turning process — for a specified amount of time, depending on the type and thickness of the wood. The PEG slowly displaces the water in the wood fibers, chemically 'drying' the wood. Unlike water, PEG won't evaporate. Consequently, the PEG-soaked wood won't shrink, distort, check, or split.

But PEG has some limitations. First of all, it's not cheap. For someone like Rude who does a lot of green turning, the expense could be prohibitive. Then you need a place to store it and a tank big enough to soak the wood. For most woodworkers with only limited shop space, this is impractical. Finally, you have to use finishes that are compatible with polyethylene glycol, since the oily PEG never dries. Your choices of finishes are limited — and somewhat expensive.

Rude employs an inexpensive, versatile alternative to PEG: plastic bags and sandpaper. Once he fishes a chunk out of storage and begins to turn it, he keeps the stock in a plastic trash bag when he's not working. (See Figure 2.) "This slows the drying process," says Rude. "Wood checks and splits because it dries *unevenly* — the surface loses water before the interior. The plastic bag keeps the surface moisture from leaving the stock. Sometimes, if I need to let an unfinished turning sit for a long time, I sprinkle a little water in the bag to *replace* some of the surface moisture."

The wood is dried on the lathe during the final sanding. Rude normally turns his pieces until they are quite thin —1/4″ or less. The friction of the sandpaper creates enough heat to evenly dissipate the moisture. A complete bowl only has 10%-15% moisture content. "This is about the same moisture content as air-dried lumber," claims Rude.

However, there are two precautions that you must take if you dry your turning in this fashion. First of all, you must use extremely sharp abrasives. If the sandpaper is dull, the wood will get too hot and the water will evaporate from the surface too quickly. Second, you must finish the turning *immediately*, preferably on the lathe. Rude suggests that home craftsmen use a mixture of tung oil and spar varnish (more oil than varnish), applied with a cloth pad or your bare hands while the turning is revolving at a low speed.

"The finish seals the wood and prevents any residual moisture from evaporating quickly," says Rude. "The finished turning will still distort slightly, but it rarely splits or checks. And the distortions that do occur make the turning much more interesting."

Turning Techniques

When Rude fishes a chunk of wood out of his pile to turn, he begins by determining the turning axis. He pares off unwanted stock on a bandsaw, then locates the centers by experimenting with a compass. (See Figure 3.) He tests several different centers, trying to decide which center will give him the best balance and make the best use of the turning stock on the lathe. "I don't always get a good center on the first try," admits Rude. "The compass helps, but you really have to mount the stock on the lathe and turn it a little before you know for sure. I sometimes have to try two or three different centers."

Rude mounts the block as a spindle turning between the drive center and the tailstock, then turns on the lathe at the *slowest* possible speed. (See Figure 4.) If the vibration isn't excessive, he pares the turning down a little with a chisel, then turns the machine off. "I check to see if I'm

Figure 1. Rude's wood storage looks like a pile of firewood. But some of the ugliest pieces of wood will often yield the most beautiful turnings.

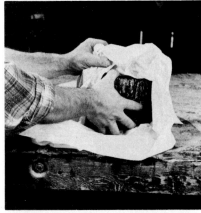

Figure 2. To prevent a chunk of green wood from drying out when you're not turning it, keep it wrapped in a plastic trash bag.

Figure 3. Experiment with a compass until you find the approximate center of a turning block.

Figure 4. Initially mount the turning block on the lathe as a spindle turning. Make sure the lathe is set to turn at its *slowest* speed.

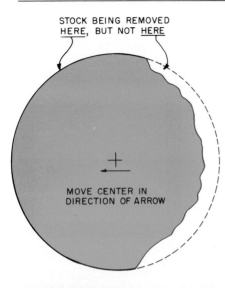

STOCK BEING REMOVED
HERE, BUT NOT HERE

MOVE CENTER IN
DIRECTION OF ARROW

Figure 5. If your center is off, you will remove more stock from one side of a turning block than the other. Relocate the center a short distance *away* from the side that's *not* being shaved by the chisel.

Figure 6. Once you've decided on a turning center, rough out the shape of the outside.

removing more stock from one side of the turning than the other," explains Rude. "If I am, then I haven't found the true center."

He dismounts the turning and moves the center 1/4"- 1/2" *away* from the side that isn't being shaved by the chisel. (See Figure 5.) He turns on the machine and tries again. After trying several different centers, he finally decides on one that suits him. He turns on the lathe (still working at low speed) and roughs out the outside shape of the turning. (See Figure 6.)

> **Tip ◆** Rude suggests that you turn at speeds between 400 and 1300 RPM. The work progresses slower, but it's safer and easier to be accurate. He does most of his work at 800 RPM.

To complete the outside shape and to turn the inside shape, Rude has to remount the workpiece on a faceplate. "When you remount the work on a faceplate," he says, "it's important that you keep the same turning centers you worked so hard to find."

To keep the centers exact, he employs a few tricks. First of all, he uses a faceplate with a mounting hole drilled and threaded clear through. He carefully measures the diameter of this hole with calipers, then turns down the base of the stock so that he has a short, round tenon. (See Figures 7 and 8.) He 'screws' this tenon into the faceplate, using it to properly center the workpiece. (See Figure 9.)

Figure 8. Turn a short, round tenon at the base of the turning. This tenon must be exactly the same diameter as the hole in the faceplate.

Figure 7. To transfer a rough turning to a faceplate, first measure the diameter of the faceplate mounting hole with a pair of calipers.

Figure 9. Mount the turning to the faceplate, inserting the round tenon in the mounting hole. This will help you keep the same turning axis that you were working with when the stock was mounted as a spindle turning.

Rude then mounts the faceplate on the lathe, and advances the tailstock to check that the work is still mounted on the proper centers. "The center might move a hair or two," he says. "Not enough to worry about, but enough that it would affect your turning if you shaped the outside *before* you mounted the stock on a faceplate. Always wait until *after* the stock is mounted on the faceplate to finish the outside." Rude leaves the tailstock in place when he finishes the outside to provide extra support. (See Figure 10.)

Once Rude turns the outside of the stock, he often finds cracks and checks that weren't visible when he began. "If you leave these go," Rude says, "they might eventually ruin your turning. You have to stop them before they get any bigger." Rude uses a substance called cyanoacrylate glue to fill the gaps. (See Figure 11.) This glue comes in two parts —the resin and the activator. Rude applies the resin first, waits a few seconds, then applies the activator. Immediately, the glue swells up and seals the cavity. In a few minutes, Rude can begin turning again.

"I imagine this type of glue is available from several different sources," says Rude. "But I only know of one." The name brand of the glue he uses is "Hot Stuff". It's available from:

Satellite City
P.O. Box 836
Simi, CA 93062

Figure 10. When the stock's mounted on the faceplate, finish shaping the outside. Use the tailstock for extra support.

Figure 11. Fill small cracks or checks with cyanoacrylate glue to keep them from getting any bigger.

Tip ◆ Cyanoacrylate glue is also useful for hardening rotted parts of the wood or adhering the bark to the turning block so that it won't come off. Rude uses this last trick quite often; the bark lining at the top of some of his bowls enhances the design. (See Figure 12.)

After he's finished with the outside of a turning, Rude tackles the inside. "The hardest part of turning the inside of a bowl," says Rude, "is knowing when to stop." It's also difficult to turn the very center of a bowl — the stock wants to catch the chisel and whip it around. To solve both problems at once, Rude mounts a drill chuck on his tailstock and drills a 1″ hole in the stock right down the center. (See Figure 13.) He measures carefully as he drills, stopping when the bit reaches the exact depth of the bottom of the bowl.

He pares away at the inside, using the hole to gauge when to stop. It's interesting to watch Rude turn the inside of a faceplate turning. He uses a roundnose chisel, ground and honed to a fairly long bevel. Most woodworkers are under the impression that a roundnose can only be used for *scraping* on the lathe, but Rude *shears*. (See Figure 14.)

Figure 12. Cyanoacrylate glue can also be used to keep the bark from separating from the heartwood. Rude uses this technique to add a decorative rim to some of his bowl turnings.

Figure 13. To help gauge the depth of a bowl turning, first drill a 1″ hole down the center. Stop drilling when the hole is as deep as you want the bottom of the bowl.

Figure 14. The inside of a bowl is usually turned with a roundnose chisel. The roundnose is a scraping tool, but by regrinding a longer bevel on the tip, you can use it to shear.

"With enough practice, you can shear with anything," reveals Rude. "It's all in how you hold the chisel."

Finally, he sands the turning. To speed this chore up, he uses a power disc sander on the outside of the turning. (See Figure 15.) Rude holds the tool carefully so that the disc rotates in the opposite direction as the turning. "Don't use too much pressure," he warns. "Keep the sander moving and back it off frequently. Remember, you don't want to overheat the turning."

Some Parting Thoughts

As Rude finishes up his first turning for the day and gets ready to mount his second, he offers a few thoughts about shapes: "I usually let the shape of the turning block dictate the shape of the finished turning — within reason."

The hallmark of his turnings are their delicacy, and for that reason he has to take several design precautions to make them more durable. "I sometimes employ a 'reverse curve' in my turnings so that the top of the bowl curves back on itself. This adds strength and prevents distortion." (See Figure 16.)

Rude has also found that the way you mount a turning may determine its final shape. He sometimes produces bowls that look, for all the world, that they were carved in an oval shape. "They're not," Rude assures us. "They're perfectly round. The oval is an optical illusion." To produce that illusion, he mounts a tree limb sideways on a faceplate and turns it. (See Figure 17.)

"I mentioned it before, but it bears repeating," says Rude. "You never know what you're going to get out of a block of wood until you actually turn it. That's what makes the lathe so exciting."

Figure 15. If you're in a hurry, you can use a power disc sander to sand the outside of a turning. Be sure to hold the sander so that the disc rotates in the opposite direction as the turning.

Figure 16. A 'reverse curve' adds strength to a bowl turning and helps to keep it from distorting.

TYPICAL REVERSE CURVE

Figure 17. To turn an oval-shaped bowl, mount a tree limb *horizontally* on the faceplate. The oval shape is actually an optical illusion.

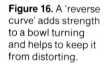

TIPS
TURNING

Making a Bastard Gouge

One of the most time-consuming chores in lathe turning is constantly having to change chisels. A turner sometimes needs to use as many as half a dozen different chisels to get the shape he's after on the lathe.

◆ For this reason, Rude invented a chisel he calls the 'bastard gouge'. (See Figure A.) Once you've practiced turning with it, you can use it as a skew, gouge, roundnose, even a parting tool. Unfortunately, you can't buy it anywhere — you have to make your own.

◆ Rude starts with bar tool stock and grinds a small hollow on the upper flat. Since most grinding wheels are flat, you may have to redress an old stone to grind this semi-circular shape. (See Figure B.) Then he grinds a 45° bevel on the sides and bottom flat, following the contour of the hollow.

Figure B. To grind the hollow in the gouge, you may have to redress an old grindstone.

Figure A. Rude's invention, the 'bastard gouge', is an extremely versatile lathe chisel. With a little practice, you can use it as a skew, gouge, roundnose, even a parting tool.

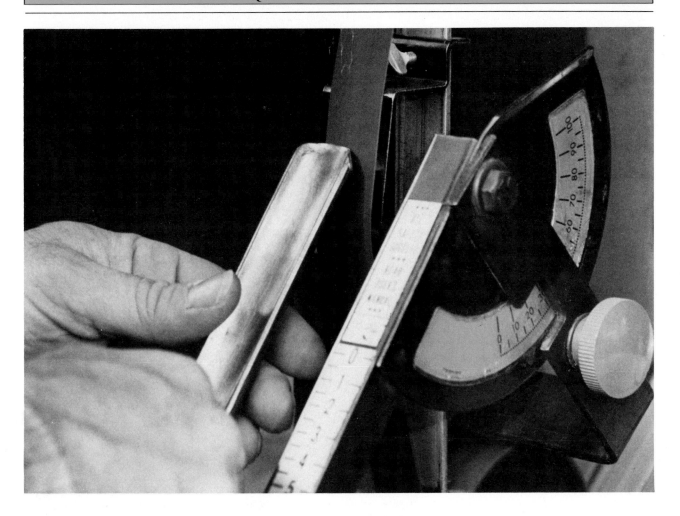

Sharpening with a Jig

Having trouble keeping your tools sharp? Use a jig — the simpler the better.

How many times have you heard this old homily before? 'It's no fun woodworking with a dull chisel.' Here's another one: 'Your woodworking takes just half the time if you keep your tools sharp.'

We've all heard these craftsman's cliches before. We know they're true. And if your sharpening skills are anything like mine, you probably feel a little twinge of guilt upon hearing them again. My chisels are never as sharp as they should be. I'm just an average woodworker, with average sharpening skills, and it takes me a long time to put a professional edge on a cutting tool — a lot longer than it takes me to just go ahead and wade into the work with an edge that's duller than it should be. Consequently, I don't sharpen my tools as often as I should.

I may get better about sharpening, though. Recently, a friend of mine showed me that a good jig and the proper technique takes all the pain and suffering out of sharpening.

By following this simple procedure, even the rankest of amateurs can achieve decidedly un-rank results with very little practice.

Selecting a Good Jig

Before I tell you about sharpening with a jig, let me introduce you to my friend: Dick Belcher of Dayton, Ohio, is an award-winning woodcarver. He's traveled extensively in North America and Europe, displaying his talents and giving seminars in carving. He's found, through years of experience, that only with a properly sharpened chisel can you get the control you need for safe and accurate woodworking. And he's also found that one of the hardest things for his students to learn is how to properly sharpen their chisels.

"It's not that they don't know how," explains Dick. "It's that most woodworkers don't do enough sharpening to develop the feel, the muscle control, or the eye needed to put an edge on a tool. You need a good sharpening jig."

I think most of us amateurs would buy that. We know we need a jig. After all, that's why they put the chisel rests on bench grinders, right?

Figure 1. The Pro-Edge jig attaches to a 1″ belt sander/grinder, as shown here. There are other jigs available that attach to belt sanders and disc sanders.

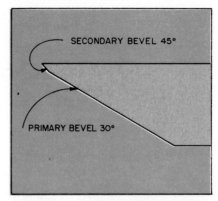

Figure 2. By 'stropping' your chisels with a leather strip after you've honed them, you put a microscopic second bevel on the edge. The stropped chisel is imperceptibly duller, but the edge will stay sharp lots longer.

SECONDARY BEVEL 45°

PRIMARY BEVEL 30°

Figure 3. Impregnate your leather strop with a jeweler's rouge or polishing compound. Use a compound in a tallow or grease base — dry compounds tend to build up static electricity. This doesn't hurt the sharpening process, but it can be uncomfortable.

Well, as I found out, it's not quite that simple. An unadorned chisel rest attached to a bench grinder may not be the world's best sharpening system. Most rests will only hold flat cutting tools with any accuracy; there's too much guesswork to sharpen a gouge. For a sharpening jig to be truly useful to the home craftsman, it should hold a variety of tools — wood chisels, lathe chisels, plane irons — at a variety of angles to the moving abrasive with absolute stability.

There are a few systems like this on the market in the home craftsman's price range, and several more you can make. Most of them attach to a bench grinder, belt sander, or sander/grinder. Dick prefers a store-bought jig called the 'Pro-Edge'. (See Figure 1.) It adapts to most makes of 1″ belt sander/grinders, and will hold any kind of chisel or plane iron. With some ingenuity, it can also be adapted to sharpen jointer knives.

As you shop for a jig — or set out to design your own — look for these essentials: There should be at least two adjustments. The jig should allow you to adjust for the cutting bevel *and* the length of the tool. It should provide an easy, stable way for you to 'roll' or tilt a tool across the abrasive so that you can sharpen gouges and skews. And it should let you change the abrasives on your machine with a minimum of fuss, *without* changing the bevel angle.

Abrasives

Just as important as having a good jig to hold the tools is having the right types of abrasives to sharpen them. A single grinding stone or abrasive belt won't do. Dick treats sharpening the same way some people treat sanding. He starts with a coarse abrasive, works down to a finer grit, then polishes the surface.

"If you're hand-sharpening with benchstones, the classic technique is to start out with a soft Arkansas stone, switch to a hard Arkansas, then polish with a leather strop or Cratex®," explains Dick. "You can get the same results on

a sander/grinder by starting with 100#, then 320#, then a leather belt."

The 100# removes any nicks in the cutting edge, but won't give you an edge sharp enough to work with. It just 'shapes' the edge. The 320# begins to sharpen the tool, and most woodworkers would be satisfied with the edge it leaves. But the leather strop polishes the metal, removing microscopic imperfections, so the cutting edge glides through the wood.

The leather also puts a second, microscopic bevel on the edge. (See Figure 2.) Since the leather gives slightly when you push the tool against it, the belt will grind a *slightly* different bevel than the abrasives. This actually blunts the edge, dulling the tool imperceptibly. But the resulting edge is stronger and will last longer than an edge that's razor sharp.

"There's very little difference between a razor edge, the right edge, and a dull edge," Dick says. "You don't want to sharpen a woodworking tool so that you can shave hairs; the edge won't last. Take some of the edge off with the strop, but not too much."

The leather belt, by itself, won't polish the cutting edge. You have to apply an abrasive such as jeweler's rouge to it. Dick used the abrasive compound that came with his Pro-Edge jig, but found it somewhat unnerving. "The abrasive was dry when it was applied to the belt," says Dick. "As I worked, a huge static charge built up. I'd go to turn the machine off and POW! My hand gets sore just from thinking about it."

Dick found that an abrasive compound in a tallow base

Figure 4. To determine the proper bevel for a chisel, pay more attention to the *length* of the bevel than the angle. Hand-held and hand-powered chisels (such as carving chisels) should have a long bevel of 1/4"–3/8". If you intend to use the chisel on the lathe or hit it with a hammer, grind a short bevel, less than 1/4".

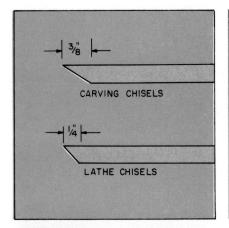

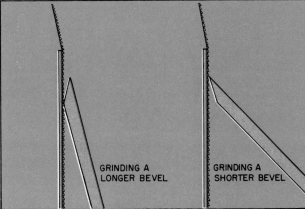

Figure 5. To reproduce the proper bevel angle for a given chisel on your grinding jig, first position the chisel so that a black shadow shows behind the edge. Then slowly readjust the bevel angle until the shadow disappears.

Figure 6. To grind longer bevels, leave some shadow. To grind shorter bevels, adjust the jig until the shadow disappears, then go a little bit further.

Figure 7. As you sharpen your chisels, dip them in water. Watch the beads of water on the edge as you work. If these start to evaporate, the metal is getting too hot.

Figure 8. The abrasive belt must travel in the same direction as the chisel is pointing.

cuts down on the static. (See Figure 3.) He uses an industrial brand called 'Formax F-122, Abrasive Belt and Grease Stick'. "But any polishing abrasive in a tallow or hard grease base would work," he claims.

Grinding the Right Bevel

The first step in any sharpening procedure is to determine the proper bevel for the cutting tool. "There's a good deal of discussion as to the proper *angle* of the bevel for various types of woods and work," Dick told me. "I find the *length* of the bevel is more important. Get the length right and the angle will be right."

So what's the proper length? Well, if you're doing a lot of hand work — pushing the chisel with your hands only, as when you use a carving chisel — then you'll want a longer bevel so that you can lay the tool down close to the work. Dick thinks that 1/4" to 3/8" is about right. If the chisel is very thick, you may even want to extend the bevel out to 1/2".

However, long bevels are weaker than shorter bevels. So if you're hitting the chisel with a mallet or using it for lathe work, keep the bevels to 1/4" or less. The extra metal will help absorb the blows. (See Figure 4.)

To adjust your sharpening jig to grind a proper bevel, first lay the tool in the jig with the machine *off*. Adjust the bevel angle so that you can see a dark line behind the cutting edge — this is the shadow the chisel throws on the belt. (See Figure 5.) Increase the angle until the line disappears. At this

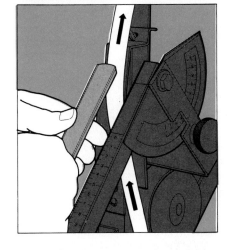

point, the jig will grind *exactly* the same angle you presently have on the chisel. If you want to grind a *shorter* bevel, continue to *increase* the angle, so that the heel of the chisel raises off the abrasive belt. To grind a *longer* bevel, *reduce* the angle until you can see the dark line again. (See Figure 6.)

Proper Sharpening Technique

The trouble with using a machine to sharpen tools is that the abrasives can cause the tools to heat up very quickly. They may turn a dark blue, or even red. Once this happens, the edge is ruined. Overheating takes the 'temper' out of tool steel and renders it too soft to hold a sharp edge.

Figure 9. A burr on the tip of a chisel will reflect a 'line of light' as you look at it head-on.

Figure 10. The last step in a good sharpening procedure is stropping the edge to remove all burrs and create a secondary bevel. Use slightly more pressure than you did when you were honing the chisel with abrasives.

To prevent this, dip the chisel in a cup of water *before* you press it against the running abrasive belt. As you apply it, use a very light pressure. Watch the beads of water on the edge carefully. As the metal heats up from the friction of the belt, the water will evaporate. When it does, take the tool out of the sharpening jig and dip it in water again. (See Figure 7.) Repeat as necessary.

Warning: The abrasive must travel 'up', or in the same direction that the cutting edge of the tool is pointing. (See Figure 8.) For some sander/grinders, this is the opposite direction that the tool normally runs. Refer to the 'Tips' section at the end of this chapter for an easy way to reverse belt direction.

Using the water to control the temperature of the cutting edge, start with the 100# abrasive. Grind the tool until you have achieved the bevel you're after and/or all the nicks have disappeared. You can tell that the nicks are gone by looking at the edge head-on in a strong light. The abrasive belt will have created a slight burr on the edge, and this burr will reflect a 'line of light' back at you. (See Figure 9.) If the line of light is even all the way across the edge, the nicks are gone.

Remove the burr with a few strokes of a wet stone or gouge slip on the *opposite* side of the bevel from the one that you were sharpening. Change to the 320# belt and repeat the process, continuing to dip the tool in water as you work. Sharpen until you see another line of light, then remove it with a stone.

> **Tip ◆** The closer you are to finishing with the abrasive belts, the less pressure this process will require. Thin metal heats faster.

Figure 11. To test for sharpness, use the chisel to cut *across* the grain of some scrap wood. If the chisel is properly sharpened, the cut will be clean and smooth. If it's not sharp, there will be slight tears.

Finally, change to the leather belt. Make sure the belt is impregnated with abrasive compound, then apply the tool to the belt. On this step, you can use slightly more pressure than you did with the abrasive belts. (See Figure 10.) With the leather, there is less danger that you will overheat the tool. And you must depress the belt just a little to create the secondary bevel.

> **Tip ◆** Once you've impregnated a new leather belt with abrasive compound, you rarely have to apply more. 'Touch it up' once every 3-6 months as a general rule. A single stick of jeweler's rouge could last a lifetime in a normal home shop.

Testing for the Proper Edge

How do you know that you've properly sharpened a chisel or plane iron. According to Dick, the best way to test the tool is to cut a scrap of wood *across the grain*. (See Figure 11.)

"If the tool is still dull in one spot, or there is a microscopic nick you didn't remove," Dick showed me, "the wood will tear. If the tool is sharpened correctly, the cut will be smooth."

How do you tell that a tool has lost the proper cutting edge after you've used it for a while — besides the fact that the work will go slower?

"Use the 'line of light' trick," advises Dick. "Periodically inspect your chisels. A nick will reflect a tiny spot of light. A blunted edge will show an uneven line of light. If you see any light reflected from the edge, it's time to sharpen them again."

Perhaps now this chore won't seem so foreboding with a good jig — and the proper technique.

Sources

The Pro-Edge jig shown in this chapter is sold through the mail from:

Prakto, Inc.
P.O. Box 1023
Birmingham, MI 48012

The Prakto folks also sell abrasive sharpening belts and leather polishing belts to fit most sander/grinders. Write for prices.

The tallow-based abrasive stick Dick Belcher uses is manufactured by the Formax Manufacturing Corporation of Detroit, Michigan. This is an industrial supplier, and they can't afford to sell one stick at a time. You may want to go in with a few woodworking friends to get together a large enough order. Or you can contact:

NASCO
901 Janesville Avenue
Fort Atkinson, WI 53538

NASCO is an arts and crafts supplier. They sell jeweler's rouge in a grease base stick.

TIPS
SHARPENING

Reversing a Motor

Sander/grinders are set up so that the belt travels *down*, holding the material to be ground or sanded against the worktable. To use this tool for sharpening, you must reverse the direction of the belt. This isn't hard; on most machines all you need to do is switch two wires at the back of the electrical motor housing. However, if you're going to be switching off between sanding and sharpening constantly, this can get to be a real pain.

◆ With a little ingenuity, you can wire your motor so that you can reverse the direction by simply throwing a switch. First, check to see that your motor is reversible. This information should appear on the housing. (See Figure A.) Use a double pole, double throw switch to actually reverse the motor leads, and an ordinary single pole, single throw switch to turn the current on and off. (See Figure B.)

Warning: Be sure that the rated amperage of the switches is equal to or greater than the amperage of the motor. And never reverse the direction of the motor while it's running. Always turn off the current first.

Figure A. Before you wire a motor so that you can reverse the direction of rotation, first check the housing to determine that the motor is indeed reversible.

Figure B. The front switch simply turns the current on and off. The back switch is a double pole, double throw switch *without* a crossover. It's used to reverse the leads.

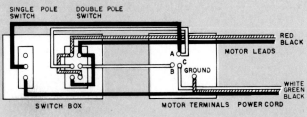

WIRING A REVERSIBLE MOTOR

Making and Installing Drawers

There's more than one way to hang a drawer.

Adrawer is nothing more than a simple box, open at the top. It's just five pieces of wood — front, back, sides, bottom — but there are so many, many ways to put them together. And there are just as many ways to 'hang' it.

How do you choose the proper drawer materials, construction, or method of installation for the project you're designing? There are no hard and fast answers. Building a drawer, like so many other considerations in woodworking design, sometimes boils down to a matter of personal taste — and what tools you have on hand.

However, the design of the drawer, the selection of materials and joinery, and the way it's hung can't be totally random. If you want the project to last, there are a few things you should consider carefully.

Wear and Tear

First, consider how a drawer is used: You pull it out of its case and push it back continually, using a handle attached to the front panel. The stress created by this pushing and pulling wears hardest on the joints between the sides and the front panel. For this reason, these are usually the strongest joints in the drawer — and the most complex.

Whatever you keep in the drawer is going to weigh down on the drawer bottom. If you jerk the drawer open,

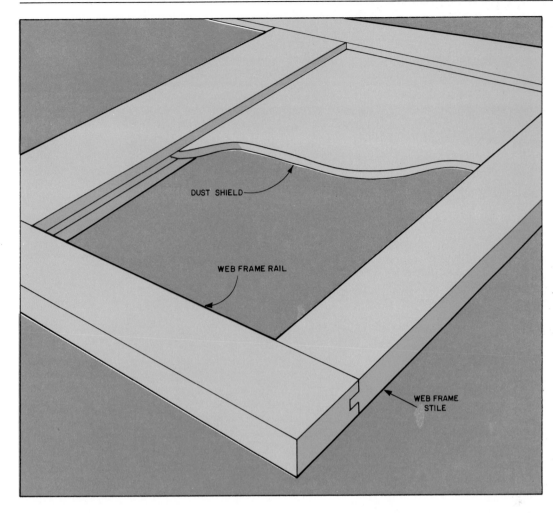

DUST SHIELD

WEB FRAME RAIL

WEB FRAME STILE

Figure 1. Dust shields between drawers keep dust and dirt from sifting down and soiling the drawer contents.

the contents will press against the back. However, these weights and pressures are applied from one direction only, and they never reach the magnitude of the stress on the side-to-front joints. Simple grooves and dadoes are sturdy enough to join other parts of the drawer.

There are other important parts of a drawer that must stand up to abuse, but these vary from drawer to drawer. These are the portions of the drawer that rub against the case, where wood slides against wood — or metal, or plastic, depending on how you hang the drawer. These parts should be made out of (or faced with) hardwood. Furthermore, the action of wood sliding against wood will create a fine sawdust that will sift down, soiling the contents in lower drawers. You may want to build barriers or 'dust shields' into a case, to separate the drawers. (See Figure 1.)

Keep all these things in mind as you work. Anticipate the wear and tear on a drawer, and choose the materials and joinery accordingly.

Materials

Not every part of every drawer needs to be made from good, expensive lumber. Most craftsmen prefer to make only the parts of the drawer that will show — usually just the front panel — from cabinet-grade wood, and the rest from 'utility' wood. (See Figure 2.) This utility wood is usually #2 or #3 pine, but it can also be plywood, scraps, anything that's cheap but sturdy.

When you choose utility wood, be careful to use something that has been dried in the same manner (and for the same length of time) as the cabinet-grade lumber in the rest of the project. For instance, much of the #3 pine lumber you buy off the rack in a building supply store has not been kiln-dried as long as, or with the same care as the furniture-quality hardwoods you can get from other sources. The differences in moisture content between the drawer parts may cause the finished drawers to warp.

Where two wooden parts slide against each other, at least one of the parts should be made from a hardwood. Usually, either the drawer sides or the drawer back will rub against some sort of guide. Traditionally, this guide is made of an inexpensive hardwood such as oak, beech, or rock maple — and the best wood for the job is maple.

Figure 2. You needn't build the entire drawer from expensive hardwoods. The sides, back, and bottom — the parts you can't see when the drawer is closed — are often made from cheaper 'utility' woods.

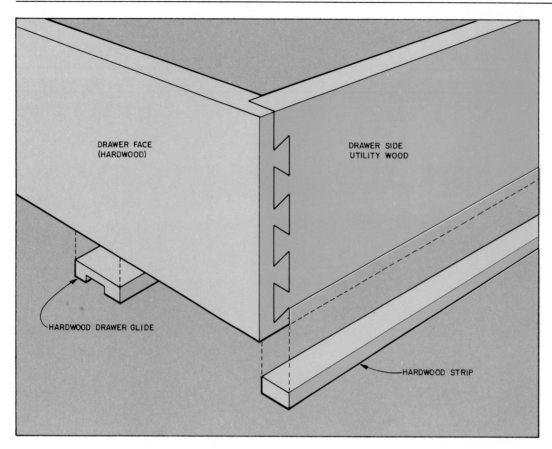

DRAWER FACE
(HARDWOOD)

DRAWER SIDE
UTILITY WOOD

HARDWOOD DRAWER GLIDE

HARDWOOD STRIP

Figure 3. To reduce wear on sliding parts, make them out of hardwood. Or face the edges that will rub with hardwood strips.

There are several reasons for this: The most obvious is that hardwood doesn't wear as fast as softwood, and a hardwood guide will last longer. Less obvious is the fact that hardwoods — particularly close-grained hardwoods such as maple — can be sanded glass-smooth. This reduces friction and improves the sliding action of the drawer. Furthermore, the sliding action will continue to polish the hardwood. The more the drawer is used the better it will work.

Guides are normally fairly small parts, and don't require a lot of hardwood. If, for some reason, you need to make the larger drawer parts out of hardwood, you can save yourself some money by simply 'facing' the sliding surfaces with hardwood. Simply glue 1/4"–1/2" thick maple strips where you want them. (See Figure 3.) Use aliphatic resin (yellow glue) to hold the strips in place.

Drawer bottoms are normally the largest parts of a drawer, and are therefore subject to the most distortion when the humidity or temperature changes. To keep this distortion to a minimum, use thin plywood or hardboard panels for the drawer bottoms. If you're a purist and insist on using solid wood, choose a close-grained wood such as pine or poplar. These are less susceptible to changes in the weather.

Tip ◆ If you're making a project that will be used to store clothes, towels, or bed linens, consider using cedar 'closet liner' for the drawer bottoms. (See Figure 4.) The aromatic cedar in this 1/4" thick chipboard will keep your clothes and bed sheets smelling fresh. In fact, a chest of drawers with cedar drawer bottoms will keep a whole room smelling fresh.

Joining the Front to the Sides

Once you have settled on the materials, decide on the most important joint in the drawer — how you will join the front to the sides. This joint will depend a great deal on what sort of drawer you're making. Drawers are classified by how they fit in their furniture case. There are three basic types: Flush drawers, lip drawers, and overlay drawers.

Flush drawers — A flush drawer is fitted so that the front of the drawer is flush with the case. (See Figure 5.) It may also be slightly recessed. But in either example, a flush drawer is 'stopped' at the back so that the drawer front lines up properly with the case when you shut the drawer.

Lip drawers — Some drawer fronts are rabbeted so that there is a 1/4"–1/2" thick 'lip' all around the outside edge of the drawer, larger than the drawer opening. (See

Figure 4. Drawer bottoms made from 1/4" thick cedar 'closet liner' keep clothes and linens smelling fresh. The aromatic cedar also discourages moths and other insects.

Figure 5. A flush drawer is mounted so the face of the drawer will be flush with the face of the furniture case.

Figure 6. The front of a lip drawer has a rabbet cut all the way around the edge. This creates a lip that overlaps the case.

Figure 7. On an overlay drawer, the front is wider (and sometimes taller) than the drawer opening, so that the entire drawer front overlaps the case.

Figure 8. Half-blind dovetails are best used to join the sides and fronts of flush drawers. They are so called because you can only see the joint from one side.

Figure 9. Use a router and a dovetail template to cut the dovetail slots and the dovetails in one operation.

Figure 10. The dovetails will fit snugly in the slots. Tap the parts together carefully with a mallet. To prevent damage to the wood, you may want to wrap the head of the mallet in a cloth.

Figure 6.) This lip overlaps the case and stops the drawer when the drawer is closed.

Overlay drawers — The front of a drawer may be cut so that entire board is wider and/or taller than the drawer opening, in order to overlap the case. (See Figure 7.) Like a lip drawer, the overlay drawer is stopped at the front.

There are many different ways to join the drawer fronts to drawer sides (more than we have room to discuss here). But not all joints work well on all types of drawers. A joint that works for a flush drawer may not be suited for lip drawers or overlay drawers. Here are three common examples:

Half-blind dovetail — The half-blind dovetail is one of the sturdiest and most widely used drawer joints, but it works best on flush drawers. (See Figure 8.) It is difficult to make on a lip drawer without special equipment, and impossible to make on an overlay drawer.

One of the reasons this joint is so popular is that it can be easily and accurately cut with a hand router and a dovetail template. This template holds the wood so that you cut both the dovetails and the slots in one simple step. (See Figure 9.) After the joint is cut, simply tap the boards together with a mallet. (See Figure 10.) There's no more work needed!

Lock joint — A lock joint is suited to both a flush drawer and lip drawer, but not overlay drawers. (See Figure 11.) It's simple to make, but requires several more steps than the router-made dovetail. However, this joint will save you some work if you're making a lip drawer. You can cut the lip and the lock joint at the same time.

Cut the side pieces first: Make a 1/4" x 1/4" dado on

the inside surfaces. (See Figure 12.) Then cut a 1/4″ groove in the ends of the front panel, forming two tenons 1/4″ wide. (See Figure 13.) The depth of this groove will depend on how wide you want the lip to be. Finally, cut the *inside* tenon on the front so that it's just 1/4″ long. (See Figure 14.) The outside tenon will become the lip.

> **Tip ◆** A tenoning jig will aid in cutting the groove in the ends of the drawer front.

French dovetail — A 'french dovetail' is a dovetail-shaped tenon cut in the ends of the drawer sides. This tenon slides into a dovetail slot in the drawer front. (See Figure 15.) The joint can be used on all three types of drawers, but it is best suited to the overlay drawer. If you cut a dovetail slot too close to the ends of a flush drawer or lip drawer, the outside edge of the joint will be very weak. There's enough room at the ends of an overlay drawer that you shouldn't have to worry about this problem.

The easiest way to cut a french dovetail is to use a portable router mounted to a router table. Cut the tenon first, just grazing the ends of the drawer sides with the router bit. Cut the inside surface first, then turn the board over and cut the outside. (See Figure 16.) Without changing the height of the router bit, cut the slots in the drawer front. If your router table will accept a miter gauge, use it for this operation. (See Figure 17.) If the drawer front is slightly taller than the drawer sides, you may want to stop the slot at one end.

Joining the Sides to the Back

You could use many of the same joints at the back of the drawer that you used on the front, but there's really no reason for it. You never see the back end, and it doesn't have to absorb the same punishment. Most craftsmen use a much simpler arrangement: The back of the drawer traditionally sits in dadoes in the sides, set back 1/4″–1/2″ from the ends. (See Figure 18.)

You may wonder why professional cabinetmakers have settled on this joint, since the design actually wastes some potential drawer space. Well, first of all, it's simple and quick to make. And the drawer back must withstand some pressure from the drawer contents pushing against it. A rabbet wouldn't do it; the dado has to be set slightly forward so that there's a 'lip' to hold the back.

Finally, many flush drawers are stopped by butting up against the back of the case. (Even some lip and overlay drawers are made to come within a fraction of an inch of the back of the case.) The extra stock at the ends of the sides gives you something you can easily sand down to custom fit each drawer just right. And if the back of the drawer happens to warp, it won't effect the overall fit of the drawer in the case.

Joining the Bottom to the Drawer

The bottom of a drawer is set in a groove that runs around the inside of the front, back, and sides — classic frame-and-panel joinery. (See Figure 19.)

In some factory-built pieces, you'll find there is no groove in the back. Instead, the back is cut smaller than the front and sides so that it extends down just to the top of the

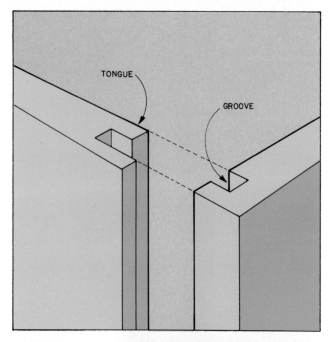

Figure 11. You can use a lock joint in either flush or lip drawers.

Figure 12. The first step in making a lock joint is to cut a dado on the inside surface of the sides.

Figure 13. Cut a groove on the ends of the drawer front, creating two tenons. A tenoning jig will prove a big help on this operation.

Figure 14. Finally, cut the tenon on the inside surface of the drawer front to the proper length.

Figure 15. A 'french dovetail' is a dovetail-shaped tenon cut in the ends of the drawer sides. This slides into a dovetail slot in the drawer front. It's mostly used on overlay drawers.

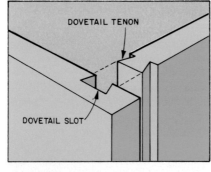

DOVETAIL TENON

DOVETAIL SLOT

Figure 16. Use a router mounted to a table to make a french dovetail. Cut the tenon with a dovetail router bit in much the same way you'd cut a tenon with a dado blade.

Figure 17. Without changing the height of the router bit above the table, cut the dovetail slots to accept the tenons.

Figure 18. Traditionally, the back of a drawer is attached to the sides with simple dadoes.

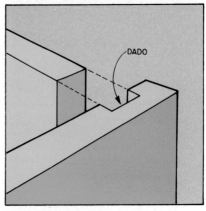

DADO

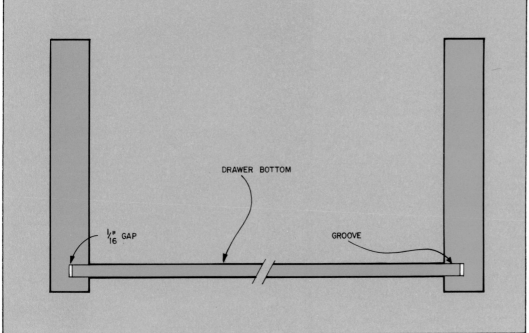

DRAWER BOTTOM

$\frac{1}{16}$" GAP

GROOVE

Figure 19. The bottom of a drawer is set loosely in grooves in the front, back, and sides.

groove. This allows you to slide the bottom in place *after* the drawer is built. The bottom is cut slightly oversize so that it can be tacked to the back with brads. (See Figure 20.) On first glance, this seems like a good arrangement; it simplifies assembly. But that's the only advantage. The lack of a back groove weakens the overall drawer. Eventually, the wood dries out, the brads loosen, and the bottom shifts every time you open the drawer.

Set the bottom panel in a groove on all four sides. *Don't* glue it in place. The bottom must be allowed to 'float' in the groove, so the panel is free to expand and contract with the weather. The panel should also be cut approximately 1/8″ undersize to give it room to move.

> **Tip ◆** If you make the bottom panel from solid wood, you may wish to leave more than 1/8″ 'slop' on some dimensions. Solid wood expands and contracts up to 1/4″ *across* the grain for every 12″ of width. (Movement *with* the grain is much smaller; only 1/10 of the cross-grain movement.)

Hanging the Drawers

How you hang a drawer does not depend so much on the type of drawer as the case it fits in. Some drawer guides are designed to be part of the case construction, to add strength and stability to the project; others are there just to hang the drawers.

There are also wooden guides that you can make yourself and drawer hardware that you can buy. Just as we didn't have the room to discuss all the various drawer joints, we won't have time to cover all the various methods of drawer installation. Instead, we'll concentrate on three wooden guides that you can make with a minimum of fuss.

Center Guides — If you notch the bottom edge of the back of a drawer, the drawer can be guided easily along a single hardwood runner that rests in the notch. (See Figure 21.) This is called a center guide. Of all the drawer installation methods, it produces the least friction since there is only one guide.

It also has several other advantages: The central runner must be mounted on a frame of some sort. This frame can be incorporated into the furniture case as part of its structure. (This is sometimes called 'web frame construction'.) If you want to stack one drawer on top of another — as in a chest of drawers — the frames separate the drawers and keep the case rigid. Thin panels or 'dust shields' can be built into the frames to keep dust and dirt from sifting down from one drawer to another. (See Figure 22.)

> **Tip ◆** If you build web frames, you may want to mount 'kickers' to the undersides of the frames, in line with the drawer sides. These kickers prevent the drawers beneath them from tipping down when the drawers are opened. (See Figure 23.)

Corner Guides — Drawers can also be guided by mounting runners alongside the bottom corners. These runners may be mounted to drawer frames, or they can be simple L-brackets installed in the furniture case. (See Figure 24.) Whether you use frames or brackets will depend on whether or not you need the frames as an integral part of the case.

Side Guides — Runners can also be mounted to slide in dadoes cut in the drawer sides. (See Figure 25.) These side guides are perhaps the simplest way to hang a drawer, but they contribute nothing to the overall strength of the case. They are best used when you have only a few small drawers to be mounted in a sturdy case.

> **Tip ◆** No matter what method you use to hang your drawers, you'll find that they'll work better if you rub the sliding parts with paraffin.

Parting Thoughts

This certainly isn't everything there is to know about drawers. As we mentioned, there's a great deal we've left out due to space considerations. However, the methods, joinery, and materials we've outlined here can be combined in various ways to make and mount sturdy, attractive drawers in almost any sort of project, large or small.

Figure 20. Sometimes, the drawer back is cut short and the drawer bottom is tacked to it. This simplifies drawer assembly, but it weakens the overall drawer.

Figure 21. A center guide rides in a notch or groove in a drawer glide. The guide is attached to the web frame and the glide is attached to the drawer bottom.

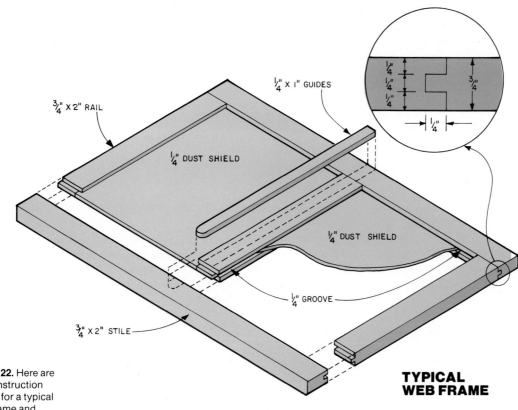

TYPICAL WEB FRAME

Figure 22. Here are the construction details for a typical web frame and center guide. Notice the dust shields.

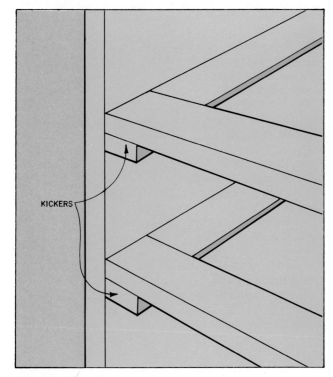

Figure 23. 'Kickers', mounted to the undersides of web frames, keep the drawers beneath them from tipping down when opened.

Figure 24. Corner guides may be nothing more than simple L-brackets installed in the furniture case.

Figure 25. Side guides support *and* guide a drawer. They rest in dadoes that are cut into the drawer sides.

Index

Popular Science Books offers a wood identification kit that include 30 samples of cabinet woods. For details on ordering, please write Popular Science Books, P.O. Box 2033, Latham, NY 12111.